Government
Commission
Communication

Recent Titles in the Praeger Series in Political Communication
Robert E. Denton, Jr., *General Editor*

Broadcasting Propaganda:
International Radio Broadcasting and the Construction of Political Reality
Philo C. Wasburn

Enacting the Presidency:
Political Argument, Presidential Debates, and Presidential Character
Edward A. Hinck

Citizens, Political Communication and Interest Groups:
Environmental Organizations in Canada and the United States
John C. Pierce, Mary Ann E. Steger, Brent S. Steel, and Nicholas P. Lovric

Media and Public Policy
Edited by Robert J. Spitzer

Cold War Analytical Structures and the Post Post-War World
Cori E. Dauber

American Rhetoric and the Vietnam War
J. Justin Gustainis

The Inaugural Addresses of Twentieth-Century American Presidents
Edited by Halford Ryan

Studies in Media and the Persian Gulf War
Edited by Robert E. Denton, Jr.

The Modern Presidency and Crisis Rhetoric
Edited by Amos Kiewe

Government
Commission
Communication

Edited by
Christine M. Miller
and
Bruce C. McKinney

Praeger Series in Political Communication

Westport, Connecticut
London

Library of Congress Cataloging-in-Publication Data

Government commission communication / edited by Christine M. Miller
and Bruce C. McKinney.
    p. cm. — (Praeger series in political communication, ISSN
1062–5623)
   Includes bibliographical references and index.
   ISBN 0–275–94223–6 (alk. paper)
   1. Governmental investigations—United States. 2. Communication
in politics—United States. I. Miller, Christine Marie.
II. McKinney, Bruce C. III. Series.
JK518.G69   1993
353.009'92—dc20   93–17118

British Library Cataloguing in Publication Data is available.

Library of Congress Catalog Card Number: 93–17118
ISBN: 0–275–94223–6
ISSN: 1062–5623

First published in 1993

Praeger Publishers, 88 Post Road West, Westport, CT 06881
An imprint of Greenwood Publishing Group, Inc.

Printed in the United States of America

The paper used in this book complies with the
Permanent Paper Standard issued by the National
Information Standards Organization (Z39.48-1984).

10 9 8 7 6 5 4 3 2 1

This book is dedicated to
the memories of
Lawrence Wayne Miller
and
Marion Grace Converse McKinney
B.A. in Speech, Northwestern University, 1941

Contents

Series Foreword *by Robert E. Denton, Jr.*   xi

Preface   xv

I. STUDYING GOVERNMENT COMMISSIONS

1. Considering Commissions Critically
   Nicholas F. S. Burnett   3

2. Rhetorical Constraints on Government Commissions
   W. David Snowball   31

3. Commissions as Organizations: Characteristics,
   Functions, and Context
   W. Timothy Coombs   51

II. CASE STUDIES

4. The Warren Commission
   Bruce C. McKinney   75

5. The 1970 Commission on Obscenity and Pornography
   Roger A. Soenksen   103

6. Factors Affecting the Decision-Making Process in the
   Attorney General's Commission on Pornography:
   A Case Study of Unwarranted Collective Judgment
   Dennis S. Gouran   123

7. The Rogers Commission Investigation
   of the *Challenger* Tragedy
   Christine M. Miller   145

8. The Senate Select Committee on POW/MIA Affairs:
   A Government Committee as Mediator
   William D. Kimsey and Rex M. Fuller   167

References   199

Index of Government Commissions   213

Subject Index   215

About the Editors and Contributors   219

Series Foreword

Those of us from the discipline of communication studies have long believed that communication is prior to all other fields of inquiry. In several other forums I have argued that the essence of politics is "talk" or human interaction.[1] Such interaction may be formal or informal, verbal or nonverbal, public or private, but it is always persuasive, forcing us consciously or subconsciously to interpret, to evaluate, and to act. Communication is the vehicle for human action.

From this perspective, it is not surprising that Aristotle recognized the natural kinship of politics and communication in his writings *Politics* and *Rhetoric*. In the former, he established that humans are "political beings [who] alone of the animals [are] furnished with the faculty of language."[2] In the latter, he began his systematic analysis of discourse by proclaiming that "rhetorical study, in its strict sense, is concerned with the modes of persuasion."[3] Thus, it was recognized over twenty-three hundred years ago that politics and communication go hand in hand because they are essential parts of human nature.

In 1981, Dan Nimmo and Keith Sanders proclaimed that political communication was an emerging field.[4] Although its origin, as noted, dates back centuries, a "self-consciously cross-disciplinary" focus began in the late 1950s. Thousands of books and articles later, colleges and universities offer a variety of graduate and undergraduate coursework in the area in such diverse departments as communication, mass communication, journalism, political science, and sociology.[5] In Nimmo and Sanders's early assessment, the "key areas of inquiry" included rhetorical analysis, propaganda analysis, attitude change studies, voting studies, government and the news media, functional and systems analyses, technological changes, media technologies, campaign techniques, and research techniques.[6] In a survey of the state of field in 1983, the same authors and Lynda Kaid found additional, more specific areas of concerns such as the presidency, political polls, public opinion, debates, and advertising.[7] Since the first study, they have also noted a shift away from the rather strict behavioral approach.

A decade later, Dan Nimmo and David Swanson argued that "political communication has developed some identity as a more or less distinct domain of scholarly work."[8] The scope and concerns of the area have further expanded to include critical theories and cultural studies. Although there is no precise definition, method, or disciplinary home of the area of inquiry, its primary domain comprises the role, processes, and effects of communication within the context of politics broadly defined.

In 1985, the editors of *Political Communication Yearbook: 1984* noted that "more things are happening in the study, teaching, and practice of political communication than can be captured within the space limitations of the relatively few publications available."[9] In addition, they argued that the backgrounds of "those involved in the field [are] so varied and pluralist in outlook and approach, . . . it [is] a mistake to adhere slavishly to any set format in shaping the content."[10] More recently, Swanson and Nimmo have called for "ways of overcoming the unhappy conse- quences of fragmentation within a framework that respects, encourages, and benefits from diverse scholarly commitments, agendas, and ap- proaches."[11]

In agreement with these assessments of the area and with gentle encouragement, in 1988 Praeger established the series entitled "Praeger Studies in Political Communication." The series is open to all qualitative and quantitative methodologies as well as contemporary and historical studies. The key to characterizing the studies in the series is the focus on communication variables or activities within a political context or dimension. As of this writing, nearly forty volumes have been published and numerous impressive works are forthcoming. Scholars from the disciplines of communication, history, journalism, political science, and sociology have participated in the series.

I am, without shame or modesty, a fan of the series. The joy of serving as its editor is in participating in the dialogue of the field of political communication and in reading the contributors' works. I invite you to join me.

Robert E. Denton, Jr.

NOTES

1. See Robert E. Denton, Jr., *The Symbolic Dimensions of the American Presidency* (Prospect Heights, IL: Waveland Press, 1982); Robert E. Denton, Jr., and Gary Woodward, *Political Communication in America* (New York: Praeger, 1985; 2d ed., 1990); Robert E. Denton, Jr., and Dan Hahn, *Presidential Communication* (New York: Praeger, 1986); and Robert E. Denton, Jr., *The Primetime Presidency of Ronald Reagan* (New York: Praeger, 1988).

2. Aristotle, *The Politics of Aristotle,* trans. Ernest Barker (New York: Oxford University Press, 1970), p. 5.

3. Aristotle, *Rhetoric,* trans. Rhys Roberts (New York: The Modern Library, 1954), p. 22.

4. Dan Nimmo and Keith Sanders, "Introduction: The Emergence of Political Communication as a Field," in *Handbook of Political Communication,* eds. Dan Nimmo and Keith Sanders (Beverly Hills, CA: Sage, 1981), pp. 11–36.

5. Ibid., p. 15.

6. Ibid., pp. 17–27.

7. Keith Sanders, Lynda Kaid, and Dan Nimmo, eds. *Political Communication Yearbook: 1984* (Carbondale, IL: Southern Illinois University: 1985), pp. 283–308.

8. Dan Nimmo and David Swanson, "The Field of Political Communication: Beyond the Voter Persuasion Paradigm," in *New Directions in Political Communication,* eds. David Swanson and Dan Nimmo (Beverly Hills, CA: Sage, 1990), p. 8.

9. Sanders, Kaid, and Nimmo, *Political Communication Yearbook,* p. xiv.

10. Ibid.

11. Nimmo and Swanson, "The Field of Political Communication," p. 11.

Preface

After twenty-four successful shuttle flights, NASA and the nation were shocked when, on January 28, 1986, the space shuttle *Challenger* exploded seventy-three seconds after liftoff, killing six astronauts and Christa McAuliffe, America's first teacher in space. At first, the nation believed that the National Aeronautics and Space Administration (NASA), after so much success, had finally been the victim of the many dangers associated with space flight. Most believed that the loss was the tragic but inevitable cost of this pursuit: in the words of Ronald Reagan, "It's all part of the process of space exploration and discovery" ("The Questions Get Tougher" 1986).

Seven years later, most are aware of the fact that faulty decision making on NASA's behalf—not fate—doomed the *Challenger*. The source of this information came from a rather unique political body, often maligned and frequently misunderstood—a governmental commission. Outside of the works of A. Platt (1971), F. Popper (1970), M. Komarovsky (1975), and D. Flitner (1986), little has been written about presidential and other governmental commissions, save the much-publicized Warren Commission. What has been written usually falls under the purview of a critique of the final report of these commissions and committees. Much less has been written about the communication of these groups while they are in session. The purpose of this book is to fill that void.

Commissions are unique and often-misunderstood political bodies. In the ideal case they are expected to provide expert, independent advice to the President or to other governmental bodies that is immediately acted upon; this is more often the exception than the norm. Since this is a book about government commission communication, it is also a book about political communication. R. E. Denton and G. C. Woodward (1990) describe four characteristics of political communication: it has a short-term orientation, it features communication based on objectives, it exemplifies the importance of the mass media in public affairs, and it is audience-centered. In briefly examining these characteristics, it becomes evident that government commission communication shares many of the same characteristics.

Commissions do not last long. Their life span is usually several months, though some last longer as a result of last-minute changes to their final reports. One measure of the effectiveness of commissions is how quickly their recommendations are adopted. Commissions that are evaluated as unsuccessful are ones whose recommendations are not accepted. A good example of this is the 1970 Commission on Obscenity and Pornography (see Chapter 6), whose final report was rejected by President Nixon.

Communication based on objectives is another implicit characteristic of government commissions. Their deliberations are directed toward some specific end, even if this end is not essentially clear to those who are responsible for seeing that the commission's charge is carried out. For example, the 1983 Task Force on Hunger was created "to minimize something [the hunger issue] the Democrats and the television networks have made into an issue" (see Chapter 2). Other commissions have had explicitly stated goals: the Rogers Commission was created to determine what went wrong with the space shuttle *Challenger* (see Chapter 7), and the Warren Commission was created to convince the American people that Lee Harvey Oswald was the lone assassin of President Kennedy (see Chapter 4).

The importance of the mass media, perhaps not as crucial a factor fifty years ago, cannot be overlooked when studying government commissions. Chairman Rogers was well aware of the media criticisms that followed the release of his commission's investigation into the *Challenger* tragedy (see Chapter 7), and he made certain that the media were not kept in the dark about his commission's final report—a mistake that cost the Warren Commission considerable credibility. One need only look at any instance in which a government commission is charged with withholding or censoring information to understand the importance of the media in commission studies.

As with any political communication, commissions have a specific audience. The audience for presidential commissions is quite clear: presidents create these commissions, and the President is the primary audience of the report. Though the U.S. Navy had considerable interest in the findings of the Roberts Commission that investigated the Pearl Harbor disaster, its final report was addressed to President Franklin Delano Roosevelt. Other government commissions that are not created by the President still have a specific audience to which their final report is addressed. In addition, secondary audiences are often implicitly or explicitly addressed throughout a given commission's life span.

The primary objective of this book is to reflect the pluralism of the study of political communication by providing general discussions of commission communication as well as critical analyses of government commissions. To accomplish this, the book is divided into two parts. In Part I, the authors discuss general characteristics of commissions and provide an understanding of methodology for analyzing commissions. In Part II, the authors look at five case studies: three analyze presidential commissions, one examines an Attorney General's commission, and the last one probes the workings of a U.S. Senate Select Committee.

PART I

Chapter 1 concerns studying commissions rhetorically. The key focus of this chapter asks why some commissions succeed while others fail. It also examines the effectiveness of commissions as they communicate to their specific audience—usually, the President. Like any communicative event, commissions and their reports function in a rhetorical environment, and that fact must be understood in the analysis of government commission communication.

Chapter 2 examines the rhetorical constraints that face government commissions. The author asks a pertinent question with respect to political communication that takes on added meaning in the wake of Iran-Contra: Do commissions practice what Plato called a "noble lie"? Is telling the truth a luxury that commissions do not have? With terms like "plausible deniability" and "political truth" common in political rhetoric, it is a question well worth examining.

Chapter 3 takes the perspective of studying commissions as organizations. The notion that commissions share many characteristics with formal organizations is posited, and common commission characteristics are discussed. Additionally, criteria are offered for evaluating the success of government commissions based on certain functions, such as the investigatory function, the symbolic reassurance function, and the policy influence function.

PART II

The first case study presented in Chapter 4 is an analysis of the decision making of the Warren Commission, which investigated the assassination of President John F. Kennedy. Irving Janis's groupthink hypothesis is used as a means of analyzing the deliberations when the commissioners had to determine how to investigate a rumor that Lee Harvey Oswald—Kennedy's accused assassin—was in fact employed by the Federal Bureau of Investigation (FBI). Additional insights are presented regarding the tenuous relationship between the Warren Commission and the FBI.

Chapter 5 examines a commission whose report was rejected by the Senate and President Nixon—the 1970 Commission on Obscenity and Pornography. The Commission, which became known as the Lockhart Commission, had the dubious task of determining if there was a relationship between the widespread dissemination of pornography in the United States and declining morality. It is usually the case that when an administration or Congress does not like a report from a commission, they ignore it. The Lockhart Commission's report didn't meet that fate; instead, it was attacked by the Nixon administration before it was even released. This chapter examines the faulty arguments used to attack the report and the three conclusions by the Lockhart Commission regarding pornography in the United States.

Following the Lockhart Commission's lead, in 1985 the Reagan administration appointed another commission to examine the effects of pornography, which became known as the Meese Commission. Like the Lockhart Commission, the Meese Commission was under attack before it released its report. Unlike the Lockhart Commission, the Meese Commission concluded that there was a cause-effect relationship between pornography and sexually violent behavior. Critics charged that the Commission's investigation was politically inspired, its conclusions were predetermined, and its recommendations created the prospect of grave infringements on rights of privacy and free expression. Central to Chapter 6 is the analysis of faulty reasoning that the Meese Commission used with respect to a cause-effect relationship between pornography and sexual violence.

Chapter 7 examines the Rogers Commission, which was created to probe the space shuttle *Challenger* disaster. The decision-making and investigatory processes used by the Commission and the constraints under which it operated are explored. Central to the analysis of the Rogers Commission is the fact that it tried to be as open as possible to the public and did not want to conduct its business behind closed doors, which would have led to media speculation about its findings. This chapter also examines the surprisingly cooperative relationship between the Commission and NASA, the organization it was investigating.

Commissions are usually created in response to some crisis or troubling event. The assassination of President Kennedy and the explosion of the space shuttle *Challenger*, two events clearly planted in the American psyche, both had presidential commissions to investigate what went wrong. However, the Vietnam War, one of the defining events in U.S. history in the second half of the twentieth century, has had no commission to investigate what went wrong in Southeast Asia. It has been twenty years since the last American troops left Vietnam, and the country has been troubled by the question of unaccounted-for POWs and MIAs. It would seem that the investigation of the fate of American POWs and MIAs would be an issue demanding investigation by a presidential commission. Yet no president to date has chosen to appoint a blue-ribbon presidential commission to examine this issue. The final chapter of this book examines why a Senate select committee and not a presidential commission was created to examine this issue. The chapter focuses on how the Senate Select Committee on POW/MIA Affairs acted as a mediator between activist groups that insisted there are still American POWs and MIAs in Southeast Asia, and the U.S. government, which has always contended that no Americans were left behind at the end of the war.

At this point an important question is raised: Why include a Senate select committee in a book about commissions? While Senate select committees do not strictly meet the definition of a commission, they can and often do operate in very similar ways. Therefore, they serve as important analogs to commissions established by the executive branch and, in the final analysis, their communication is no less important, and no less political, than governmental commissions.

The preparation of this book has been a two-year project that began as a panel for the Commission on Governmental Communication at the 1990 Speech Communication Association Convention in Chicago. The authors would like to thank Bob Denton for his encouragement to begin this project. We would also like to thank the following people for their help in the preparation of this book: Mike McDaniel, Patsy Odom, Stephen Pullum, Harold Weisberg, and Maggie Fuchs. We also gratefully acknowledge the resources extended to us by our respective universities.

Part I

Studying Government Commissions

1

Considering Commissions Critically

Nicholas F. S. Burnett

In what may be the earliest references we have to the practice of criticism, Aristophanes, in his classic *Frogs*, suggests that two standards must be considered paramount by the critic. The first is "skill in the art" and the second is "wise counsel for the state." Over 2,000 years later, we could do far worse than borrowing from the Greek playwright as a starting point for consideration of how to critically evaluate the rhetoric of government commissions. The first standard allows us to recognize that the primary product of government commissions is their rhetoric; the second standard suggests to critics a most contemporary notion—that they need not confine their comments to parochial views of rhetoric as merely style, figure, or trope. While government commissions are often responsible for policy generation and are, in fact, integral parts of the governing apparatus of the nation, they are important, in and of themselves, as symbolic acts. Their recommendations should be analyzed not merely as policy output but as attempts by the government or its agents to portray the world in a particular way and to privilege a particular view of reality.

The purpose of this chapter is to introduce a framework for the study of the rhetoric of government commissions. It will begin with a rationale for considering government commissions as an appropriate object of study. After enumerating the distinguishing features of government commissions, the chapter will feature an extended discussion of the logic of approaching government commissions as rhetorical artifacts. Finally, three case studies are briefly considered in order to demonstrate possible approaches to the rhetorical criticism of government commissions.

WHY STUDY COMMISSIONS?

The easy answer is that we should study them because they are intrinsically interesting. In the past ten years, major government commissions have investigated and reported on police brutality, the *Challenger* disaster, the status of children, government waste, obscenity and pornography, funding for the arts, hunger, organized crime, and chemical warfare. Not all government commissions are engaged in such high profile controversies; during the same time period, government commissions have also studied the future of Arctic research, pay scales for government employees, and the optimum number of people in an airline crew. Nonetheless, we are drawn to government commissions because they deal with the great issues of the day. Political scientist David Flitner (1986) has suggested that "commissions reflect their eras and some of the most volatile, unavoidable issues extant. . . . [T]he commissions have played a part in raising awareness, setting new terms of debate, and bringing about changes in attitudes" (195).

The intense public controversy surrounding the release of the final report of the Attorney General's Commission on Pornography (also known as the Meese Commission) in July 1986 serves as a case in point. Standing, ironically, in the main foyer of the Department of Justice beneath the nearly naked figure of Lady Justice, Edwin Meese received the almost 2,000-page report that called for citizen mobilization against adult bookstores and vigorous prosecution of the organized crime element running the pornography business in the United States. The Commission's whirlwind of public hearings, testimony from mystery witnesses, and tours of adult bookstores had made headlines for months prior to the release of its final report. The anti-censorship forces had been called to action by the American Civil Liberties Union (ACLU) and the National Coalition Against Censorship. Barry Lynn of the ACLU traveled around the country creating headlines as a one-man "truth squad," criticizing everything from the choice of commissioners to the differential treatment of its witnesses. There is little doubt that issues related to the control of pornography and the larger question of its social impact had become focused at this point in the mid-1980s. The Meese Commission served as the lightning rod for the discussion of these important issues.

A second reason to study commissions is that they demonstrate both the advantages and problems of governing in an open society. At times in this nation's history, issues have developed that seemed to be almost too important or too sensitive for the normal governmental processes. The Warren Commission was established to investigate the assassination of President Kennedy at a time when confusion and fear reigned. Shaken by the riots of the summer of 1967, President Johnson sought to demonstrate that the federal government had mobilized in response and established the Kerner Commission to investigate the causes of the riots. Lacking an independent mechanism for investigating the causes of the beating of Rodney King and the role of the police department in Los Angeles, Mayor Tom Bradley asked Warren Christopher to head an independent investigatory commission. The report, issued just over four months later, found extensive evidence of widespread racism in the department and a lack of accountability in matters of police brutality. In each of these cases, because of the need to go outside of normal governmental structures for answers, the shortcomings of the political system to address certain kinds of problems come into bold relief. In the case of Los Angeles, the absence of civilian review in the police department served not only as the impetus for the Christopher Commission but as the basis for important policy changes in the structure of Los Angeles city government as well.

A final reason to study commissions has to do with their sheer numbers and influence. Although the use of commissions at the federal level can be traced to President George Washington during the Whiskey Rebellion in 1794, the first president to make extensive use of commissions in their present form was Theodore Roosevelt. In an attempt to educate the American people and the Congress about the importance of acting to preserve the country's natural resources, Roosevelt appointed a Public Lands Commission, an Inland Waterway Commission, and a National Conservation Commission. So taken was Roosevelt with the work of the latter group that in transmitting its report to Congress, he called it "one of the most fundamentally important documents ever laid before the American people" (Flitner 1986, 13).

The social unrest of the 1960s and 1970s merely accelerated a trend at the federal level toward using commissions. Both Presidents Johnson and Nixon, faced with enormous social upheaval, turned to the opportunities afforded by commission creation. The decade from 1963 to 1973 saw the establishment of such weighty advisory panels as the President's Commission on the Assassination of President Kennedy (the Warren Commission), the President's Commission on Law Enforcement and the Administration of Justice (the Katzenbach Commission), the National Advisory Commission on Civil Disorders (the Kerner Commission), the National Commission on the Causes and Prevention of Violence (the Eisenhower Commission), the Commission on Obscenity and Pornography (the Lockhart Commission), the President's Commission on Campus Unrest (the Scranton Commission), and the National Commission on Marijuana and Drug Abuse (the Shafer Commission), among others. During 1989, the last year for which reasonably accurate figures were available, the General Services Administration (GSA) reported that over 1,000 advisory committees were operating at all levels of the federal government with forty-nine of these directly advising the President (U.S. General Services Administration 1990, 1). As these figures suggest, however, defining what is and is not a government commission needs to be discussed.

DEFINING COMMISSIONS

Because so little has been written on commissions from a communication perspective, it makes sense to survey the extant work in the social sciences for clues to the definitional problem. The literature from political science has struggled with the prospect of defining government commissions. While precise definitions for so fluid an institution may be difficult, Thomas Wolanin, in his study of presidential advisory commissions from Truman to Nixon, isolated six essential characteristics. He defined a commission as "(1) a corporate group created by a public act, (2) which is advisory to the President, (3) all members of which are appointed directly by the President, (4) which is ad hoc, (5) at least one member of which is public, and (6) whose report is public" (1975, 7).

Wolanin's definition is probably more exacting and exclusive than we need for the present study, but a few characteristics are worth mentioning for our purposes. His insistence on a corporate group suggests that the commission must not merely be a working group within a government agency or department, but have an independent existence and identity. From a rhetorical standpoint, the ability to identify the source of a message and, as a result, discuss its credibility and ethos is critical. An advisory body is one that has no direct power to enforce its suggestions or policy recommendations; it must do its work by persuading others to adopt its recommendations and by making its report to the public. Sometimes the audience of the report may be the general public; in other cases, it may be profitable to look to the singular audience of the President. Under Wolanin's criteria, however, not all commissions are commissions. The Interstate Commerce Commission and the Federal Communication Commission carry the correct name, but their permanent standing and their ability to promulgate administrative regulations on their own accord would eliminate them from consideration in these studies. In 1986, as a response to a series of terrorist events involving Americans, George Bush chaired the aptly named Vice President's Task Force on Combatting Terrorism. It issued a thirty-three-page report detailing some of the government's responses to these threats. For our purposes however, it does not meet Wolanin's criteria because all of the members were drawn exclusively from within the administration. No members of the public were included.

Alan Dean (1969) has suggested a similar list of characteristics in his discussion of ad hoc commissions for policy formation. Dean suggests that such bodies are: temporary, composed of multiple members, limited in scope to a particular area of inquiry, given official status, purely advisory, and composed in whole or in part of private citizens (101–102). Such commissions, Dean argues, are the analogs of the British Royal Commissions in England or the official commissions of inquiry in Canada. He also recognizes that the same model for policy formulation is sometimes used at the state and local level as well.

David Flitner (1986), while adopting most of Wolanin's framework, describes presidential commissions functionally as "investigatory bodies, generally without statutory bases, which within a defined purview are directed to seek out all relevant information, sift it, piece it together, arrive at conclusions, and, on the basis of their conclusions, make recommendations for legislative and/or social action" (16).

Neither Wolanin nor Flitner would suggest that the internal advisory groups commonly found in various government agencies are sufficiently similar to the examples discussed thus far to merit their inclusion. Nor would we want to extend the net of this investigation to include those bodies. Although there exists a Tea Tasting Board and a Federal Condor Advisory Committee (Tutchings 1979), their significance is marginal.

With the exception of Dean's brief reference, the primary political science literature on commissions does not extend the discussion to non-federal commissions. For our purposes, that is a significant oversight. Two rhetorically significant state and local commissions come to mind: the Cuomo Commission on Trade and Competitiveness, and the Independent Commission on the Los Angeles Police Department. The Cuomo Commission was established in late 1986, ostensibly to investigate the place of New York State in the global economy. Populated by some of the same policy advisors appointed to Bill Clinton's cabinet, the Cuomo Commission (1988) was more likely a well-crafted public relations effort designed to position Mario Cuomo and his economic theories in a position to have a major influence in the national Democratic scene. The Independent Commission on the Los Angeles Police Department, also known as the Christopher Commission, was initiated shortly after the Rodney King incident in April 1991 to investigate the extent to which structural problems in the police force training and supervisory systems were responsible for the reactions of the officers involved in the beating. Neither of these commissions is federally based and yet each is potentially an important object of study. The fact that the majority of the extant literature focuses on presidential commissions should not deter us from considering these other bodies. Each commission was ad hoc; each had a clear investigatory mandate outside of the normal governmental structures; each consisted of members of the public appointed by the appropriate executive branch leader; neither had the authority to do any more than make recommendations; and both commissions concluded with the issuance of a very interesting public report.

Wolanin's definitional scheme is useful as a guide to the kinds of investigatory and advisory bodies most appropriate for our purposes here. While it is likely that presidential or federal executive branch commissions may hold the most allure for critics, we should recognize the possible importance of subnational commissions for rhetorical critics. Even investigatory committees of the Congress, while not specifically meeting all of the criteria of Wolanin's definition, may operate as analogs to commissions established by the executive branch.

Another method of characterizing commissions is by function. Though the reasons for commission creation are often subject to speculation, both Wolanin and Flitner, in the two most comprehensive recent treatments of government commissions, suggest a variety of possible motives for commission creation. The first is to engage in policy analysis. Of the ninety-nine commissions he examined between 1945 and 1973, Thomas Wolanin proclaims that "the stated goal for every presidential commission is to be a policy analyst" (1975, 13). This seems to be the primary purpose for over half of the commissions he examined and was a clear secondary purpose for the rest. Either because of the intractable nature of the problem or the crisis it may have precipitated, commissions offer a forum outside of the traditional governmental arena to bring in the best and the brightest to deal with an important social issue.

Wolanin labels a second function "window dressing," an unfortunate label because it trivializes its importance. He suggests that this function is designed

to help sell or market a proposal to which the President is already committed. Commissions created with this in mind are expected to facilitate the acceptance of a presidential initiative by other political actors, usually Congress and the federal bureaucracy, whose consent is required for authoritative action. The President has already decided what to do in these cases, and the commission is meant to help him to do it and, to a certain extent, to tell him how to do it. (15)

Building a consensus for political action by placing the imprimatur of a blue-ribbon commission remains a legitimate function in an open society where even the best of policy proposals often languish for lack of a constituency. Certainly the Meese Commission and its focus on a regulatory scheme for controlling pornographic material gave license to Meese's Department of Justice to aggressively enforce obscenity laws. Federal prosecutions increased by 400 percent in the years following the Meese Commission's enthusiastic support for the strict control of erotic materials (Demac 1990).

A third purpose for commissions suggested by Wolanin involves long-range education. To the extent that commissions help to place issues on the public agenda, they can be instrumental in educating the public. Wolanin illustrates this function with reference to President Kennedy's Panel on Mental Retardation (1961–1962), which

spotlighted and made legitimate this formerly taboo problem. This legitimization and symbolic elevation of a problem to the status of a "national goal" . . . is a minimal purpose for almost every commission. Creating a commission is a tangible expression of the President's concern for a problem and an indication that he believes that the Congress, the bureaucracy, the parties, and the public should also be concerned. (1975, 21)

Crisis response is the fourth purpose suggested by Wolanin; though it was quantitatively less significant in the sample of government commissions he studied, it is, nonetheless, a critical function for these bodies. Following the assassination of John F. Kennedy, the nuclear crisis at Three Mile Island, and the ill-fated flight of the space shuttle *Challenger,* the response by the government was to appoint a commission to help neutralize the crisis in confidence. Flitner (1986) suggests that commissions can

represent a symbolic tool with which the President communicates awareness of a situation that is of concern to his constituency, reassures the disaffected that they will not be ignored, and responds to the sense that he must do *something*. Commissions are one place to start doing something, especially when there may be potential danger in leaving a problem unattended any longer. (20)

Flitner uses the term "symbolic reassurance" to describe this function of commissions. Often, there are unreasonable expectations about what a President can actually do in the face of a national crisis. Following the shootings of Martin Luther King, Jr., and Robert Kennedy, President Johnson, desperately unsure of what to do, turned once again to a commission for answers. He created the National Commission on the Causes and Prevention of Violence, asked Milton Eisenhower to serve as chairman, and in the process, triggered what may have been one of the most thorough and thought-provoking inquiries into all phases of violence. The broad-ranging report included a historical overview, a discussion of the role of firearms and the media in promoting the acceptability of violence, and eighty-one recommendations for dealing with the social conditions conducive to violence (Flitner 1986, 36).

A final purpose for the creation of commissions could be considered the converse of crisis management. What Wolanin terms "issue avoidance," less charitable critics might call sandbagging. One way to deal with an intractable problem confronting a president (or other chief executive) may be to consign it to the ignominy of an underfunded, unpublicized commission. While delay may be viewed as a kind of negative action, it may also have a beneficial effect. One advantage of a crisis-related commission is that it offers something of a cooling-off period during which the emotions of the moment can be quelled, allowing rational analysis to proceed. George Sulzner has suggested that "the ability of a national governmental study commission to channel controversy into more objective settings, which may cool heated emotions somewhat, further promotes political pacification" (1974, 216). He warns, however, that the pacification "has a utility of limited duration. When it becomes apparent to the advocates of change that a study commission is being used as a tool for policy procrastination, their previous pleasure is likely to become active criticism" (Sulzner 1974, 216).

How can we define commissions? The literature from the field of political science suggests that governmental, ad hoc advisory groups, with independent status, whose members include private citizens and who make their findings public, qualify for commission status. They need not be found exclusively at the federal level; in fact, they may be found at all levels of government. They are incorporated with the purpose of formulating policy options, providing symbolic reassurance, educating the public, or mobilizing support. Commissions may be instituted to delay action but often that delay will serve the important function of providing a cooling-off period.

Throughout all of these discussions, it should be apparent that much of the work of government commissions can be analyzed from a rhetorical perspective. Commissions offer a view of the world along with suggestions for improvement. If the view presented is not compelling, if its final report is not persuasive, if it fails to provide the symbolic reassurance that the government is acting in the public's best interest, if its attempts at mobilization fail, then the failures may be linked to the rhetorical inadequacies of the commission, its report, or its strategic choices. For the same reasons, when commissions succeed we need to know why.

STUDYING COMMISSIONS RHETORICALLY

In suggesting that we think about studying commissions rhetorically, I want to make clear that our interest is not a hegemonic one. It is not the intention of this chapter to suggest that the *only* productive approach to the study of commissions is one based in communication and rhetorical theory. My interest is not to supplant the studies done in sociology, public policy, or political science but to supplement them. Rather than try to answer the question posed by both Wolanin and Flitner or, more recently, by Tutchings—are commissions effective in accomplishing their stated goals?—we might more profitably ask the question: Why is it that some commissions fail while others succeed?

Consider, for example, two important commissions of the late 1960s. Although its final report sold 30,000 copies in three days and 1,600,000 copies from March to June 1968, the Kerner Commission remains a case of mixed results. The final report so enraged President Johnson that he withheld comment for an entire week and then "praised only the scope of the *Report* and the energy and dedication of the commissioners" (Flitner 1986, 109). Aides described Johnson as furious with Kerner's conclusions, in particular its discussion of white racism and its recommendation that the government spend $30 billion for new social programs (Flitner 1986, 110–11). Despite the icy reception offered by Johnson, the Kerner Commission Report had a profound effect on the discussion of race relations in America. Its final report was adopted as a text in high school, college, and police-community relations classes around the country (Flitner 1986, 153, 157).

While the Kerner Commission may have been one of the most written-about government commissions in history, there has been no attempt to discuss its rhetorical choices. Coming so close as it did to the elections of 1968, commissioners must have known that this conclusion would enrage a president still considering reelection:

This is our basic conclusion: Our nation is moving toward two societies, one black, one white—separate and unequal. . . . What white Americans have never fully understood—but the Negro can never forget—is that white society is deeply implicated in the ghetto. White institutions created it, white institutions maintain it, and white society condones it. (*Report of the National Advisory Commission on Civil Disorders* 1968, 1, 16)

Success or failure, the Kerner Commission and its rhetorical choices remain largely uninvestigated from a rhetorical perspective.

The second commission from the late 1960s with curiously mixed results was the Commission on Obscenity and Pornography. After two years of independent research, the Commission came to a decidedly unpopular conclusion—that there was little scientific evidence suggesting a causal relationship between viewing pornographic materials and anti-social behavior. As a result the Commission went further to suggest that with certain exceptions the laws restricting consenting adults from receiving these materials should be repealed. Although lauded by social scientists as the most comprehensive study ever done on the effects of pornographic materials, the response from the political community was stony silence. Nixon's response was unambiguous: "I categorically reject its morally bankrupt conclusions and major recommendations. So long as I am in the White House, there will be no relaxation of the effort to control and eliminate smut from our national life" (Flitner 1986, 113).

A lengthy Minority Report, authored by Charles Keating, Jr. (yes, the Savings and Loan Keating), and the Rev. Morton Link, kept the Commission's report from speaking with a single voice. Denouncing the Danish solution of decriminalization of pornographic materials, Keating railed in his statement against the majority's conclusions:

What is rotten in Denmark is already positively putrid in this country—and all this only in anticipation of the release of the soft-line Majority Report! . . . I can only comment that if the majority . . . has its way . . . we will witness complete moral anarchy in this country that will soon spread to the entire free world. (*Report of the Commission on Obscenity and Pornography* 1970, 615)

It was not until the report of the Attorney General's Commission on Pornography in 1986 that the government had the authoritative ammunition to carry on a protracted war against the proliferation of pornography.

Why did the 1970 Commission on Obscenity and Pornography fail to move the political establishment? Is there any way they could have delivered their conclusions in a manner more likely to facilitate their acceptance? Could the final report of the Kerner Commission, so exacting and blunt in its condemnation of white, middle-class racism, have been crafted in such a way as to prevent a hardening of attitudes and a polarization of views? Was Johnson's response inevitable given the conclusions the Commission sought to present? Are these two instances of "failure" in fact failures at all? These are the kinds of questions to which a rhetorical critic may reasonably attend.

How, then, do commissions function rhetorically? Roderick Hart (1990) has suggested a number of senses in which rhetoric functions.

Applying some of these to the rhetoric of government commissions should yield some insight that allows for a more educated answer. Hart suggests that, among other things, rhetoric distracts. He notes that

we do not just give away our attention, so it takes rhetoric at its best to side-track us. . . . [T]he rhetor constantly requests listeners to think about this topic, not that one; to consider this problem, not those they are currently thinking about; to try out this solution, not that endorsed by the opposing speaker. In this sense, rhetoric operates like a good map. (22–23)

Among other ways, commission rhetoric distracts by trying to narrow the latitude of choices that the audience has by controlling the definition of the problem being confronted (for example, were the riots acts of violence or responses to a racist society?). Commissions can also distract audiences by establishing the acceptable criteria for a solution (such as privileging the rights of consenting adults over the government's interest in control-ling erotica).

Hart next suggests that rhetoric enlarges. His description almost seems to be written with commissions in mind:

[M]odern persuaders are the heralds of old. They move among us singing the siren song of change, asking us to open our worlds a bit and to study a new way of looking at things, to consider a new solution to an old problem (or an old solution to a problem we did not know we had). Rhetoric oper-ates like a kind of intellectual algebra, asking us to equate things we had never before considered equatable. (1990, 25)

By equating decriminalization with control, the 1970 Commission on Obscenity and Pornography asked (perhaps unsuccessfully) for a radical change in America's approach to dealing with pornography. By encourag-ing novel associations of ideas in some cases and careful instances of dis-association in others, rhetoricians and government commissions do their best to shift frames and reconstruct reality for their audiences.

Another important function suggested by Hart is the naming power of rhetoric. He notes that naming "helps listeners become comfortable with new ideas and provides listeners with an acceptable vocabulary for talking about these ideas" (1990, 26). In tackling the dizzying complexity of eco-nomic theories associated with international trade and competitiveness, the New York State Cuomo Commission labeled the nation's approach to economic growth in the first half of the twentieth century as "the American Formula." Responsible for unprecedented economic growth and astounding increases in worker productivity, the American Formula is a label that sanctifies past practices but sets the stage for the Cuomo Commission's list of recommendations and points us toward, predictably enough, "the *New* American Formula." It is a strategy "based on a new insight: in a global economy, our consumption will depend upon increasing our production. Therefore, America needs a producer strategy in which both the public and private sectors learn to work together in a productive partnership" (*The Cuomo Commission Report* 1988, 236). The complex array of the Cuomo Commission's specific recommendations are all given coherence and legitimacy with the application of a label that would seem to suggest that the New American Formula is the logical successor to the policies that encouraged the explosive economic growth in the first part of this century.

Finally, from Hart's list we find that rhetoric empowers. It gives voice to the disgruntled and forces rhetors to be flexible in adapting to their audience. Hart writes:

Social power, then, often derives from rhetorical strength. Grand ideas, deeply felt beliefs, and unsullied ideologies are sources of power too, but, as Plato has told us, none of these factors can be influential without a delivery system, without rhetoric. Purity of heart, honest intentions, and a spotless record of integrity are assets to a political speaker, but they are hardly enough to sustain a campaign unless they are shared with the voters. (1990, 27)

No matter how accomplished its experts, no matter how passionately it may endorse a set of recommendations, a government commission must still communicate that message to its audience. Whether narrowly conceived as the chief executive who created the commission or more broadly considered as the public, the audience for a government commission's rhetoric faces an empowered constituency determined to present its view of the world, a view most profitably presented when adapted to the values and beliefs of the audience.

Why study government commissions rhetorically? As with any study of rhetoric, the critic attempts one of three broadly conceived goals: first, to understand the success or failure of the rhetorical act; second, to advance our understanding of rhetorical theory by studying a significant artifact through the lens provided by the theory; and third, for ideological reasons, to investigate the systematic bias possible as the language of government commissions functions either to perpetuate the existing relations of domination in a society or to provide an alternate vision of society able to transcend that domination. By investigating the ways in which government commission rhetoric distracts, enlarges, names, and empowers, critics contribute powerfully to our understanding of human relations.

ASSESSING GOVERNMENT COMMISSIONS RHETORICALLY

To this point, we have provided a rationale for studying government commissions and for studying those commissions rhetorically. What we are still lacking, however, is a guide to proceeding with the critical enterprise. Before laying out such a guide, a few caveats and confessions are in order. First, what follows is a preliminary step in the rhetorical analysis of government commissions. It is not meant to be an exhaustive listing of relevant concepts or methodologies. Second, I remain firmly committed to pluralistic approaches to rhetorical criticism. Although it is likely that critics will find some approaches more useful than others, the featuring of any given method in this chapter is not meant to serve as an argument for the exclusion of others. Finally, this section is meant to share possible points of entry into the rhetoric of government commissions; it is not meant to straightjacket prospective critics with prescriptive formulae. With that in mind, the critic concerned with a comprehensive analysis of the rhetoric of any particular government commission may want to address some or all of the following elements.

The Socio-Political Background of a Commission

Any government commission exists within a particular socio-political milieu with which a critic must contend. For example, discussing Theodore Roosevelt's Commission on Public Lands in 1903 makes sense only insofar as one is familiar with the attitude of the public toward conservation, Theodore Roosevelt as a leader, and the other issues of the day contending for the public's attention. Given the various motives an executive may have for creating a commission, it seems prudent for the critic to go beyond the stated goals for its establishment to see if other motives were even more important. Hart, in a discussion of the assessment of speech situations, suggested that a thorough analysis would include an analysis of power, ego needs, social obstacles, the speaker's priorities, the audience's priorities and the speaker-audience relationship (1990, 68–69). An analysis of the social and political climate of the mid-1980s at the time of the Meese Commission would include an appreciation for the dynamics of the religious right, the reception of the previous commission on the subject of pornography, the changes in the types of erotic materials available to the public (no doubt more violent and graphic than those common twenty years earlier), and the political priorities of the Reagan administration and its relationship with the American public.

The Commission's Charge

A unique element in the establishment of a commission involves the public document that gives it life. The commission's charge, issued by the agency or official with the authority to convene such a body, expresses the official list of expectations and goals for the commission. It may include specifically what is or is not relevant material for the commission's study as well as what form the final report ought to take. The charge from the Independent Commission in Los Angeles (the Christopher Commission) is typical:

The Commission's work will be primarily prospective, focusing on needed changes to the department's methods of selecting, training, promoting, and disciplining its officers. The Special Commission will not adjudicate individual complaints. That is the job of the Police Commission, the Chief and the LAPD. The Special Independent Commission may, however, consider particular cases in order to determine the existence of a pattern, practice, or general condition. The Commission will also consider recommendations for possible charter amendments, new laws and steps that the Mayor, the City Council, the Police Commission or the Chief should take. (*Report of the Independent Commission on the Los Angeles Police Department* 1991, Appendix 1)

Beneath the bureaucratic prose, an important restriction was placed on the Commission. It was not the task of the Christopher Commission to determine whether or not the individual officers in the Rodney King case had overstepped the boundaries of excessive force. Rather, it sought to place the incident in the broader context of an analysis of training, recruitment and supervisory practices, and the effectiveness of the citizen complaint system presently used by the Los Angeles Police Department (LAPD).

Sometimes a commission can do its best to fulfill a charge and still be rebuffed by the politician who formed it, simply for doing its job. In his charge to the Kerner Commission on Civil Disorders, President Johnson urged, in the most passionate terms, that the Commission follow their hearts to the truth. He urged the Commission to "let your search be free. Let it be untrammeled by what has been called the 'conventional wisdom.' As best you can, find the truth, the whole truth, and express it in your report. I hope you will be inspired by a sense of urgency, but also conscious of the danger that lies always in hasty conclusions" (*Report of the National Advisory Commission on Civil Disorders* 1968, 296–97). When the Kerner Commission came back with the fundamental conclusion that "our Nation is moving toward two societies, one black, one white— separate and unequal," Johnson felt betrayed. Be careful what you wish for; sometimes you get what you want!

The Commissioners and Commission Staff

It is particularly important for a critic to investigate the people appointed to a commission as a prelude to any discussion of the commission's credibility or ethos. Although they are constrained in their actions by the commission's charge and their fellow commissioners, individuals may still have considerable influence. In the case of the Meese Commission, liberal critics scrutinized each of the appointments and, even before the release of the final report, complained that the deck had been stacked (Demac 1990). In particular, they were appalled that the majority of the commissioners already seemed to have publicly stated positions on the question of the harm of pornographic materials. Even more alarming to some critics was the appointment of Henry Hudson, a former U.S. Attorney and head prosecutor for Arlington County, Virginia, with a reputation for vigorously (and even recklessly) enforcing anti-obscenity statutes. When Father Bruce Ritter, a Catholic priest who served as the head administrator for Covenant House, a runaway shelter in New York City, and James Dobson, the president of a group called Focus on the Family, were also included, liberals fretted that the die had been cast and the religious right had the Commission firmly in its corner.

The tendency for commissions to become known informally by the last name of their chairperson also speaks to the importance of ethos. When newly sworn-in President Lyndon Johnson appointed Chief Justice Earl Warren to his commission to investigate the assassination of John F. Kennedy, he hoped to establish the commission's credibility as beyond reproach. As yet another example of the power of naming, this practice sometimes takes on the variation of being named for the political leader who formed the commission; thus the Meese Commission and the Cuomo

Commission draw their informal names not from their chairs but their conveners. It might be interesting to inquire why the Meese Commission did not come to be called the Hudson Commission and why the final report of the New York State Commission on Trade and Competitiveness carries Cuomo's moniker and not that of Lewis Kaden, the Commission chairman.

Another line of inquiry relevant to commission membership popular in the political science field has to do with an analysis of the types of people appointed to commissions. Terrence Tutchings (1979), for instance, analyzed the ninety-nine major commissions appointed between 1945 and 1973. He came to the none too surprising conclusion that of the 1,269 commissioners listed for these bodies, nearly two-thirds were clearly identifiable as members of what Thomas Dye has called "America's governing elite" (38–39). Any suggestion that commissions might be a significant force for change in a society would no doubt be tempered by the fact that so many of their participants would seem to have a vested interest in maintaining the status quo. It may be that who is not represented on government commissions is as important as who is.

In addition to the commissioners themselves, government commissions are often supported by a huge army of lawyers, technical consultants, and administrative assistants, all of whom report to the executive director of the commission. After the chair of the commission, the executive director may wield the greatest power. Responsible for coordinating and hiring the staff, the executive director is responsible for much of the day-to-day work of the commission. To the extent that a commission may be underfunded or understaffed, a critic may need to evaluate the competence of the support staff in order to get a complete picture of the constraints under which the final report was produced.

Finally, understanding the commission membership may give a critic schooled in communication theory a better grasp of the potential for conflict in commission deliberations. David Flitner has suggested that there are powerful forces operating on commissions to achieve unanimity (1986, 87–89). That conflict, Flitner notes, "may be restrained by a desire for unanimity growing out of the belief that a united front conveys more legitimacy than does a fragmented one" (88). When commissioners are unable to maintain consensus, the subsequent fracturing may lead to opposing coalitions, rancor, the development of minority reports, and even attempts at sabotage. To the extent that commission meetings and hearings are open to the public, additional data on the dynamics of the conflict may be available.

The Final Report

In many senses, observers of government commissions participate in a metonymic fallacy that the final report *is* the commission. That fallacy is compounded when critics attend only to executive summaries or lists of recommendations. While the final report may be the most important "text" the commission may produce, it is not the only data that a critic using a communication perspective could examine. The executive order or public law creating a commission often contains a provision requiring that the commission make an interim or preliminary report. Staff studies authorized by the commission are often released in advance of the final commission report. In the case of the National Commission on the Causes and Prevention of Violence (the Eisenhower Commission), the task force on historical and comparative approaches to violence released its landmark study, *The History of Violence in America*. In addition, the Eisenhower Commission released a well-publicized task force study on the violence that took place during the 1968 Democratic National Convention in Chicago.

Government commissions also release technical and staff reports depending on their budget and the perceived importance of the data. The 1970 Commission on Obscenity and Pornography had sufficient funding to sponsor independent research by prominent social scientists on the question of the effect of viewing erotic materials. Their studies were published by the commission in technical reports. Seventeen years later, the Meese Commission, which critics claimed was severely underfunded, sponsored no new research and released only its own voluminous final report of over 1,900 pages.

In one sense, the final report should be the primary focus of a rhetorical critic. Hart has argued that

a message is the visible record of a complex interaction. The rhetorical critic focuses heavily on message cues, because that is all that is left after a dynamic human encounter has occurred. Often, the message itself contains only the slightest traces of this complexity and so the critic must "put back" such elements to make the message/situation as whole as possible. (1990, 73)

Because commissioners know that their final report will be their most widely read, most publicized product, a critic would pay special attention to the strategic choices, the language, and the arguments of the final report.

Assessing Commission Impact

While the enterprise of rhetorical criticism has grown beyond the absolute necessity of determining effect, assessing the impact of a government commission is a logical object of study for political scientists and rhetorical critics alike. The political science literature takes the issue of commission impact to be the defining issue in determining worth. Although the popular press may have at times presented a less than charitable view of the work done by commissions, both Flitner and Wolanin have argued that commissions perform a valuable policy function in government. Flitner's conclusion is worth noting:

Commissions have become a tool by which the President and Congress seek information and advice. They collect facts on a grand scale, sometimes in an unprecedented manner, and render the considered opinions of their members regarding the subject at hand and what should be done about it. Beyond this, responsibility moves to others. *Commissions can compel only through their words.* (1986, 195, emphasis added)

Wolanin's conclusion is even more positive. He notes that typically commissions "received presidential support and were very often an important contribution to proposed or implemented changes in federal policy. Commissions also have a broad and significant impact as educators of the general public, government officials, the professional community, and their own members" (1973, 193).

More contemporary government commissions may have met with less enthusiastic support; nonetheless, assessing effect solely by counting the number of recommendations that ultimately find their way into policy may be an unnecessarily narrow interpretation of effect. As Wolanin suggested, the educational mission of commissions is significant and perhaps underappreciated. In order to assess the effect of government commissions, the critic needs to have a full appreciation of the goals the commission was intended to fulfill. If the actual goal of the creation of a commission is to divert attention, to delay or to avoid action, then implementation of commission recommendations may actually be judged, from the chief executive's perspective, to be a failure.

THE RHETORICAL CRITICISM OF GOVERNMENT COMMISSIONS

There is no single rhetorical theory or critical methodology that would be intrinsically more valuable than others in the study of the rhetoric of government commissions. It would be folly to suggest that any single approach could provide critics with an interpretative lens that would be, in all cases, superior to others. The artifacts simply vary too widely in structure, tone, and argumentative strategy for there to be any unified theory that would accommodate all of them. The case studies in this book exemplify how a pluralistic approach can yield important critical insights.

For that reason, I remain strongly committed to the notion of critical pluralism. Because an important goal of this book is to encourage other critics to see government commissions as a fruitful area of study, I think it would be productive to examine brief examples, critical vignettes if you will, as a way of demonstrating some possible avenues of analysis. These vignettes are not intended to be complete critical analyses, but rather introductory probes, the rhetorical equivalent of a pilot test. In the two cases that follow, I will establish some of the background necessary for the critical exercise and then make some preliminary assessments about each commission's rhetoric.

The Christopher Commission: An Argumentative Analysis

The entire nation was sickened by the videotape broadcast of members of the Los Angeles Police Department beating what appeared to be a defenseless Rodney King following a high speed chase through the San Fernando Valley in southern California. The videotape, shot by George Holliday in the early morning of March 3, 1991, recorded officers of the LAPD administering fifty-six baton strokes as well as numerous kicks to King's head and body.

In the wake of widespread community outrage and calls for the resignation of Chief of Police Daryl Gates, two separate investigations were launched. On March 27, in response to growing criticism of his actions and the Department's efforts to investigate its officers, Gates issued a ten-point plan that included the appointment of a five-person investigatory panel to be headed by retired California Supreme Court Justice John Arguelles. Just four days later, Mayor Tom Bradley announced the formation of the Independent Commission on the Los Angeles Police Department to be headed by Warren Christopher, a former Deputy Attorney General and Deputy Secretary of State in the Carter administration. More important, Christopher had served as the vice chairman of the McCone Commission that had investigated the 1965 Watts Riots. Three days later, Arguelles and Christopher issued a joint statement agreeing to merge the two investigations. They intended to "proceed on a fully independent basis, with funding and staffing from private sources. . . . Our operations will be fully integrated, so as to enable us to proceed with maximum efficiency and without wasteful duplication" (*Report of the Independent Commission on the Los Angeles Police Department* 1991, Appendix 1). The Commission was charged with investigating the selection, training, and disciplining of police officers. In addition, they were asked to investigate the effectiveness of the citizen complaint system and the appropriateness of new City Charter provisions on the appointment, removal, and disciplining of the Chief of Police. Just three months later, the Christopher Commission's final report was delivered to Mayor Bradley and the people of Los Angeles.

The report is remarkable, first and foremost, for the enormous amount of work it seems to represent. Appendix II includes a list of commission and staff activities detailing the fact that attorneys serving as counsel to the Commission contributed more than 16,000 hours of work, and accountants and statistical consultants contributed more than 9,000 hours. Those figures seem frightfully large until one discovers the list of tasks completed during the Commission's fact-finding phase—nearly 700 interviews with LAPD officers, government officials, experts in the field, and community and religious leaders. The Commission and its staff reviewed over 100,000 pages of computer-generated transcripts from patrol car Mobile Digital Terminals (MDTs), over 1,200 personnel complaints, hundreds of case files on use of force reports, and personnel packages for 700 police officers. In addition, over 8,000 letters from the general public and computer databases with tens of thousands of records of use of force reports and personnel complaints were also investigated. This enormous mobilization, accomplished in just twelve weeks, seems almost too impressive. That the Commission felt compelled to share the specifics of its tasks in such detail suggests to this critic that the Commission was extremely sensitive about its credibility and how its task was to be accomplished.

Among the central claims of the Christopher Commission is that LAPD departmental culture and the lack of an effective disciplinary system have contributed to significant problems of racism, ethnic prejudices, sexism, and anti-gay bias. The report finds significant problems with the department's recruitment and training practices and a philosophy of policing that creates "a siege mentality that alienates the officer from the community" (*Report of the Independent Commission* 1991, xiv).

Most compelling, however, is the Commission's insistence that these problems are widespread: there are "a significant number of LAPD officers who repetitively misuse force and persistently ignore the written policies and guidelines of the Department regarding force" (ix). No indictment could be more compelling or plainly argued: it is stark and without qualification. The Commission goes on, however, to chronicle just how widespread the misconduct was. By invoking the power of technology to analyze the problem of brutality, the Commission hoped its findings in this area would take on added credibility:

The Commission's extensive computerized analysis of the data provided by the Department (personnel complaints, use of force reports, and reports of officer-involved shootings) shows that a significant group of problem officers poses a much higher risk of excessive force than other officers:— Of approximately 1,800 officers against whom an allegation of excessive force or improper tactics was made from 1986 to 1990, more than 1,400 had only one or two allegations. But 183 officers had four or more allegations, 44 had six or more, 16 had eight or more, and one had 16 such allegations. (*Report of the Independent Commission* 1991, x)

The Commission continues the "small group of problem officers" argument by noting that of the 6,000 officers involved in use of force reports from January 1987 through March 1991, more than 4,000 had fewer than five reports each but that sixty-three officers had twenty or more reports each! In its most understandable terms, the Commission notes that the top 5 percent of the officers (ranked by number of reports) accounted for more than 20 percent of all reports (*Report of the Independent Commission* 1991, x).

This is both a powerful and a dangerous argumentative strategy. Even as the Commission made arguments about the Department's structural problems and the pervasive culture of racism it allows, they are also making an argument that allows for the absolution of the majority of the Department and sanctions the scapegoating of the small group of "problem officers" as the real villains. The commissioners may find themselves to be the victims of their own statistical prowess. While their statistical consultants and the use of computerized databases allowed for the review of an enormous amount of data in a remarkably short period, it also guaranteed that the review would be superficial, well removed from the specifics of each event. To pass over the fact that 1,400 officers had only one or two allegations of excessive use of force on their way to singling out the small number that seemed completely out of control, the Commission essentially allows for the dismissal of the sins of the 1,400. In their zeal for quantitative thoroughness and precision, they have lost the qualitative information that might allow for an understanding of why police officers become abusive and how the behavior can be changed. The fact that an officer may have beaten a citizen to within an inch of his or her life—but only once or twice!—does not make the incident any less serious or the officer any less dangerous.

The strategy of focusing on the "problem officers" is further discredited by reports that fifteen months after issuance of the Christopher Commission report, the vast majority of the officers identified as involved in the most citizen complaints and excessive force charges were still on the force, still in jobs in which they have direct contact with the public ("LAPD's Unaddressed Problems" 1992). The Commission's report has had an impact in Los Angeles, albeit not in the way the city may have intended. One consequence of the report and its exacting documentation has been its usefulness for plaintiffs bringing damage suits against Los Angeles for police brutality. Paradoxically, even as the city is taking steps to understand and eliminate police brutality and excessive force, it may find itself increasingly vulnerable to lawsuits as the patterns of disciplinary negligence and widespread racism are documented with compelling precision. Donald Cook, a civil rights attorney involved in litigating police brutality suits, explained that: "It is a great piece of evidence—really trustworthy, credible evidence of what we have been saying for years" (Connelly 1992, B1). He was confident that the Christopher Commission report would not only enable him to win more suits, but that the evidence of negligence would additionally increase the size of the jury awards he was likely to win. Were the members of the Independent Commission on the Los Angeles Police Department in a Catch-22? If they are less than completely forthcoming on the scope and depth of the police brutality problem, they may risk the charge of a whitewash. If they release all the relevant data on the LAPD's problems, they may jeopardize the financial integrity of the city by making it overly vulnerable to opportunistic lawsuits.

A complete analysis of the argumentative strategy of the Christopher Commission awaits further study. Indeed, this Commission offers critics, using any number of approaches, a fruitful area of study. A closer look at the logic and power of the statistics presented in the report might offer the traditional-minded critic a surfeit of data. A dramatistic critic might explore the Christopher Commission's careful constellation of terms employed whenever it seeks to express disapproval. We know, for instance, from one member of the Commission that the language of the final document represented a substantial weakening of the outrage expressed in earlier drafts (Wilkinson 1991, B1). Scholars interested in organizational conflict might attempt to determine how the three Gates-appointed commissioners functioned as the Commission came to its conclusions. In short, critics should look at the Christopher Commission as an artifact capable of supporting inquiry using any number of critical approaches.

The Ideological Dimensions
of the Meese Commission Report

Even before the final report of the Attorney General's Commission on Pornography was released, it was being savaged by critics around the country. As detailed elsewhere in this book, nearly every aspect of the Commission's work was subject to attack—the qualifications and alleged biases of the commissioners, the motives of the Attorney General, the lack of funding, the lack of time, the differential treatment of witnesses, as well as what may be the most damning indictment against a government commission—the charge that the findings were preordained (Demac 1990). If the Commission's recommendations were a response to ideological pressures rather than the result of a commitment to open and honest inquiry, then it is appropriate to ask: In what ways does the Meese Commission function ideologically? Before answering that question, we need to consider briefly a framework for investigating rhetoric and ideology.

The literature associated with ideology is vast and often difficult to penetrate. For rhetorical critics, one of the most lucid discussions comes from John Thompson (1984) in his *Studies in the Theory of Ideology*. Thompson's approach is intrinsically related to rhetoric because he locates the study of ideology in the study of language:

Hence to study ideology is, in some part and in some way, to study language in the social world. . . . It is to study the ways in which the multifarious uses of language intersect with power, nourishing it, sustaining it, enacting it. . . . The theory of ideology invites us to see that language is not simply a structure which can be employed for communication or for entertainment, but a social-historical phenomenon which is embroiled in human conflict. (Thompson 1984, 2)

Language should be the focus of a study of ideological processes, because, Thompson argues, "it is primarily within language that meaning is mobilized in the interests of particular individuals and groups" (73). To conduct an ideological analysis therefore can be defined as "the study of the ways in which meaning serves to sustain or alter relations of domination" (Burnett 1989, 127).

Simply announcing the critic's intention to focus on the ideological power of language does not suggest a framework for analysis. Fortunately, Thompson, drawing heavily on the work of Anthony Giddens, has identified three central processes through which ideology operates in the social sphere:

In the first place, relations of domination may be sustained by being represented as legitimate. . . . A second way in which ideology operates is by means of dissimulation. Relations of domination which serve the interests of some at the expense of others may be concealed, denied, or blocked in various ways. . . . A third way in which ideology operates is by means of reification, that is, by representing a transitory, historical state of affairs as if it were permanent, natural, outside of time. (Thompson 1984, 130–31)

While Thompson is careful to qualify that these modalities are neither exhaustive nor necessarily mutually exclusive, they are nonetheless important strategies through which ideology operates. The task before us, therefore, is to attempt to discover if these processes are operating in the writings of the Meese Commission.

The forces of domination in a society operate far more successfully and efficiently if those who are being dominated either do not realize they are being oppressed or come to believe that such domination is necessary and natural. Conversely, it may be necessary to attempt to de-legitimize any threats to the existing order by casting them as unnatural or dangerous. This "naturalization of domination" forms the core of legitimation strategies.

In a sense, as long as government commissions maintain a positive public ethos, legitimation can be an inherent feature of their operation. Government commissions and the experts they employ help to privilege a certain set of facts, a particular perspective on the world. Whether or not the audience ultimately comes to share that view is, as W. David Snowball demonstrates in the next chapter, a measure of their legitimation. One could argue that the Meese Commission has come to legitimate the kind of evidence-free, conclusionary insistence of harm that Charles Keating, Jr., presented in his dissent to the 1970 Commission on Obscenity and Pornography. The voluminous report, the dramatic testimony of the victims of pornography, the field trips to the adult bookstores, the hundreds of pages of graphic summaries of plot lines and enormous lists of titles of pornographic books, magazines, and films all work together to give the reader the overwhelming impression that our society is being inundated by this material. "Of course this material is dangerous," one can imagine some censorship advocate saying, while waving a copy of the Commission's report, "This 2,000-page government report proves it!"

Chapter 9 of the Commission's report serves as a specific example of legitimation techniques. This 303-page chapter purports to be an analysis of the imagery found in magazines, books, and films in "adults only" pornographic outlets. For over one hundred pages, the titles of 2,325 magazines, 725 books, and 2,370 films are simply listed with no attending analysis or description. To what end? What is to be gained by knowing that patrons at the neighborhood adult bookstore might find the latest issue of *Rubber Quarterly*, a paperback entitled *Brenda's Eager Surrender*, or a video called *Vixens of Kung Fu*? The remaining 200 pages are filled with graphic synopses of plots and story lines of various pornographic materials found in these stores. The descriptions are so graphic in fact that if the materials on which they are based could be legally restricted, one would probably have to enjoin the Commission's chapter as well. The morbid interest displayed by this chapter's inclusion in the report is quite remarkable. I would argue, however, that it has a powerful function of legitimation. By providing stark lists of titles and clinical descriptions of the action on videotapes or in magazines, whatever artistic, aesthetic, cathartic, or educational qualities these materials may have is destroyed. This chapter, in its own way, makes these materials even more sordid and lewd than they may already be. It de-legitimizes any potential for pro-social effects that these materials may have, effects that the 1970 Commission on Obscenity and Pornography sought to investigate and chronicle. In so doing, it reinforces and legitimates the Commission's conclusions about the necessity of controlling obscenity. By ripping these materials from their context, the Commission succeeds in eviscerating any complexity or nuance that might be present. I certainly do not want to be understood as arguing that all literature or films branded as pornographic contain some lofty artistic value. But decontextualizing any message, reducing it to a title or a lifeless description, has a powerful delegitimizing function. How much easier would it be to censor Robert Mapplethorpe's photography if we did not have to actually confront it and instead could simply judge it by its description? Even a powerful non-obscene work like Picasso's *Guernica* can be made to seem mundane and unimportant by reducing it to mere description, without interpretation or context.

Dissimulation, the second of Thompson's modalities, is the presentation of a sectional or individual interest as more universal. Dissimulation occurs when a speaker's individual interests are advanced at the expense of the audience's interests such that the audience is encouraged to misunderstand who would benefit from such a particular argument or point of view. Critics of the Meese Commission have argued that this is exactly what was operating as conservatives reached out to form a rather bizarre alliance with some feminists around the issue of pornography. Carole Vance, writing in *The Nation*, explained:

If the Meese Commission gets its way, it will be because it has launched a novel propaganda offensive that superficially uses the rhetoric of social science and feminism—*though not their substance*—to disguise the traditional right-wing moral agenda. As part of its ideological warfare the commission uses vague but powerful words . . . to unite what it hopes is a broad constituency in an unthinking but culturally overdetermined reaction that links sexuality and its surrogate, sexual images, with harm to women and death. (1986, 1)

This strategy of conciliation toward feminists did not escape notice even within the Commission itself. Acknowledging the conflicting views among feminists on the issue of pornography, three of the women on the Commission joined in a carefully worded statement that proclaimed:

We respect, however, the rights of all citizens to participate in legal activities if their participation is truly voluntary. We reject any judgmental and condescending efforts to speak on women's behalf as though they were helpless, mindless children. . . . We consider both the limitation of choices and sexual exploitation to be degrading attacks on the basic value and dignity of women. (*Report of the Commission on Obscenity and Pornography* 1970, 194)

The strategy of dissimulation is being practiced to the extent that the Meese Commission attempted to speak for women or to represent the Commission's views as those of the majority of women.

Of Thompson's modalities, reification may well be the most difficult of the three processes to apply to rhetorical analysis. The process of reification involves preventing the historical and mutable character of a culture from being identified as such. If the dominant interests in a culture are intimately tied to preservation of the status quo, then it is in their best interest to represent the status quo not merely as the latest instance of that culture but rather as "the way things have always been." Charles Keating, Jr., in his dissent to the 1970 Commission on Obscenity and Pornography, argued that the progress of Western Civilization has always depended on the suppression of sexually-oriented materials and that societies that have loosened those taboos have self-destructed (*Report of the Commission on Obscenity and Pornography* 1970, 578–79). By presenting history as a history of repression, Keating engaged in the reification of the existing laws against sexually explicit materials and was able to cast the majority's recommendation of deregulation as a radical policy option.

Thompson further explains that reification involves "representing processes as things, deleting agency and constituting time as an eternal extension of the present tense: all of these are so many syntactic ways to reestablish the dimension of society 'without history' at the heart of historical society" (1984, 137).

In the case of the Meese Commission, the existence of the 1970 Commission on Obscenity and Pornography is mentioned only briefly. Rather than dealing with the specific historical context for research on sexually explicit materials, the Meese Commission merely argues that our society has undergone tremendous technological changes since 1970 and that, though providing no proof, it finds that "it would be surprising to discover that these technological developments have had no effect on the production, distribution and availability of pornography" (*Attorney General's Commission on Pornography* 1986, 225–26). While recognizing that our culture may have changed somewhat in the intervening sixteen years, what is not so clear is the recognition of the Meese Commission's burden of rejoinder—that is, the Commission's responsibility to account for and respond to previous claims. In fact, it explicitly rejects any such responsibility (*Attorney General's Commission on Pornography* 1986, 225), and claims instead to be working "from a different perspective" (224–26). Indeed, one could argue that the different perspective it is working from is one that selects and quotes only from those sets of facts and scientific studies that support its point of view. Edward Donnerstein, perhaps the leading researcher in the country on the effects of viewing sexually explicit materials, felt that the Meese Commission had seriously mischaracterized the nature of his conclusions (Demac 1990, 47).

By presenting its report as "state of the art" research related to sexually explicit materials, the Meese Commission has eliminated the context for evaluating its claims and positioned itself to be *the* authoritative source on the question of effects and the role of government in restricting these materials. This exercise in reification in turn enhances the ideological impact of the work.

Other scholars may find various elements of the Meese Commission worthy of study. The Commission's discussion of and categorization scheme for defining sexually explicit materials would be a delightful artifact for a Burkean critic. Commissioner Frederick Schauer's careful explication of obscenity law and the legitimacy of governmental suppression would no doubt fascinate students of the First Amendment. Further attention needs to be directed to the rhetoric of the report itself and not simply to the various frailties of the Commission membership or funding. Critiques of this sort are made infinitely more compelling when the critic can point to evidence in the text where such problems have surfaced.

CONCLUSION

My goal in this chapter has been to initiate a discussion on critical approaches to the study of government commissions that feature communication. In providing a discussion of the goals of government commissions my intention was to provide critics with benchmarks by which they could begin to assess these panels and their role in American society.

The discussion of the various elements of government commissions is intended to provide prospective critics with initial points of entry into their analysis, not an exhaustive guide to all of the dimensions of government commissions that might be studied from a communication perspective. Finally, I have presented two critical vignettes designed to spark discussion and encourage further study into the realm of government commissions.

2

Rhetorical Constraints on Government Commissions

W. David Snowball

[R]esearch indicates that most presidents heed and act favorably
on the reports they receive from their commissions. (Bledsoe
1989, 151)

It is apparent that the findings and recommendations of
Presidential Commissions are not respected at the top levels of
government. (Mack 1975, 145)

[It's just] part of government by fire brigade. (Etzioni 1968, 18)

[I]t is a kind of Alice in Wonderland. (K. Clark, National
Advisory Commission on Civil Disorders 1968, 29)

Plato would have approved thoroughly of presidential commissions.
While we most frequently associate Plato with an anti-rhetorical stance
and with an unyielding philosophical purity, there is more complexity to
his vision than that. Plato separated the discovery of truth from the
rhetorical process. In contemporary terms, he believed that good leaders
came to understand what was in the best interest of the state without
resorting to any sort of public give-and-take on an issue. Once the leader
knew what was needed, he or she would use the instruments of mass
communication to convey the appropriate conclusions to an inattentive
public (Plato 1956, 273–74). Some things, though true, were far too
dangerous to be allowed to fall into unauthorized hands; these should be
"altogether suppressed." Failing that, such things should be told "to a

select few under oath of secrecy, at a rite which requires, to restrict it still further, the sacrifice not of a mere pig but of something large and difficult to get" (Plato 1941, 377–78). In her extended meditation on lying, Sissela Bok (1978, 176) recounted the context for one of Plato's discussions: Plato "used the expression 'noble lie' for the fanciful story that might be told to the people in order to persuade them to accept class distinctions and thereby safeguard social harmony" (Bok 1978, 176). Bok went on to excoriate Plato for his repeated defenses of governmental lying. As she compared passages in *The Republic*, she reached the unshakable conclusion that Plato endorsed active, frequent, unreined deception. Although translators differ sharply on the exact meaning of several passages, the interpretation most consistent with the general tenor of Platonic thought is somewhat more generous to Plato than Bok is. While Plato's ideal state is paternalistic, Plato's argument is not for a self-serving lie on the part of the ruler; rather, he argued for the moral legitimacy of a plausible rhetorical construction of reality that might dispel social tension. The most generous of Plato's translators, F. M. Cornford, rendered the discussion this way:

Again, a high value must be set on truthfulness. If we were right in saying that gods have no use for falsehood and it is useful to mankind only in the way of a medicine, obviously a medicine should be handled by no one but a physician. . . .[I]f anyone, then, is to practise [sic] deception, either on a country's enemies or on its citizens, it must be the Rulers of the Commonwealth, acting for its benefit. (Plato 1941, 389)

By Cornford's reading, made during the first years of World War II, Plato is not advocating either brainwashing or propaganda, but rather something closer to allegories and parables by which to catch the attention and spark the imagination (Plato 1941, 106). Thus, a passage that is frequently translated as permitting a "noble lie" becomes a "convenient fiction . . . a single bold flight of invention, which we may induce the community in general, and if possible the Rulers themselves, to accept." Such a carefully constructed story might, over the course of years and generations, "have a good effect in making them care more for the commonwealth and for one another" (Plato 1941, 414–15). This concession to the pragmatic needs of rulers is particularly striking in Plato's case, since his epistemology links the notion of truth so tightly to the notion of reality (Plato 1941, 382).

We can start with Plato because, as the parent of the systematic study of political theory, he framed half of all of the debates political scientists have ever held. Though he was appalled by it, Plato understood the unchanging dynamics of human interaction and sought to construct a system that could channel our chaotic energy into a constructive course. Part of the process of control, as Plato explained it, was the selective control of information and the strategic framing of social issues. This was precisely the role that necessitated the Republic's noble liars. Are, then, our presidential commissions today's noble liars? Plato's criteria for such a judgment were simple: Did they deceive, out of absolute necessity, for the good of the people as a whole? Keeping in mind the special nature of "noble lies," we will ultimately be able to conclude that the commissions and the Presidents who appoint them are certainly committed to "convenient fictions," though the nobility of their acts must increasingly be questioned. Our argument will proceed in two steps: discussing the nature of presidential commissions, then analyzing the major rhetorical constraints under which they operate and by which the commissions' credibility is constrained.

THE NATURE OF PRESIDENTIAL COMMISSIONS

Given Plato's insistence on the importance of good stories in creating understanding, we should begin with the story of one contemporary commission to help flesh out our abstract claims. The nature and limitations of the commission process are strikingly illustrated by the President's Commission on Urban Families, which was created in 1992. The official version of reality was presented by President Bush at a fund-raising dinner in May 1992:

And I had a meeting with the National League of Cities. I mentioned this in the State of the Union. Key mayors, Tom Bradley of Los Angeles, a mayor from a tiny—a Republican mayor from a tiny town in North Carolina, and all size city mayors from in between. One from Plano, Texas. And they came to me and said we've been thinking what we can do about the cities and we think that the single most important problem is the demise, the dissolution, the decline of the American family. And I just can't tell you what an impact that made on me. They weren't saying, send us all this money. . . . they asked me to appoint an urban commission, a commission on the American family, which as you may recall I did announcing John Ashcroft of Missouri and Mrs. Strauss, the former mayor of Dallas to be the co-chairs of that committee. (Bush 1992a)

In his 1992 State of the Union address, Bush described the mayors' revelation that families were in trouble and were threatening the vitality of cities as "something striking" (Bush 1992b, A18).

Bush's speeches often contained references to the Commission, though these were rarely more than a sentence long and were generally buried near the end of the presentation. In a March 1992 address to the National League of Cities, whose leaders had approached Bush about the Commission (in the speech Bush calls them "your executive board of directors, or whatever group it was—I've never been sure with whom I was dealing, but they were all big shots, believe me"), the Commission received a three-sentence mention, which appeared 208 lines into a 229-line transcript ("Remarks" 1992b). These comments about the Commission were shorter and less prominent than, for example, his usual reminder that:

[I]t's also been said that what happens in your house—this was a quote by the famous Silver Fox that lives with me in the White House, Barbara Bush—It's also been said that what happens in your house—and this is the way she put it, and I think it's very relevant—is more important than what happens in the White House. ("Remarks" 1992b)

This is consonant with Bush's observation made to a meeting of religious broadcasters that "We need a nation closer to the Waltons than the Simpsons" (Goodman 1992, 65). The President generally credited the Commission's timing to the maturation of the issue; that is, the mayors "were right to ask [for the appointment of the Commission], because it's time to determine what we can do" ("Bush Calls" 1992, A17). Bush's comments on the subject have avoided mention of any previous studies or commissions that might have been able to inform the government's policy toward families.

A series of facts not presented by President Bush casts a somewhat brighter light on the new Commission's appointment. According to the National Academy of Sciences, between 1983 and 1988 the federal government generated twenty-two studies and commission reports on the state of families and children in America. A study by Barbara Dafoe Whitehead, of the Institute for American Values, concluded that these commissions failed to "influence public policy or even shape public opinion in any lasting way" ("Why Children's" 1991, 20). Under pressure from Senator Lloyd Bentsen, though, Reagan and Bush acquiesced in the creation of a new Commission on Children, chaired by Senator Jay Rockefeller. The 32-member Commission (including representatives of the White House) was formed, held hearings, commissioned research, and submitted a unanimous report to the President in June 1991. Chairman Rockefeller reported that:

[W]e made some history when diverse groups—Republicans, Democrats, liberals, conservatives, and just every imaginable ideological point you could think of, . . . reached consensus and . . . unanimously adopted a blueprint for action. We don't [know] when that has happened on behalf of children and families before in this nation. (Rockefeller 1991)

The report, nonetheless, disappeared without a trace: there is no evidence of any public comment by the President on the Commission, the report, or any of the issues it addressed anywhere in the *Weekly Compilation of Presidential Documents*, the *New York Times*, the *Congressional Record*, the *Congressional Quarterly,* or the enormous *Nexis* database. A single sentence-long comment by spokesman Fitzwater, three weeks after the report's release, represented the extent of the White House response.

The President was approached in January 1992 by members of the National League of Cities; contrary to his fond recollection, the mayors wanted $3 billion in aid. Funds for the request were to be transferred from the Pentagon to rebuild America's "human infrastructure—children and families" ("Yet Another Study" 1992, 20). This was not the first opportunity Mr. Bush had to study this exact question. In 1989, former Republican staffer Leonard Garment and the director of the Rockefeller Institute, Richard Nathan, proposed a national commission on the urban poor to the White House. The proposal was summarily rejected (Cohen 1992, A23). By 1992, however, Mr. Bush was under pressure from sagging approval ratings, especially with regard to his domestic policy. The President had to do something.

The mayors asked for billions. They got a presidential commission.

The Commission was announced in the President's State of the Union address. At the same time, the President made his first appointment; he appointed a reliable political ally, Missouri Governor John Ashcroft, to co-chair the Commission. Ashcroft's appointment triggered immediate consternation, in part because of his conservative Republican ideology, which had seldom been associated with sympathy for urban families, and in part because of a series of executive actions he had taken as governor: a 70 percent reduction in preschool programs, a 20 percent cut in child abuse programs, elimination of 400 children from child abuse treatment, and a refusal to fund food assistance to low-income pregnant women and children ("Missouri Urban Families" 1992). The Governor had proposed the creation of a Division of Children's Services to consolidate existing programs. His appointment was generally seen as a prelude to a cabinet-level position (possibly Housing or Education) in a second Bush administration (White 1992).

The Governor was unclear about the Commission's charge, noting only that it was "to build character and the kinds of values that we want families to provide" ("Missouri's Governor" 1992), and the Commission languished. It was not officially created by the President until the swearing-in of the commissioners on March 12, at which time Ashcroft admitted he was still undecided about the Commission's focus (Bush 1992a). Its executive director was not selected for another two months, on May 16. And the Commission did not hold its first official meeting for almost a week after that ("Task Force" 1992). This meant that four months of the Commission's statutory eleven-month life had passed before it convened. We might speculate that the Commission may have been even less expeditious had not the May 1992 Los Angeles riots sharply focused the electorate's attention on urban decay and unrest. The Commission's first expert witness recommended a variety of the same programs urged by the Commission on Children and rejected sub silentio by the President a year before ("Task Force" 1992).

The story of the Commission's creation gives us ample reason to suspect that truth-seeking was not the Commission's prime objective. If this were an honest attempt to confront a serious problem, we would have expected a much different history. There would have been some recognition of the work that had gone before and some attempt to explain why another commission was called for. There would have been a budget that allowed for research rather than recapitulation. There might even have been a meeting of the Commission before a third of its life had passed. Instead, the story of the founding of the Commission suggests more the presence of convenient fiction than inconvenient fact.

This brief look at the Commission on Urban Families can help us understand more clearly the nature of the beast. As it is used here, the term "presidential commission" refers to a small subset of all of the government's advisory bodies. Professor Nicholas Burnett's masterful essay offers a series of clear delineations that will be useful here (see Chapter 1). A presidential commission is composed of private citizens appointed by the President on an ad hoc basis, often in response to a crisis. A number of these features influence a commission's credibility, so we will look at them in somewhat greater detail.

Commissions are composed largely of private citizens and government assistants on loan from different agencies. The ideal commission would represent a broad cross section of the population, and there is considerable effort made to achieve a diverse membership. Writing over twenty years ago, Frank Popper made roughly the same point in his study of a half-century of presidential commissions, which generally include:

at least one businessman, labor leader, lawyer, educator, editor, farmer, woman, Negro, Protestant, Catholic, Jew, Easterner, Midwesterner, Southerner, Westerner, federal government official, congressman, member of a previous administration, enlightened amateur, and friend of the President. (1970, 15)

In one idiotic outburst, former Secretary of the Interior James Watt was able to revel in the diverse membership of the 1983 Commission on Federal Coal Leasing while simultaneously demeaning the members. Watt commented that "we have every kind of mix you can have . . . a black . . . a woman, two Jews and a cripple" (Baruch 1983a, 549). While the Commission on Urban Families might not be able to claim such a mix, it did include an easterner, midwesterner, southerner, westerner, white, black, Hispanic, city official, private expert, minister, and friend of the President ("New Panel" 1992).

About 60 percent of all commissioners represent some sort of national elite; most commissioners have been either attorneys or academics who temporarily provide their expertise to the government (Bledsoe 1989, 144). These professions are overrepresented, in part, because of their expertise. They are also overrepresented because the practitioners of these professions can free up the substantial blocks of time needed to serve on commissions. Such flexibility is a luxury denied to citizens in most professions, who would have great difficulty in scheduling extensive travel and meeting time while at the same time pursuing their careers. This has raised a serious concern: that we have created a class of professional commissioners who shift constantly between the public and private sectors. Jason DeParle sarcastically suggested that:

[T]hose ideally suited for the job include university presidents, former ambassadors, former ambassadors who are now university presidents, governors, former governors who are now university presidents, Wall Street bankers, and other kindred spirits—like Theodore Hesburgh, John Gardner, Milton Eisenhower, Tom Watson, John J. McCloy, any Rockefeller. (1983, 43)

While such selection is not coincidental, neither is it strictly intentional. As one frustrated aide to President Johnson put it, while looking for qualified individuals "the same damn names turn up time after time" (Wolanin 1975, 85).

The commissioners' status as important outsiders influences the commission in a variety of ways. First, it may increase the prestige and perceived credibility of the final report by providing the imprimatur of distinguished private citizens. Second, it may limit the ability of the commissioners to actually serve on the commission. Most commissioners serve on their commission while simultaneously holding their regular jobs; as a result, commission meetings typically occur on weekends, rarely occur more than once each month, and routinely suffer from the absence of 25 to 50 percent of the commissioners (Bledsoe 1989, 144–46). This sort of scheduling problem might account, in part, for the delay observed with the Commission on Urban Families. Finally, it means that each commissioner comes to his or her appointment with a fairly clearly defined set of outside interests and, potentially, a constituency to be appeased.

Each individual commission is not a permanent feature of the government. There are, of course, presidential commissions that are permanent elements of the bureaucracy. Examples of such permanent advisory boards include the Committee for the Preservation of the White House and the President's Commission on White House Fellowships (U.S. General Services Administration 1990, 33). The commissions with which we are dealing are often referred to as "ad hoc commissions" and typically exist for one to three years (Bledsoe 1989, 143). These time limits also constrain, to an extent, the ability of the commission to produce a reasoned response to its problem area. Acquiring professional staff, especially if it is through the graces of an uncooperative federal agency, can gobble up weeks. Learning the ropes, coordinating schedules, framing study questions, and performing related activities all slice into the commission's limited life span.

As a result, commissions generally depend on existing research rather than having the luxury of commissioning their own studies. Ashcroft explained that the Commission on Urban Families, for instance, would "tap into previous studies and the work of other commissions" ("Task Force" 1992). With perhaps unintended understatement, Annette Strauss, co-chair and former mayor of Dallas, defended the process by reminding listeners that "We're not going to reinvent the wheel. A lot of good work has been done" ("Task Force" 1992). One unexpected effect of the Commission's short life span is that it diminishes the documentary support for and quality of proposed solutions. As Paul Peterson, director of governmental studies for the Brookings Institution, explained:

Documentation requires days of reading, gathering, and assessing information, followed by hours of careful writing and editing. But while a good staff can document a problem, it cannot gather evidence to assess proposed recommendations until these are agreed on by the commission. Unfortunately, a commission typically agrees on its proposals only at the end of its term of office. By that time it is too late to look at the evidence. (1983, 9)

As a result, carefully documented problems frequently are paired with amorphous solutions that are not susceptible to implementation.

A commission relies on the force of words for its effectiveness. The basic function of an advisory commission is to offer advice; the laws and proclamations creating such commissions have never delegated to such groups the power to act upon their own recommendations. As a result, the ability of a commission to understand and to adapt its arguments to an audience becomes a prime element in determining its effectiveness.

A presidential commission is appointed by and reports to the President. But presidential commissions, as Professor Burnett documents, are not the only investigatory and advisory bodies worthy of examination. The commission structure has proven so valuable that virtually every department and agency in the federal government has its own advisory commissions whose expertise ranges from the highly technical to the remarkably odd. Such nonpresidential federal commissions include the Board of Tea Experts, the Winegrape Varietal Names Advisory Commission, and the International Screw Threads Standards Commission (U.S. General Services Administration 1990). In any recent year, the federal government has sponsored approximately a thousand advisory commissions, with a cumulative budget of about $80 million and 21,000 commissioners (DeParle 1983, 42; U.S. General Services Administration 1990). Of these, about fifty are presidential advisory commissions. During 1989, the President established thirteen new commissions, reauthorized two, and oversaw the termination of four (U.S. General Services Administration 1990, 33).

Finally, a presidential commission addresses issues that are socially or politically exigent. Presidents appoint commissions because things have gone wrong. Two different types of failings generally precipitate the formation of a commission. The first is an external failing; that is, something outside of the government goes seriously awry. The range of issues confronting the commissions newly minted in 1989 illustrates this point: commissions were established to report on the semiconductor industry, law enforcement, the Martin Luther King federal holiday, economic development of the Mississippi Delta, federal salaries, AIDS, rural development, children, drug-free schools, migrant education, superconductivity, aviation security and terrorism, and catastrophic nuclear accidents (U.S. General Services Administration 1990, 33). The second sort of failing is an internal failing; that is, the normal functioning of government is diagnosed as being inadequate and incapable of resolving the external failing without help. *Time* magazine's longtime correspondent on government affairs, Hugh Sidey, pointed out that "a presidential commission usually signals a failure of the normal governmental machinery" (Sidey 1983, 14). It is, as such, both an indictment of the government and a response to the indictment.

These, then, are the faces of our (potentially) noble (potential) liars. What we need to do next is understand the pressures that might force noble citizens to conclude that noble lies are their only recourse.

MAJOR RHETORICAL CONSTRAINTS ON PRESIDENTIAL COMMISSIONS

There are two predominant complaints raised about presidential advisory commissions. The first is that they never really do anything. They form, they talk, they huff, they puff, they issue a glossy report, and they disappear. The second is that they are little more than diversions. At their best, they produce a dignified ratification of what the President believed all along. At their worst, they become a pawn of the President in a cynical game of diverting public attention and defusing pressure for sweeping changes. To critics, the whole process seems immoral and deceptive since the process of open inquiry promised at the commission's inception is never fulfilled.

The validity of these criticisms is open to some dispute, since they tar all commissions with the same broad brush. It is clear, as Professor Burnett points out, that there are subsets within the realm of presidential commissions and that some of these subsets function quietly and effectively. For our purposes, though, a more important function of these objections is to highlight the rhetorical nature of these bodies.

Whether they are written by journalists, pundits, scholars, or social scientists, virtually every analysis of presidential commissions begins with the question, "why?" That is, what is the reason for appointing a commission? These answers are typically couched in lists of reasons. By far the most famous was authored by political journalist Elizabeth Drew in 1968:

(1) To obtain the blessing of distinguished men for something you want to do anyway. (2) To postpone action, yet be justified in insisting that you are working on the problem. (3) To act as a lightning rod, drawing heat away from the White House. (4) To conduct an extensive study of something you do need to know more about before you act, in case you do. (5) To investigate, lay to rest rumors, and convince the public of the validity of one

particular set of facts. (6) To educate the commissioners, or to get them aboard on something you want to do. (7) Because you can't think of anything else to do. (8) To change the hearts and minds of men. (Drew 1968, 45–47)

While other lists express different perspectives on the function of the commissions (see, for example, DeParle 1983, 43–46), no subsequent list has offered any significant insight beyond Drew's.

It is possible to distill the reasons offered in these lists into two basic categories. Sulzner refers to the categories as "conflict-managing" and "problem-solving" (1974, 207). Baruch's terms are "legitimizing" and "fact-finding" (1983a, 549). In either case, they recognize two distinct functions served by commissions. The first function is rhetorical; that is, to convince people that something is being done about a problem. The second function is practical; that is, to actually do something about a problem.

At one time, a balance existed between these two functions. As we look at the record of the commissions appointed from the 1950s through the 1970s, there were a fair number whose recommendations on controversial questions became written into law; these ranged from racial integration of the armed forces to the passage of civil rights acts, from creation of an all-volunteer military to reform of federal welfare programs. These commissions were the creatures of activist presidents who saw a powerful role for the federal government in shaping America's future. While often the President and his commissioners knew in advance what conclusions the commission needed to reach (for example, support of the racial integration proposals of the 1950s), they did at least know that the commission's recommendations might enter the public debate.

As the ideology of the American Presidents changed in the 1980s and early 1990s, the commissions' balance was lost. Presidents who branded the federal government as "part of the problem" had little enthusiasm for an activist government. The great mass of the people, only tepidly involved in the affairs of the polis in the best of times, drifted farther and farther from active attendance to the public good and into a preoccupation with their private affairs. This transformation left little room for visionary leadership and little need for the practical functions of presidential commissions. The process was reduced, as others have put it, to "blue smoke and mirrors" (Germond and Witcover 1980).

Given the validity of our indictment, we can conclude that commissions have become increasingly fictive creatures; that is, they are more concerned with rhetorical tasks than any others. They exist as part of the web by which Presidents create the "convenient fictions" of the day. The commissions are part of a symbolic game; their creation, machination and fruition are bounded by and responsive to the rhetorical needs of their President. Our argument here should not be read as a wistful longing for the good old days when men were men and commissions were taken seriously. It is undeniably the case that commissions have, since their origination in the first Washington administration, served the needs of the President. It is clear that they have always been servants of the President, and not vice versa. Even thirty years ago it was common wisdom that presidential commissions existed mostly to fill the libraries with their offspring ("the libraries of America groan with tomes from such advisory groups pronouncing on the great issues of the day," according to *Time* correspondent Hugh Sidey). But it is disastrously fallacious to read the commissions of the 1990s largely or solely in light of the theoretical literature of the 1960s and 1970s. Rather, we need to remember that these commissions are part of a larger political system and that as this system mutates, so too must the commissions change.

Our argument up to this point is that commissions function as pawns in a rhetorical game. The next task we should undertake is to understand the kinds of rhetoric that are involved in this process.

First, the creation of the commission is a type of rhetoric. The notion that the mere act of creation is rhetorical is certainly not new. Kenneth Burke, for example, long ago discussed the notion of "Administrative Rhetoric," which was, he claimed:

[M]ost clearly illustrated by Machiavelli's *The Prince*. The concept of Administrative Rhetoric involves a theory of persuasive devices which have a directly rhetorical aspect, yet include operations not confined to sheerly verbal persuasion. One example will suffice. It is a variety of what I would call the "bland" strategy. It goes back to the days when the German Emperor was showing signs of militancy—and Theodore Roosevelt sent our fleet on a "goodwill mission." Ostensibly paying the Emperor the compliment of a friendly visit, the President was exemplifying his political precept, "Speak softly and carry a big stick." (Burke 1966, 301)

There are, of course, many more contemporary examples of the politician's mastery of administrative rhetoric; these range from kissing babies and shaking hands at a factory gate to attending state funerals and hosting state dinners (Golden, Berquist, and Coleman 1989, 338–39). In a world where actions speak louder than words, these performances can be among our most powerful rhetorical ploys.

The appointment of a commission is, itself, such a rhetorical act. Elizabeth Drew expressed the most common motivation for appointing a presidential commission: "because you cannot think of anything else to do but you know you had better do something" (1968, 45). David Flitner argues that the mere existence of a national commission "represent[s] a symbolic tool with which the President communicates awareness of a situation that is of concern to his constituency, reassures the disaffected that they will not be ignored, and responds to the sense that he must do something" (1986, 19). This observation goes some length in explaining the President's appointment of the Commission on Urban Families. There is, manifestly, no reason for an additional commission on children and families if we conceive of a commission as a fact-finding body. The President has access to two dozen preceding reports and hundreds of staff experts. The commission has neither the time, the expertise, nor the resources to generate a significant addition to the sum of human knowledge on the problem. Even if they were to generate substantial new insights, there seems no recent precedent for expecting their recommendations to inform policy.

We might argue that the rhetorical advantage of appointing a commission has largely been destroyed by the very factors we have just discussed: the overuse of the process and the inattention of the electorate. That may, in one sense, be true: the President is unlikely to reap major political gains directly from the appointment of a commission. He may, however, gain substantial advantage by denying the issue to his opponents; that is, it is difficult to get a disconnected public mobilized around an issue when the President is able to point to the undeniable grandeur of a blue-ribbon commission and to call for prudent examination before precipitous action.

This is precisely the pattern followed in the case of the Reagan administration's 1983 Task Force on Hunger. The Task Force on Hunger was created "to minimize something the Democrats and the television networks have made into an issue," according to a senior Reagan advisor. Senate Republican leader Robert Dole learned about the commission on TV. After two weeks it had neither members nor staff ("Boom in Blue Ribbons" 1983, 18). The final report waffled seriously on the question of hunger:

We have not been able to substantiate allegations of rampant hunger. We regret our inability to document the degree of nonclinical hunger because such lack of definitive quantitative proof contributes to a climate in which policy discussions become unhelpfully heated, and unsubstantiated assertions are then substituted for hard information. ("Excerpts from Final Report" 1984, A16)

Many of the panel's recommendations resembled proposals already made by Mr. Reagan but rejected by Congress ("Antipoverty" 1984, A17). Despite the fact that the Commission's chief finding was that they did not know what the facts were and their chief recommendations were presidential retreads, we are forced to conclude that the Commission was successful since it accomplished precisely what the President needed: it defused a volatile issue during the approach of an election. The Commission on Urban Families seems to fall into the same category: Mr. Bush had interest neither in doing anything about the problem of urban families nor in surrendering an issue to his campaign opponents. The commissions, thus, may continue to serve as a valuable rhetorical tool despite their sundry weaknesses.

The task of commissions, then, becomes paradoxical. As part of the rhetorical act of creating the commission, the President perforce appoints individuals who have a strong stake in the issue. And, having been charged with confronting a great problem, the commissioners generate pressure on themselves to succeed. But success is measured by the advice that reaches the President: if the advice moves the President to action, the commission has succeeded. If the President remains unmoved, the commission has failed. The rhetorical problem for the commission becomes reading this very special audience of one. It needs to find fault (since, as we have noted, the appointment of a commission arises out of failures) without embarrassing the President. It needs to propose solutions that conform with what it learns and that are, at the same time, consonant with the President's vision.

Commissions have used a number of rhetorical strategies to complete these tasks. Several deserve particular note: adopting a president's rhetorical stance, suppressing unacceptable evidence, and issuing unanimous reports.

Commission members usually know where a president stands on the issues that they have been asked to confront. On some occasions, commission chairs are quite open in discussing the relationship with the President's beliefs. One clear illustration of this argument was Mr. Reagan's Task Force on Arts Funding, which was created amidst furor concerning a recommendation for a 50 percent reduction in the budget of the National Endowment for the Arts. Very early in the commission's inquiry, Charlton Heston, the commission's chair and a close friend of the President, commented:

In the President's opinion, the national endowments have been an effective mechanism for fostering the arts and humanities in this country. We have come to the same conclusion ourselves. Our preliminary examinations indicate that the endowments, however they might be streamlined or made administratively more efficient—and I don't know how that might be—remain the primary structure for fostering the arts and humanities in this country. ("Panel" 1981, C12)

When questioned about the issue that had prompted the commission's founding (i.e., whether the budget should be substantially reduced), Mr. Daniel J. Terra (Reagan's Ambassador at Large for Cultural Affairs) and Mr. Heston answered that the group was not assigned to deal with federal financing. "The task force," Mr. Heston said, "is well aware that Congress is going to end up with a considerably smaller sum of Federal money for the arts and humanities" ("Panel" 1981, C12).

This sanguine public position appeared somewhat at odds with the commission's internal conclusion. One staff member reported:

Most of the members would have recommended higher funding than the president wanted, and when the president appoints you, you don't want to turn around and kick him in the butt. Besides, it wasn't necessary to come up with any policy findings. The commission was supposed to act as a lightning rod. (DeParle 1983, 41)

While it is rare that the servility of a commission to the President's agenda is publicly announced, it is not rare that the commission knows what is expected of it. This is sometimes the case because the President's stance has been widely publicized (as in the case of the National Bipartisan Commission on Central America), because the commission members are directly involved in the issue, or because the President tells them (for example, the letter appointing members to President Kennedy's commission on federal salaries notified the members that the President fully intended to submit a particular salary proposal to Congress during the following January and that their input was needed before the President "firmed up" the package—see DeParle 1983, 45). They are, as a result, under pressure to express new ideas in old words; that is, to make changes seem harmonious with the President's interests and agenda. This desire is sometimes driven to an embarrassing extreme, as when the Task Force on Private Sector Initiatives made a stirring twelve-minute video-tape to show Reagan in the White House theater. In response, Mr. Reagan gratefully asked, "How do you talk with a grapefruit in your throat?" and gave a gold-plated tire gauge to the chairman, to measure private sector accomplishments ("Expert Advice" 1983, 4).

More typically, commissions merely try to parallel a president's arguments and statements. Commentators on the Kerner Commission, for example, were struck by the Johnson-esque tone of the report:

Such language could just as well have rolled off the tongue of the President of the United States to a national television audience. President Johnson had been making similar statements for a long time, even prior to his election to office in 1964. Nor were the commission's recommendations for government action, though ambitious and extensive, considered radical. Mostly they are extensions of what the federal government already was doing. (Herbers 1988, 20)

Despite having solutions that were explicitly crafted to appeal to the President's sensibilities (Herbers 1988, 21) and despite public interest so intense that the Kerner Commission report sold at the rate of 100,000 copies per day during the week after its release ("Studying the Study" 1968, 16), a single rhetorical miscue doomed the proceeding. In creating the Commission, Mr. Johnson gave them the sort of clear mandate that we often assume all commissions should receive:

[T]his matter is far, far too important for politics. Sometimes various Administrations have set up commissions that were expected to put the stamp of approval on what the Administration believed. This is not such a commission. We are looking to you, not to approve our own notions, but to guide us and to guide the country through a thicket of tension, conflicting evidence and extreme opinion. So, Mr. Chairman and Mr. Vice Chairman, let your search be free. Let it be untrammeled by what has been called the "conventional wisdom." As best you can, find the truth, the whole truth, and express it in your report. (National Advisory Commission 1968, 537)

It appears, unfortunately, that the commissioners may have incautiously decided to believe the President and thus made their great mistake. The Kerner Commission report turned out to be insufficiently glowing in describing President Johnson's efforts on behalf of black Americans. The President, always sensitive to criticism, was remarkably irritated. As a result, he maintained a stony silence about the Commission and its recommendations for nearly a week after the report's release. When he did answer a reporter's question about the Commission, he praised the Commission but faintly, for its thoroughness. And, in an aside, he grumbled that, "They always print that we don't do enough. They don't print what we do" ("Guilty or Not?" 1968, 46). Thereby snubbed by the President and denied a spot on the media agenda, the *New York Times* Washington correspondent wrote, "the report was thus filed away to gather dust in the archives as America tried to forget about the riots and the troubled ghettos" (Herbers 1988, 21–22).

Sometimes the best efforts of a commission to accommodate its recommendations to a president's desires fail for no reason better than changing times. A committee may be appointed to address an issue whose political salience has faded substantially by the time the report is released. As an example, the Final Report of the National Commission on Technology, Automation, and Economic Progress (a blue-ribbon commission of labor leaders and industrialists) was originally scheduled for presentation by the Commission to Mr. Johnson in a public ceremony at the White House, midweek. This would have maximized the visibility of the report by giving the national media both the time to cover the issue and the visual opportunities presented by the White House. The presentation was shifted, with a two-day notice, to Saturday (a "dead" news day), a date rejected by the Commission members because it offered insufficient time to arrange their schedules. It was then shifted to a Monday, which turned out to be the day of a crippling snowstorm that closed the federal government. The report was finally released on the next Thursday at the end of Bill Moyers's daily news briefing without prior notice, without Commission members present and without a symbolic meeting with the President (Bell 1969, 118–19). The report, as a result, joined the list of those missing and presumed dead. "The irony in all this is that the Commission had made truly strenuous efforts to reach a consensus in order to gain the strongest possible support for its recommendations" (Bell 1969, 119), but changing economic conditions had diminished the urgency of the problem and rendered the Commission expendable.

Life for commissions that directly cater to the President's predilections is uncertain. Life for commissions that contradict the President is (in Hobbes's words) "short, nasty, and brutish." The most famous "runaway" commissions called for legalization of pornography and marijuana and were, in the words of one White House aide, "dead on arrival." More recently, the Reagan administration disavowed major portions of the Kissinger Commission's recommendations before they were even written. Spokesman Larry Speakes said Reagan was inclined to ignore calls for tying aid to rights, got grief from all sides for that comment, punted back to the position that the President will "have an open mind," then undercut that by later recalling the President's veto of legislation that would have imposed just such requirements (Smith 1984, A18). The report ultimately offered to the President contained the dissents of three Commission members, all Republicans and all city or county officials, who rejected the recommendations (as did the President).

To get around the prospect of offending the President by presenting reports that contain unpalatable facts, commissions may choose to suppress or selectively interpret the findings of their professional staffs. A variety of examples support this claim. In the case of the Civil Disorders Commission, which had dispatched individual teams to research particular disturbances, "The study team on San Francisco State, for example, having found 'instances of police overreaction,' then discovered that these details had been omitted from the final version of their report" ("Rhetoric of Evasion" 1969, 370–71). In the case of a presidential commission on organized crime, G. Robert Blakey of Notre Dame prepared a report sixty-three pages long on organized crime links to public officials in Illinois. Under intense political pressure from Illinois officials, the commission chose to reduce Blakey's report to four footnotes. Specific allegations documented (and deleted) included: law enforcement and judicial corruption, racket influence in the legislature, and the names of Mafia officials ("Official Cover-up" 1967, 103). Finally, fully half of the twenty committee researchers for the Advisory Committee on Television and Social Behavior felt that their research had not been adequately reported by the Committee (Madden and Lion 1976, 44). The complaint was raised most forcefully by Dr. Monroe Lefkowitz, the principal research scientist at the New York State Department of Mental Hygiene and the author of one of the technical reports, who claimed the report's use of data was "erroneous . . . overqualified and . . . potentially damaging to children and society" (Madden and Lion 1976, 44).

Finally, reasoning that there is strength in numbers, commissions strain to produce unanimous results. Each commission report begins with a letter of transmittal, a one- or two-page message from the commission (or, more commonly, its chair) to the President. These letters typically contain three elements: first, words of praise for the President. The President's Task Force on Victims of Crime, for example, averred that "you led this nation into a new era. . . . [C]itizens from all over the nation told us again and again how heartened they were that this Administration had taken up the challenge" ("Victims of Crime" 1982). Second, letters of transmittal include a recapitulation of the commission's charge and major findings. Third, while the letters virtually never mention the commission's recommendations, they almost always note that the recommendations were unanimously reached. Of the several dozen commission reports surveyed for this chapter, only two admitted to nonunanimous recommendations. Others skirt the issue by focusing on areas where unanimity was reached. The transmittal letter for the President's Commission on Industrial Competitiveness reported reaching "unanimous agreement on the importance of competitiveness to the American people, the seriousness of the challenges we face from abroad and the thrust of the action items recommended in this report" ("Global Competition" 1985, v). Similarly, the President's Commission on Americans Outdoors could claim only that "we were able to objectively consider the problems and adjust our individual views to achieve general agreement" ("Americans Outdoors" 1987, i).

While no one knows how many of the various commission reports are unanimously supported, anecdotal accounts indicate that many commission reports are the products of last-minute compromises on both findings and recommendations. Consensus in the final report increases its credibility or legitimacy but can often be achieved only by fudging on the most controversial claims; for example, on the strength of evidence linking pornography to antisocial behavior in the Meese Commission or the probability of a single bullet in the Kennedy assassination (Bledsoe 1989, 150). As sociologist Robert Merton pointed out, "the principal group-induced pressures were generally for compromise. As one observer summed this up, there is apparently nothing like an implacable deadline, as distinct from an ideology, to move a task-oriented group towards consensus" (Merton 1975, 161). The option of minority and dissenting reports further heightens pressure on the commissioners to eliminate their most controversial findings in order to protect the credibility of their less contentious ones (161).

Commissioners, by and large, attempt to keep up a brave public face and typically claim great success for their undertakings. In the short term, they cite approving presidential statements as signs of success; in the longer term, they may be able to point to legislative action consistent with their recommendations. There is, of course, considerable reason to be skeptical about the claimed successes of the commissions in getting their recommendations adopted. In part, recommendations are reflections of expected action. In part, the adopted actions tend to be symbolic. For example, the Grace Commission offered 2,500 cost-cutting measures, of which over half (1,300) were adopted. While that average seems impressive, the savings realized by the measures adopted (only $38 million) represented less than one one-hundredth of one percent of the total savings ($425 billion) that Grace claimed was possible (Bledsoe 1989, 151). Nonetheless, J. Peter Grace "proudly gives the Grace Commission, known as the President's Private Sector Survey on Cost Control, a score of 9.9 on a scale of one to ten for effectiveness" ("Obscure Honor" 1985, 132).

None of these observations lead to the conclusion that commissions move lightly or quickly to deceive. Indeed, all the evidence points to the opposite conclusion: the deception occurs mostly as part of adaptation to their single audience member and his biases. The reason for the adaptation is not to deceive for the sake of deception but, at worst, to deceive for the sake of action. The commissioners construe evidence and construct reality in such a way as to alleviate harm to the people, though this alleviation may be mediated by the need to propose the modest actions best adapted to a president of modest ambition. In so acting, the commissions (if not the President) may earn the accolade "noble."

CONCLUSION

In the best of times, commissions can be counted on to provide no more than one version of the truth. That version is limited because commissions are limited: by the time and staff available, by a lack of power to require action, by the needs of the political system, by the human fallibility of the commissioners themselves, and by the personalities of the Presidents who appoint them. In good times and bad, some few commissions still manage to "speak truth to power." But it is this charge, of speaking to power, that presents the ultimate challenge to the credibility of commissions. As an institution, commissions can be no stronger than their President will let them be. A President who has no tolerance for inconvenient truth virtually ensures that his commissions will deliver convenient fiction.

Commissions are, then, rhetorical creatures capable only of "deeds done in words." The ultimately rhetorical nature of advisory commissions was aptly summarized by the Brookings Institution's Bruce Peterson:

Commissions do have their functions in American politics, but fact-finding, rigorous analysis, and policy development are usually not among them. Commissions are best suited to dramatizing an issue, resolving political differences, and reassuring the public that questions are being thoughtfully considered. Oscar Wilde said it best: "On matters of grave importance, style, not sincerity, is the vital thing." (Peterson 1983, 11)

3

Commissions as Organizations: Characteristics, Functions, and Context

W. Timothy Coombs

Commissions are common in politics, and they often affect policy decisions. Oddly, little is known about how commissions work beyond their basic structure and actions. One way to gain new insights into commissions is to examine them as organizations. An organization is characterized by the consciously coordinated activities of people (Kreps 1991), and the previous chapters provide proof that commissions are made up of people engaged in consciously coordinated actions. As organizations, commissions possess unique characteristics and operate within a sociopolitical context, contend with constituencies, and pursue certain functions. This chapter details commission characteristics, constituencies, and functions while noting the impact of context. The end result should be a greater illumination of how commissions operate.

COMMISSION CHARACTERISTICS

A textbook definition of a commission fails to do justice to the richness of the concept. Commissions are best defined by their essential characteristics—those factors that distinguish them from other political bodies. An analysis of the commission literature revealed five essential characteristics: (1) commissions are temporary; (2) commissions are charged to address some problematic issue; (3) commissions are advisory; (4) commissions are considered to be "outside" or independent of the government; and (5) commissions are composed of people who are perceived to be highly qualified and objective (Flitner 1986; Wolanin 1975; Zink 1987). Explication of the five essential characteristics sets the stage for a detailed discussion of commission variables.

Temporary

Commissions are temporary because they have a finite time of operation. Commissions have a prescribed start and end date; uncommon is the commission that is not given a deadline (Wolanin 1975). A commission begins when some political actor (the President, Congress, a governor, a mayor, the attorney general, etc.) announces its creation. A commission ends with the delivery of its final report to its creating entity. Typically a commission is given a fixed time in which to conduct its research (Flitner 1986). The length of a commission's life ranges from three months to over thirty-six months, with 11.6 months being the average life span of a commission (Wolanin 1975). For example, the President's Commission on Campus Unrest lasted three months, while the National Commission on Marijuana and Drug Abuse lasted twenty-six months (Flitner 1986).

This temporary nature is a limiting factor. A commission's effectiveness suffers when it is not given sufficient time to research its issue and to advocate its report. A commission may have to take shortcuts and make compromises in order to deliver its report on time. For instance, James Short, a member of the Eisenhower Commission, felt that time pressure during the investigation led to an incomplete picture of the violence and that the Commission's research was not systematic. Last, it should be noted that a commission has little time to advocate its recommendations because a commission ceases to exist after the delivery of the report (Flitner 1986).

Investigatory

Commissions are created and given a charge that indicates what problematic issue is to be addressed. The charge may be modified by the commission but the basic issue remains the same. The charge tends to be vague, giving commissioners some latitude to redefine the problem and to focus their investigation as they see fit (Wolanin 1975). All commissions share this directive to investigate; since investigation is also a function of commissions, the nature of the investigatory process will be detailed in a later section. Suffice it to say here that investigating a problem is a defining characteristic of a commission.

Advisory

Commissions are created to investigate a problematic issue and offer a course of action for resolving that issue. The commission's final report contains recommendations for how best to address the issue (Wolanin 1975). However, any commission's recommendations are merely advisory. Commissions have *no power* to enact their recommendations—to create public policy. Commission recommendations serve only to advise the commissioning agent, such as Congress, the federal bureaucracy, or the city government. For example, the Christopher Commission (1991) recommended changes in the Los Angeles Police Department in July 1991. Those recommendations included the resignation of Police Chief Daryl Gates, a revision and strengthening of the police commission, the resignation of five members of the police commission, and the creation of a new system for monitoring citizen complaints (Turque and Foote 1991; Willwerth 1991). However, the Commission could not enact those recommendations (Dunne 1991). In fact, few of the recommendations had been implemented at the time of the 1992 riots that followed the verdict of the police brutality trial stemming from the Rodney King beating. The slow pace of reform could have only added to the frustration created by the trial decision. Ultimately, it is solely within the purview of the commissioning agent to make public policy, and that agent may ignore or accept the recommendations put forth by a commission. Therefore, the advisory nature of commissions serves to limit a commission's ability to affect public policy decisions.

Outside/Independent

Commissions are expected to be outside of and therefore independent of the government. There are very subtle differences between being outside and being independent. Being outside is a physical state. A commission is outside the federal government if its membership includes people from the private sector or state and local government. Moreover, a commission is physically outside of the governmental structure since it can only advise policy makers and has no permanent position within the government's organizational chart. In contrast, independence is a state of being. A commission cannot be independent if its membership owes strong allegiance to its commissioning agent.

Qualified and Objective

Commissioners are expected to be experts on the issue under investigation (Flitner 1986; Wolanin 1975). Commissions are to be composed of the "best and the brightest." Commissioners with weak credentials can hurt a commission by raising the hint of a political appointment. When people see an unqualified person on a commission, they assume that the appointment is political and may have been made in order to pursue the goals of the commissioning agent. Qualifications serve to imply objectivity (Marver 1979).

The ideal commissioner has no preconceived notions about how the issue should be resolved. Commissioners are supposed to come into the investigation with an open mind (Flitner 1986). Extremists are not made commissioners specifically because they would be biased (Wolanin 1975). Commissioners are selected with an eye toward balancing various stakeholders in the issue—every major faction should be represented. But the people who become commissioners are to leave their previous affiliations behind. Such objectivity promotes careful research and the selection of the "best" course of action for resolving the issue. Bias is often reflected in dependence; a commissioner cannot be objective if he or she is dependent in some way on the commissioning agent. There is a bond between outsidedness, independence, qualification, and objectivity. All are factors that can affect the ability of a commission to accomplish its objectives.

KEY COMMISSION VARIABLES

Analysis of the literature on government commissions reveals three variables that appear to be critical to the operation of commissions: (1) context, (2) constituencies, and (3) functions. The context represents the larger socio-political realm in which the commission operates. Constituencies are those groups that become involved in the commission's issue. Some have a passing interest, while others are targets for the actions of the commission. Functions represent what the commission was created to accomplish.

Context: The Environment

Just as commissions are embedded within the governmental system that creates them, so too do commissions exist within a socio-political context. Commissions reside within a stream of social issues and political issues that populate the American political system. Explication of the commission's context involves unpacking its multiple levels and the multiple points in time when context is most salient to a commission. (See Chapter 2 for additional information concerning commission environment and constraints.)

Multiple Context Levels

The socio-political context of commissions can be divided into the micro and macro levels. On the micro level are the event(s) or demand(s) that triggered the creation of the commission. Commissions are established as a "response to some perceived need or demand that would normally fall within the responsibilities of routinely constituted government agencies" (Tutchings 1979, 17). For example, the Kerner Commission was created to address the problem of riots and civil disorder in the United States, while the Task Force on Food Assistance was created to determine if hunger existed in America (Lipsky and Olson 1977; Coffey 1983).

The Kerner Commission was formed in response to a series of events. Other times when a commission is formed, one event may trigger a crisis and require urgent action. The Rogers Commission addressed a crisis when it examined the explosion of the space shuttle *Challenger* (Miller 1988). The Task Force on Food Assistance was a response to demands by hunger advocates and Congress that hunger in America was on the rise (Hoffman 1983; Pear 1983b). In sum, on the micro level, commissions are formed in response to some high-visibility demand or need.

The three commissions just mentioned also can be located in a larger series of political events—the macro-level context. The Kerner Commission was part of the larger debate over civil rights in the United States; the Task Force on Food Assistance was assembled during a time when the Reagan administration was trying to overcome a callous image prior to a reelection bid; and the Rogers Commission held hearings during a time when the Defense Department was in need of shuttles for deploying parts for the Strategic Defense Initiative (SDI) (Lipsky and Olson 1977;

Mohr 1986; Pear 1983c). One should not discount the impact of the macro and micro levels of context on the operation of a commission.

Multiple Points in Time

The life span of a commission is punctuated by three points in time: (1) its creation; (2) the period of investigation; and (3) the release of the commission's final report (Flitner 1986; Popper 1970; Wolanin 1975). A commission receives its greatest amount of public attention when it is created (Wolanin 1975). The issue under investigation is a current political topic of interest to significant political constituencies (Tutchings 1979). There is political interest in the issue compounded with media coverage of the commission (Flitner 1986; Sulzner 1971). Consider the fanfare that marked the creation of the Rogers Commission, the Warren Commission, and the Christopher Commission. Each commission received extensive media coverage in the major newspapers in the United States (Miller 1988; McKinney 1985; Dunne 1991).

Following its creation, a commission sets about the task of researching the problem. The media generally ignore a commission during this time. There are a few exceptions, such as the Rogers Commission, which had testimony from its hearings published in the *New York Times* ("Key Sections" 1986).

A commission's final report is its last official act. As with the commission's creation, the final report has the *potential* to capture media coverage and political interest in the commission's topic. There are, however, no guarantees of media coverage or public interest in the commission's activities. Numerous commissions go unnoticed when their final reports are delivered. The National Commission on Technology, Automation, and Economic Progress and the President's Water Resource Policy Commission both generated little interest in their reports (Wolanin 1975).

The exceptions to interest in a commission's investigation and final report are largely a function of the socio-political context. Political attention stayed riveted on the Rogers Commission because its issue remained current during the entire life cycle of the Commission. Commissions such as the National Commission on Technology, Automation, and Economic Progress, and the President's Water Resource Policy Commission ended in obscurity because their issues somehow lost political salience. Either the life cycle of the issue had been completed or some other political issues burst onto the scene and superseded the commission's inquiry. The Commission on Technology saw its investigation complete its life cycle; by the time the report was made public the issue of unemployment had faded away. The report of the President's Water Resource Policy Commission was swept aside by the beginning of the Korean War (Wolanin 1975). The final section of this chapter elaborates upon the constraining impact of the context and notes how the same constraining factors may also energize an issue.

Constituencies: Those Publics Involved in the Issue

Various groups or publics will have an interest in the issue a commission investigates. Some of these publics press for the creation of the commission, while others simply become attracted to an active political question. A commission must be aware that it can have multiple and conflicting constituencies focused on its activities. Commissions are also composed of people representing all major factions associated with the issue (Wolanin 1975). Simply put, "Every commissioner represents a constituency" (Popper 1970, 15). The concept of multiple constituencies, therefore, operates on two different levels. On one level are the various constituencies that have a stake in the issue. On another level are the commissioners who are a part of the commission and who retain linkages to their original groups. Each of these levels requires explication.

Stakeholder: Outside Constituencies

Commissions are created because there is political interest in an issue. More specifically, some constituencies place pressure on the federal, state, or local government to address an issue (Tutchings 1979). The constituencies that prompt the creation of a commission can be placed into one of two categories: (1) government, and (2) special interest groups (Tutchings 1979; Wolanin 1975).

The government constituency may be composed of the President, the federal bureaucracy, Congress, governors, mayors, or city councils—government officials. Government officials may create a commission to address issues generated by a crisis (e.g., the Rogers Commission), personal concern (e.g., the Commission on Competitiveness), or the need to have an issue disappear (e.g., the Task Force on Education).

Special interest groups are the other key constituency that can pressure for the creation of a commission. The term "special interest" is used here to mean any group of people who come together to pursue a shared goal. For example, the National Association for the Advancement of Colored People (NAACP) was one of the forces behind the creation of President Truman's Civil Rights Committee. Sometimes a special interest is really a single individual, as with Eunice Shriver's efforts to create the Panel on Mental Retardation and John D. Rockefeller III's work to create the Committee on Population and Family Planning (Wolanin 1975).

The identification of outside constituencies is only half complete when the driving forces behind the creation of a commission are examined. Once a commission begins to address an issue, more constituencies appear as all stakeholders in the issue may be drawn to the commission's activities. Stakeholders are any group that can be affected by the resolution of an issue or that can affect the resolution of an issue (Brummer 1991; Freeman 1984). The number and types of stakeholders vary as a function of the issue. Still, it is possible to isolate major categories of the stakeholder constituencies.

The attentive public represents those people who demonstrate a serious interest in the issue (Grunig and Hunt 1984; Nimmo 1978). This group follows the issue and any action taken on the issue very closely. The attentive public may have no real stake in how the issue is resolved; their interest may be purely vicarious in nature. Much of the U.S. population watched the Christopher Commission's investigation of the Rodney King beating even though they lived outside of Los Angeles and were largely unaffected by events that transpire there. To the degree that an issue can be affected by public opinion and public pressure, the attentive public can affect the issue's resolution (Reich 1988). Activist groups can utilize the attentive public to place additional pressure on policy makers. The attentive public is typically reached through the media since Americans receive their political information from the media (Berg 1972; Turner 1980). This means that the media also have some power in affecting how the issue is to be resolved.

The phrase "affected public" is used to denote a special subset of the attentive public: any nongovernmental group that may be affected by the issue but may not have converted that relationship into active interest. Groups may be affected by an issue but take no active role in trying to influence the resolution of the issue (Kelman 1987). The Task Force on Food Assistance can be used to illustrate the concept of an affected public. People dependent on federal food assistance programs, private food sources, and the hungry all were potentially affected by the hunger issue under investigation by the Task Force. Many of these groups did not vocalize their concern in the form of activism. By default, the groups became part of the attentive public rather than an activist public. Furthermore, the affected public may not even be attentive—they may choose to ignore the issue completely instead of following its progress in the media.

The government actors and activist groups both affect and are affected by an issue's resolution. The power of each group to influence an issue varies by problem area. However, political actors (especially the President) generally have more power than activist groups in the policy-making arena (Gans 1979; Paletz and Entman 1981; Tuchman 1978). The reason for this power imbalance is that governmental actors control more resources than activist groups when it comes to policy making. More resources means more power for the governmental actors (Gamson 1975; Jordan 1990; Smith 1990).

Moreover, each of these groups is affected by the issue's resolution. Whoever presses for the creation of a commission seeks to have the issue resolved in a certain way. As a result, the governmental actors or the activist groups may all win or lose on the issue. For example, President Reagan "won" with his Task Force on Education because a potentially damaging 1984 campaign issue was diffused by the Commission (Vibbert 1984).

The commission's final report is the clearest manifestation of external constituencies. The creator of the commission always receives a copy of the final report. Still other constituencies have an interest in and a desire to read the final report. Thus, a commission must decide which constituency (or constituencies) will be the primary target for its final report. The Kerner Commission illustrates constituency selection: its final report was written for the white middle class and American blacks, not the President and the Congress who created it (Flitner 1986).

Internal Constituencies

Constituencies are internal as well as external when commissioners bring vestiges of their own reference groups to the commission. The commissioners are to be credible representatives of the constituencies but not extremists who would preclude the commission from reaching consensus (Wolanin 1975). The commissioners are expected to drop their individual interests and adopt a perspective that reflects the nation's interests (Popper 1970).

It is assumed at times that commissioners rather easily shed their constituency roles and adopt the commissioner role. Wolanin (1975) maintains that commissioners develop an esprit de corps that places commission concerns above constituency concerns and permits decision by consensus. An examination of the literature on small-group communication reveals that membership in a group does not mean automatic commitment to that group and one's role in it (Weick 1979).

The concept of internal constituencies is a natural outgrowth of the commissioner's "linking pin" role. Someone who serves as a linking pin belongs to two groups, and this dual membership facilitates the transmission of information from one group to another. Typical examples of linking pins are public relations personnel and recruiters, as they interface between the organization and the public (Kreps 1991). Commissioners collect information from various groups and bring that information back to the commission, thus making commissioners linking pins. Warren Commissioner Howard Willens played the linking pin role when he acted as a liaison between the Justice Department and the Warren Commission (McKinney 1985). Linking pins are forced to play multiple roles, which may promote role conflict. The enactment of one role may conflict with another role (Organ 1971; Spreitzer, Synder, and Larson 1979). Advocating the commission's perspective may conflict with a commissioner's constituency interests.

In the literature on group communication, role conflict is described as similar to the concepts of divided loyalty and partial inclusion. Multiple roles often reflect the fact that people belong to multiple groups. A person with multiple group membership has "divided loyalties and dispersed commitments" to the various groups (Putnam 1988, 73). Weick (1979) refers to this as partial inclusion and notes that people do not invest all of their behaviors in one group but instead disperse their interests among multiple groups. So it is reasonable to expect conflict between members of a committee who represent various external groups. Even though directed not to, people may view problems and advance solutions based upon their external group loyalties rather than their committee loyalties (Putnam 1988; Putnam and Stohl 1990). Similarly, a commissioner's loyalty to his or her constituency may override his or her loyalty to the commission.

The potential for divided loyalty and role conflict always exists in commissions since commissioners are selected precisely because they represent various and conflicting constituencies. There are both assets and liabilities to role conflict. As an asset, role conflict introduces multiple perspectives to the commission. Multiple perspectives lessen the potential that groupthink will develop by adding diversity of opinions and reducing the chances for creating too much cohesion (Janis 1982). As a liability, role conflict can lead commissioners to advocate strongly the perspective they bring with them into the proceedings to the detriment of the commission's assigned task. Clinging strongly to outside roles can prevent commissioners from identifying with and pursuing the goals of the commission (Simon 1976). Moreover, role conflict can lead to ineffective enactment of a role and to tension (Getzels and Guba 1954; Johnson and

Stinson 1975). For a commission, role conflict could be translated into poor enactment of the commissioner role and high levels of tension within the commission. Role conflict may have a curvilinear relationship to the performance of the commission. Too little or too much role conflict may hurt the group, while moderate amounts may facilitate the commission's operation.

Commission Functions

The prescribed function of a commission is investigation, but it is wrong to think investigation is the only function of the commission. Two distinctly political functions also are associated with commissions: symbolic reassurance and policy influence. This section details these three commission functions and probes how the functions are related to one another.

Investigatory Function

When people think of what commissions do, they typically conjure up the investigatory function. For example, people recall the Rogers Commission solving the *Challenger* mystery or the Warren Commission examining President Kennedy's assassination. References to the investigatory function are understandable given that commissions are structured to examine problems. A review of the commission's charge, inquiry activities, and final report illustrates the investigatory nature of commissions.

As noted earlier, a commission begins with a charge. That charge assigns the commission to investigate a specific problem and triggers the inquiry that comes to occupy the commission's time. Experts are called in, hearings are held, and commission members may travel to the field to conduct inspections (Marcy 1945; Tutchings 1979; Wolanin 1975). The inquiry culminates in a report that contains the information collected by the commission and articulates its recommendations for redressing the problematic issue under investigation (Flitner 1986; Wolanin 1975). The quality of this research is often exemplary. The National Commission on Marijuana and Drug Abuse was hailed as producing "the most comprehensive compilations of research on drug use and abuse ever made by the United States government" (Flitner 1986, 42), while the Kerner Commission's report became a mainstay in academic studies of protests (e.g., Jenkins and Eckert 1986).

The Task Force on Food Assistance is a good illustration of the investigatory features of commissions. On September 8, 1983, the Task

Force was created with the following charge: "The Task Force shall analyze Federal and other programs intended to render food assistance to the needy and shall make recommendations to the President and the Secretary of Agriculture with respect to how such programs may be improved" (*Public Papers of the Presidents* 1983, 1212). Following the charge, the Task Force held hearings on hunger and food assistance programs. Members also made trips to various cities to collect additional data from the field (United States Congress 1984). On January 10, 1984, the Task Force delivered its final report containing its findings and eighteen recommendations for resolving the issue (Pear 1984). Each of these activities exemplifies how a commission can fulfill its responsibility to investigate.

A commission's legal life and investigatory function end with its final report, but a commission's functions may be far from over at that point. Other political actors (e.g., the President, Congress, mayors, governors, or activist groups) can use the report to pursue further political objectives. President Johnson used the Commission on Law Enforcement and Administration of Justice to pursue reforms in the justice system. Johnson used the Commission's findings in ten separate presidential messages (Wolanin 1975). The National Council on Crime and Delinquency, the Anti-Defamation League, and the National Urban Coalition all used the final report of the Commission on the Causes and Prevention of Violence to further their own political objectives (Flitner 1986). Commissioners may even pursue additional goals after the final report is delivered. The additional political objectives are the symbolic reassurance and policy influence functions of commissions. These two functions may occur after or during the investigatory process.

Symbolic Reassurance Function

Commissions are extremely useful in reassuring the public that a problematic situation is being addressed. M. Edelman (1967) refers to this phenomenon as symbolic reassurance. The creation of a commission is often perceived as a meaningful action and reassures people that a problem is being handled (Flitner 1986; Sulzner 1971). Whatever the impetus behind the commission's creation, a commission can convey the perception that a problematic issue is being addressed in a significant fashion.

The purpose of the symbolic reassurance function is to create quiescence among publics. Flitner (1986) observed that a commission "reassures the disaffected that they will not be ignored" (19). Those who are disaffected often become quiescent because the creation of a commission convinces them that their demand for action has been addressed.

Quiescence is important to political actors; they need resignation by some publics as well as the support of other publics if they are to implement their plans of action successfully (Edelman 1967).

There is both a positive and a negative side to quiescence. On the positive side, quiescence can allow for a decision to be postponed in order to conduct more research and/or to let emotions subside (Flitner 1986). The Christopher Commission utilized the tactic of postponement. Emotions were high after the release of the videotape of Rodney King's beating. The Christopher Commission allowed decisions (e.g., the need for a new police commissioner) to be made about the Los Angeles Police Department after the initial outrage had ebbed and after additional research into the operation of the LAPD was conducted (Dunne 1991).

On the negative side, quiescence can be used to avoid taking any substantive action to solve a problem. A major criticism of commissions is that they provide an easy way for government agents to avoid taking concrete action (e.g., allocating funds) on an issue: a problematic issue arises, the government officials appoint a commission, and all is forgotten, since people now believe the issue is being resolved (Flitner 1986; Wolanin 1975). A result of this criticism is the use of the term "task force" instead of "commission" in naming the body. "Task force" implies action, while "commission" has come to imply inaction (Safire 1968; Shafritz 1988).

Indeed, commissions can and have been used to defer action (Flitner 1986; Sulzner 1971; Wolanin 1975). Tutchings (1979) refers to symbolic reassurance as the rhetorical action of commissions. President Reagan did not appoint the Task Force on Food Assistance because he wanted more time before acting on the hunger issue. Rather, Reagan used the Task Force in an attempt to silence hunger advocates who were critical of his food assistance cuts. Silencing the hunger advocates would serve to improve Reagan's 1984 reelection bid (Coombs 1990). As is the case with this example, commissions reassure publics with rhetorical action— they talk about the issue but cannot take action to change policy; such action remains the domain of political actors.

Policy Influence Function

The symbolic reassurance function emphasizes a commission's goal of quiescence, since changing policy is not directly within its purview. However, a commission does have the ability to influence policy. The policy influence function emphasizes substantive action and arousal. Substantive action refers to changes in policies resulting from acceptance of the commission's recommendations. Such policy changes may include alterations in administrative procedures for the federal bureaucracy, the introduction and passage of new legislation in Congress or state legislatures, or revisions of municipal policies (Burke and Benson 1989; Popper 1970; Tutchings 1979). Arousal is the opposite of quiescence; with arousal comes support for and interest in a policy proposal (Edelman 1971). Commissions have the potential to influence policy by arousing publics. The policy influence function is premised on the ability of commissions to educate publics and to mobilize support for policies.

Commissions are capable of educating publics by informing them about issues and ways to resolve the issues. "[C]ommissions appear capable of making others aware of a problem and of expanding the number of people who have heard of the solution advocated by the commission" (Wolanin 1975, 36). The Kerner Commission exemplifies this educative power. Although viewed as controversial by some, the Kerner Commission exposed people to the race-based social inequities that exist in the United States (Flitner 1986). Both attentive publics and policy makers (i.e., the federal, state, or local political agents) can be subject to the commission's educational influence. "In most cases commissions are capable of capturing the attention of at least the policy community in question, and they are often capable of reaching a much more extensive public as well" (Wolanin 1975, 35). The publicity surrounding the commission's activities makes people aware of the issue, while the content of the final report educates people as to how the issue could be resolved (Flitner 1986). It follows that the agenda-setting ability of the media helps to account for the ability of commissions to increase awareness and to educate.

The basic premise behind agenda setting is that publics tend to rate as important those issues that appear the most in the media (McCombs and Shaw 1972; Iyengar and Kinder 1987). But research on agenda setting has progressed beyond the basic level of issue awareness. One advancement has been in the level of information various publics learn from the media. Publics are not only made aware of an issue but they learn various causes of the problems addressed and ways to resolve the problem (Benton and Frazier 1976; Graber 1982; McCombs 1977). For commissions, media coverage of the final report makes people aware of the issue and of the commission's recommendations.

A second advancement resulting from research on agenda setting has been the creation of a connection between media, public, and policy agendas. There is some evidence to support the idea that the media can move an issue onto the public agenda and then onto the policy agenda (Leff, Protess, and Brooks 1986; Molotch, Protess, and Gordon 1987). The implication for commissions is that media coverage for their investigatory actions and final report *might* eventually prompt policy makers into taking substantive action on the commission's issue, possibly implementing their recommendations. This resource is not available to all commissions. As noted earlier, many commissions release their final reports and receive little or no media coverage. Still, some commissions do benefit from media coverage of their final reports. The benefit is the awareness created among the public, an awareness that has the potential to be translated into policy action. For example, the Rogers Commission and the Kerner Commission received extensive media coverage in the major U.S. newspapers (Miller 1988; Flitner 1986).

The possibility of implementation of commission recommendations is furthered by the public mobilization power of commissions. Commissions are recognized as having the ability to mobilize public opinion in support of policy proposals (Flitner 1986). Popper (1970) suggested that this mobilizing ability is derived from a commission's ability to crystallize ideas and that commissions do so more effectively than any other element in the American political system. A commission's crystallizing power comes from the experts assigned to the commission. Typically, the commissioners are very familiar with the current literature and are able to take diverse information and distill it into clear policy proposals rather than vague solutions (Marver 1979).

Implicit in the ability to mobilize is the ability to persuade publics to accept a policy proposal. As Wolanin observed, "Commissions are also particularly capable of persuading others to accept as authoritative their findings and recommendations" (1975, 41). In turn, the persuasive power of commissions is derived from the legitimacy of their recommendations. When commissions make recommendations, publics generally view the recommendations as viable policy options. Commissions make ideas more respectable and plausible, and they bolster public confidence (Flitner 1986; Popper 1970; Sulzner 1971; Wolanin 1975). Commission recommendations derive their acceptability from the membership and decision-making processes of the commission. The final section of this chapter explores more fully the effect of membership and decision making on commission legitimacy.

Just as political actors (i.e., the President, members of Congress, governors, or mayors) use commissions to reassure (gain quiescence), commissions can be used by political actors to change policies (generate arousal). The Commission on Budget Concepts led to changes in the federal budget process, while the National Advisory Commission on Libraries resulted in the passage of legislation that created a permanent federal advisory board for libraries (Wolanin 1975). Any of the constituencies pressing for the creation of a commission can utilize the commission to achieve policy objectives. Even the commissioners can use the policy influence function of commissions.

Murray Edelman's treatment of politics as symbolic action is a helpful perspective from which to view the functioning of commissions. When commissions engage in their investigatory function, the commissioners become political actors who engage in actions that can create arousal or quiescence among the publics (Edelman 1971). Commissions create quiescence when the symbolic reassurance function is employed. The policy influence function is utilized by commissions to create arousal. While the investigatory function may be the defining aspect of a commission, it serves as a vehicle for the symbolic reassurance and policy influence functions of commissions. Constituencies, characteristics, and context all interact when attempts are made to evaluate a commission's fulfillment of its functions.

EVALUATING COMMISSION SUCCESS

This final section seeks to synthesize the earlier discussions of commission characteristics, constituencies, and functions. The synthesis is accomplished by articulating how constituencies and characteristics affect the success or failure of a commission. This discussion is organized around the three functions of commissions. For each function, a measure of success is posited along with a discussion of the constituencies and characteristics needed to successfully complete the function. The section ends with a return to the overriding concern of the contextual variable.

Investigatory Function

The success of the investigatory function can be measured by determining whether appropriate procedures were followed during the investigation and whether the commission produced a legitimate set of recommendations. The constituency involved with the investigatory function is very broad and includes all publics demonstrating an interest in the issue. Therefore, all constituencies can have a stake and can play a part when judging the effectiveness of the investigatory function.

The procedural nature of the investigatory function makes membership, the investigatory process, and the final report essential characteristics. The commission's membership must appear representative and objective. A biased commission is believed to create an unfair investigation (Flitner 1986; Marver 1979). The various constituencies involved with the issue must be represented and the commissioners must be perceived to have open minds about the issue's resolution (Marver 1979; Wolanin 1975). Commissioners themselves recognize the importance of maintaining impartiality. A commission must collect information from a variety of perspectives. Ignoring a salient viewpoint leads to a charge of bias, usually from the constituency whose view was slighted. The commission's report must reflect the input of all commissioners. A report that ignores some commissioners' ideas will be labeled as biased.

Bias is to be avoided since it taints the entire investigatory function and weakens the commission's results. A commission must meet procedural expectations of objectivity and representativeness to be an investigatory success. If successful, the various constituencies will regard the commission's recommendations as legitimate. The Kerner Commission and the Task Force on Food Assistance illustrate success and failure of the investigatory function. The Kerner Commission had quality commissioners, engaged in lengthy hearings of key people, and reached consensus on its recommendations with no supplementary statements. In the end, the recommendations of the Commission were generally praised (Flitner 1986). The Task Force on Food Assistance, on the other hand, was considered biased because a majority of the commissioners disliked food assistance programs and the final report ignored minority viewpoints. In the end, the commission's recommendations were ridiculed (Rich 1984).

Symbolic Reassurance Function

The success of the symbolic reassurance function can be measured in terms of whether an issue is forgotten. If the issue moves off of the media, public, and policy agendas without substantive action being taken, the publics have been symbolically reassured. Symbolic reassurance is a tool political actors use to silence constituencies who are agitating for action (Flitner 1986). The constituencies of the symbolic reassurance function are defined as those groups who push for action on an issue. It follows that government actors and activist groups are the primary constituencies for the symbolic reassurance function. Attentive publics may become a constituency under the right circumstances. The symbolic reassurance function tries to prevent attentive publics from forming, but if the publics are attentive *before* the commission is created they cannot be ignored.

Creating a commission is the symbolic act of a government actor who hopes it will reassure the agitating constituencies. Evidence suggests that merely creating the commission is enough to lead many publics to forget an issue, since the publics believe the government is now taking action to resolve the issue (Tutchings 1979).

The composition of the membership and the enactment of the investigatory process are important factors in the pursuit of the symbolic reassurance function. As with the investigatory function, constituencies are reassured by an objective and representative commission engaged in an open investigation. A commission must avoid the appearance of bias in either its membership or its investigatory actions.

The final report may become irrelevant to the symbolic reassurance function. Publics should be reassured by the creation of the commission, thereby making the final report nonessential. According to the symbolic reassurance function, the creation and start of the commission should make the constituencies forget the issue. Therefore, the report is released in obscurity if the symbolic reassurance function succeeds. However, the final report can also be used to demonstrate that action has been taken. The report then becomes a symbolic act of the commission's work.

Two commissions created by President Reagan show the success and failure of symbolic reassurance. The Task Force on Education was a success, since the education issue disappeared from all agendas after the Commission went to work (Vibbert 1984). The Task Force on Food Assistance backfired, because the Task Force's appointment and investigatory actions served to intensify media coverage and public and policy interest in the hunger issue (Coombs 1992). The symbolic reassurance function can be pursued by political actors but relies heavily on appointments to the commission and the investigatory actions of the commission for its success.

Policy Influence Function

The success of the policy influence function is measured in terms of commission recommendations becoming public policy. According to this standard, if the recommendations fall on deaf ears, the commission has failed. The measure of success restricts the constituencies of the policy influence function to the federal, state, and local bureaucracy, along with activists. The governmental bodies actually have the power to create public policy decisions. Activist groups cannot make public policy but they can stimulate the policy actors to take action (Crable and Vibbert 1985; Gamson 1975).

The policy influence function may be utilized by commissioners themselves or by other political actors. The pursuit of the policy influence function is facilitated by two sets of factors. The first set of factors includes membership, the investigatory process, and the final report. (The three elements of the investigatory function help to establish the legitimacy of the commission's recommendations. The previous section on the investigatory function details how these three elements promote legitimacy for a commission's recommendations.)

The second set of factors includes follow-up activities by commissions, external support for the commission, and the media. These three factors all attempt to place pressure on the policy-making bodies. The objective is to create strong public sentiment on an issue, which in turn pressures policy makers to take action on that issue.

The commission uses follow-up activities to maintain interest in the issue and place pressure on policy makers. Follow-up activities are designed to keep the commission's issue on the agenda and to attract external support. Such activities can take a variety of forms. The Katzenbach Commission on Law Enforcement sponsored conferences and grants as follow-up activities; the Kerner Commission used press briefings for the three major networks and a book contract with Bantam Books to reprint the final report; and the Eisenhower Commission released each chapter of its final report separately, resulting in twenty front-page stories in the *New York Times* and *Washington Post* (Flitner 1986).

External support supplies additional legitimacy and power to the commission recommendations. Activist groups, the attentive public, and government agents at any level can all lend additional clout to a commission's recommendations. For example, the League of Women Voters pushed for the Kerner Commission's recommendations; President Johnson advocated the recommendations made by the President's Commission on Postal Organization; and members of Congress pressed for the Population Commission's recommendations (Flitner 1986; Wolanin 1975). These additional constituencies show power in numbers, a characteristic that is important in the policy-making process (Cobb and Elder 1972).

Large numbers are one of the resources used to affect the policy-making process. Policy makers cannot afford to ignore large numbers of their constituents. Therefore, if many people support an issue, usually it is taken up by policy makers (Pross 1986; Smith 1990). Moreover, an ally pushing recommendations from within the government has proven to be valuable in policy making as well (Jenkins and Eckert 1986; Jenkins and Perrow 1977).

The media serve to amplify both the follow-up activities and the external support. Media coverage garners the attention of the attentive public.

In turn, the public support for the issue creates added pressure on policy makers to place the issue on their agenda (Manheim 1987; Molotch, Protess, and Gordon 1987; Page and Shapiro 1983). For the policy acceptance function, all the resources are used to press the policy maker to accept the recommendations.

Contextual Variable

The previous synthesis of characteristics, constituencies, and functions is somewhat sterile—a sterility derived from ignoring the contextual variables associated with the life cycle of an issue and the continually changing stream of political events. Issues have a natural life cycle driven by public interest (Bitzer 1968). As publics become interested in an issue, the issue rises on the political and social agendas. Eventually interest fades and the issue moves off of the agenda. The issue life cycle occurs naturally and at times is difficult to alter (see Crable and Vibbert 1985; Eyestone 1978). The implication is that the symbolic reassurance function becomes easier and the policy influence function more difficult at the end of an issue's life cycle. The reverse is true when the issue is at its zenith. It is difficult to raise interest (push for policy changes) with an ebbing issue and hard to ignore (gain quiescence on) an issue at the peak of its public attention.

Furthermore, the flow of political events can have an impact on an issue's life cycle. Another political event may supersede the commission's issue. To some degree, the success of the symbolic reassurance and policy influence functions is constrained and enabled by the issue's life cycle and the flow of political events. Unforeseen contextual factors may subvert or empower the careful plans of political actors trying to use commissions to achieve other political goals.

CONCLUSION

This chapter has attempted to shed new light on commissions by examining their characteristics, functions, constituencies, and context. All are important factors affecting a commission's operation. Commissions can be guided by multiple functions. The function being pursued by the commission dictates which constituencies and characteristics become most salient to the commission. All of these activities transpire within and are shaped by the socio-political context surrounding the commission. By examining how these four factors interact, new insights are gained into the operation of commissions. Those insights involve how context, characteristics, and constituencies are utilized to execute the various functions of commissions. The end result is a more detailed understanding of how commissions work.

Part II

Case Studies

4

The Warren Commission

Bruce C. McKinney

In September 1964 the President's Commission on the Assassination of President Kennedy—more commonly known as the Warren Commission—released the *Warren Report,* which was the official account of the assassination of President John F. Kennedy in Dallas, Texas, on November 22, 1963. Almost as soon as the *Warren Report* was released, it was involved in controversy regarding its conclusions about the assassination. Critics from both the public and private sector demanded another investigation. At a 1991 symposium on the assassination, one frequent *Warren Report* critic, Dr. Cyril Wecht, suggested that the one-volume *Warren Report* and twenty-six volumes of *Hearings* be reclassified in all libraries as a work of fiction.[1] Oliver Stone's movie *JFK* has brought the assassination to the public's consciousness once again.

There are many arguments about the assassination of President Kennedy, and perhaps the truth about the assassination may never be known. The Warren Commission's investigation focused on a self-professed Marxist, Lee Harvey Oswald, who worked in a building along the motorcade route where Kennedy was assassinated. Oswald was arrested by the Dallas Police eighty minutes after the assassination and was charged at 1:30 A.M. on November 23 with the assassination of Kennedy. At 11:21 A.M. on November 24, Oswald himself was gunned down by Jack Ruby on national television as he was being transferred from the Dallas city jail to the Dallas county jail. He died at 1:07 P.M. in Parkland Memorial Hospital. The public might have accepted the idea that Oswald was the lone assassin, but when Ruby, another loner, penetrated the gauntlet of Dallas Police officers and shot Oswald, "almost immediately speculation arose that Ruby had acted on behalf of members of a conspiracy who had planned the killing of President Kennedy and who wanted to silence Oswald" (*Report of the President's Commission* 1964, 333).

Kennedy's successor, Vice President Lyndon B. Johnson, acted to restore some sense of national order. He sought "to avoid parallel investigations and to concentrate on fact-finding in a body having the broadest national mandate" (*Report of the President's Commission* 1964, x). On November 29, 1963, Johnson authorized the formation of the Warren Commission via Executive Order 11130.

The charge given the Commission by Johnson was to "uncover all the facts concerning the assassination of President Kennedy and determine if it was in any way directed or encouraged by unknown persons at home and abroad" (*Report of the Select Committee* 1979, 257). An article in the *New York University Law Review* stated that the Commission was needed because "in the face of . . . universal, unceasing clamor of facts, everyone with any grounds for doing so decided to investigate" (Cushman 1965, 477). This included the Dallas Police, a court of inquiry under the authority of the Dallas Magistrate's Court, a Grand Jury investigation under the Dallas County Court, the FBI, and the New Orleans District Attorney's Office (Cushman 1965).

In order to fully understand the nature and purpose of the Warren Commission, one must recognize that it was first and foremost a presidential commission that shared similarities with other presidential commissions, yet its investigation of the murder of the President was a task that set it apart from any other commission formed by a president. An examination of the Warren Commission's similarities with and differences from typical presidential commissions is presented to shed light on these aspects of the Warren Commission. Following this discussion, the relationship between the probe conducted by the Federal Bureau of Investigation and the Chief Justice's inquiry will be chronicled. Finally, the Commission's deliberations will be scrutinized to evaluate its decision-making processes.

THE WARREN COMMISSION
AND OTHER PRESIDENTIAL COMMISSIONS

Unlike Senate select committees and other governmental commissions, presidential commissions are created by the President, who selects commissioners with help from the White House staff. Popper (1970) identifies four major reasons why presidents create commissions: (1) to show concern about a problem, (2) to educate the nation, (3) to obtain new policy ideas, and (4) to mobilize support for presidential programs. According to Popper, the Warren Commission was probably a gesture on the part of President Johnson to "inspire and restore national confidence" (1970, 9) by showing that he was aware of public distress following the assassination of President John F. Kennedy and the murder of his accused assassin, Lee Harvey Oswald, two days later.

Cushman (1965) claims that Johnson created the Warren Commission to satisfy public demands about controversies surrounding the assassination. A memorandum from Deputy Attorney General Nicholas deB. Katzenbach to Johnson aide Bill Moyers three days after the assassination left little doubt about the true purpose of the Commission: "The public must be satisfied that Oswald was the assassin; that he did not have confederates who are still at large; and that the evidence was such that he would have been convicted at a trial . . . [so that] [s]peculation about his motives ought to be cut off."[2]

One may argue that the dominant purpose of the Warren Commission was not to investigate Kennedy's assassination, but to assure the nation that Oswald was guilty and to restore national confidence, a claim first advanced by H. Weisberg (1965) and E. J. Epstein (1966). By creating the Warren Commission, Johnson was showing the nation his personal concern over the assassination, be it for personal or political motives. However, the charge of the Commission—to investigate Oswald as Kennedy's assassin—begged the question and created controversies surrounding the event that persist to this day. Cushman offers his own succinct conclusion about this purpose: "Surely the injection into our system of justice of an agency [Warren Commission] based on such a preconception poses a threat to impartial justice worthy of the most careful consideration" (1965, 503).

The Warren Commission shared many similarities with other presidential commissions. First, presidential commissions are made up of commissioners who are "all well known, busy people, some of whom are unable to attend all of the meetings" (Popper 1970, 7). Like other presidential commissions, the Warren Commission had a full-time executive director to supervise the daily Commission operations. J. Lee Rankin performed this role in the Warren Commission, though he was referred to as the Commission's General Counsel. The executive director typically recruits a full-time staff, "usually composed of young lawyers and governmental employees" (Popper 1970, 7). This is exactly what Rankin did.

In his selection of the commissioners, Johnson followed the norm of presidential commissions via bicameral balancing: an equal number of senators and representatives. He also followed the rule of bipartisan balancing: one Democratic senator (Richard Russell), one Republican senator (John Sherman Cooper), one Democratic representative (Hale Boggs), and one Republican representative (Gerald Ford). The Commission's chair, Chief Justice Earl Warren, was a Republican; this may have been Johnson's way of ensuring that no one could claim that he was influencing the Commission through a Democratic chair. Rankin, Allen Dulles (former director of the CIA fired by Kennedy), and John J. McCloy (former president of the World Bank) were all Republicans, but along with Cooper, Rankin, Boggs, and Ford they met the general composite sketch of members of presidential commissions. They all had very successful careers, and their work on the Warren Commission was not seen as a stepping stone to advance their careers—all were in their fifties or sixties at the time of their appointments, and their backgrounds were "extraordinarily skewed in composition in favor of the best educated and professionally well established" (Popper 1970, 19). Additionally, all of those selected held law degrees.

In selecting the membership of the Warren Commission, President Johnson saw to it that both conservatives and liberals were represented, as well as the intelligence community. The motivation for doing this, along with his bipartisan balancing, is best stated by Weisberg:

Thereafter the GOP could have no complaints, nor the conservatives, nor, with Warren as the Chairman the eastern intellectual community, nor with the liberal republican Cooper, that faction, nor with the spooks [CIA], etc., with Dulles. In all ways [it] was [an] extraordinary [decision] and I think unprecedented. [It was] LBJ at his political astutest. (Weisberg 1985)

When the commissioners *did* meet, their attendance was poor. The Commission only met a total of thirteen times, and only Warren and Rankin attended all of the meetings. Russell (who did not want to serve on the Commission) missed six meetings, Boggs missed five, McCloy missed three, Ford missed two, and Dulles and Cooper each missed one. While all of the Commission members were busy men, it is curious with respect to the magnitude of the task at hand that they did not have a better attendance record.

The make-up of the staff of the Warren Commission was no more unique than other presidential commissions: the staff members were younger and less known than the commissioners; most were in their thirties; their service to the Commission was a full-time job. And, like other presidential commissions, they did most of the work. The commis-sioners themselves were merely a policy-making group who directed the nature of the investigation but did little investigating themselves. Rankin posed as a mediator between the commissioners and the staff in his prescribed role as the executive director. The staff was also responsible for writing the Commission's final report, which had to be approved by the commissioners; some chapters of the final report went through as many as twenty drafts before the commissioners approved them.

This may seem ironic since presidential commissions suffer from the inability to act on their conclusions. Popper claims that now-retired Navy Admiral Hyman Rickover, when testifying in 1959 about Defense Department Committees to the House Committee on Governmental Operations, made an observation that applies to presidential commissions as well:

The members of [these committees] have no responsibility, but take the liberty of making recommendations and then running off somewhere else and getting on some other committee on another subject and making more recommendations. . . . They come around, talk for a little while, make a recommendation, and go back and play golf or whatever they do. . . . They have a paper responsibility to make a certain recommendation, but once they make that recommendation, they cheerfully disband and go on and get on some other committee. (Popper 1970, 53)

Commissions must also operate by consensus, which may, in turn, cover up differences between the members. In the Warren Commission members could not agree as to whether or not Governor John Connally and President Kennedy had been hit by the same bullet. Half the Commission members believed that both men had been hit by the same bullet, while the other half felt that two separate bullets had hit each man, which would indicate that Oswald did not act alone (Popper 1970, 33). Ford wanted to state that there was "compelling evidence" that both men were hit by the same bullet; Russell wanted the report to read that there was only "credible evidence" for such a conclusion. According to McCloy, in order to reach a consensus, the "battle of the adjectives" began. The Commission finally adopted "persuasive evidence" that indicated both men had been hit by the same bullet; yet this never answered the original question of how many bullets struck each man (Epstein 1966, 130).

There are many other criticisms of presidential commissions dealing with inattentive memberships, lack of cohesion, political nature, size, lack of experience, deadlines, and lack of constructive dissent (Popper 1970). Many of these same faults may be found in the Warren Commission. Though it shares many characteristics with past and present presidential commissions, the consequences of the Warren Commission's findings continue to attract more attention than any other presidential commission—no other commission has investigated the assassination of a president.

Though the Warren Commission was similar to most presidential commissions, it did have one purpose that sets it apart from most other presidential commissions: it was investigating the "wrong-doing by an individual"—Lee Harvey Oswald—and was seeking to assess blame to Oswald. However, the Commission could not punish anyone; it could only make recommendations to President Johnson. The only similar commission in U.S. history was the Roberts Commission created by President Franklin Roosevelt to investigate the Pearl Harbor disaster: it sought to assign blame for the failure of the American forces to be prepared for the Japanese attack. This Commission, headed by Chief Justice Roberts, was the only other presidential commission headed by a Chief Justice of the United States. Both the Roberts and the Warren Commissions sought and received subpoena powers from Congress to ensure that witnesses would attend hearings and present evidence. Most other presidential commissions have not had, nor have they had the need for, the power of subpoena.

Similar to other presidential commissions, the investigation of the Warren Commission was not a legal process like that of a court; it did not have the same restrictions. Witnesses and those investigated did not have the same rights as they would have had in a court of law. In the Commission's hearings there was no judge, and though witnesses could be represented by counsel, counsel could not cross-examine witnesses or offer evidence contrary to the Commission's findings (Weisberg 1965, xiv).

Another unique aspect of the Warren Commission was that those agencies that carried out its investigations (chiefly the FBI and, to a lesser extent, the CIA and the Secret Service) were not employees of the Commission, but had responsibilities to those who employed them. The Commission's investigation was supposed to be independent, but it decided to rely on federal agencies as its investigators. This paradox was to haunt the Commission in years to come. On one hand, it would not base its findings on the FBI reports; on the other hand, it would use the FBI as its chief investigative agency. Since both the Secret Service and the FBI were responsible for Kennedy's protection (and were criticized in the *Warren Report*), representatives of these agencies and their employers had a personal involvement in the investigation that may be seen as a conflict of interest. The Secret Service had failed to protect the President adequately—many of them were out drinking well past 2:00 A.M. the night before the assassination—and the FBI had failed to notify the Secret Service about Oswald's presence in Dallas before the assassination (Marrs 1989). As Weisberg concludes, "The situation was unfair to the agencies, which did not create it, and could have burdened them with impermissible conflicts and temptations, no matter how unconsciously" (Weisberg 1965, x–xi).

THE WARREN COMMISSION AND THE FBI

Before the Commission was formed, the FBI let it be known that it felt that its report on the assassination was sufficient and that a presidential commission was not necessary. FBI Director J. Edgar Hoover claimed that a presidential commission would turn into a "three ring circus" (Kurtz 1982, 24), but he was most likely fearful that such a commission might find flaws in the FBI's hasty investigation. An intra-Bureau memorandum from Cartha DeLoach of the Crime Records Division to John Mohr, Hoover's assistant, reveals that the FBI was trying to kill a story in the *Washington Post* about the formation of the Commission. The *Post* was planning an editorial on the necessity of such a body to investigate the assassination. DeLoach was trying to convince Al Friendly, the Vice President and Managing Editor of the *Post*, that Hoover believed such a commission would "create further confusion and hysteria."[3] DeLoach asked Friendly to kill the editorial, which he agreed to do. But the editor of the *Post*, Russ Wiggins, could not give the FBI a definite "yes" regarding the elimination of the editorial. DeLoach commented that "[t]his, of course, is the usual 'hog wash' on the part of Wiggins who cannot be trusted and usually attempts to run opposite to good judgment in order to satisfy his own ego."[4]

When the FBI realized that Johnson would create a presidential commission, the FBI made sure that Johnson's presidential statement announcing the formation of the Warren Commission met with Hoover's approval. When the draft of this statement was prepared and circulated to the FBI, Hoover's written comment was, "The president discussed this with me and I am in accord."[5]

In the early meetings of the Warren Commission one sticky issue surfaced: whether or not to make public the FBI's already completed *Summary Report* about the assassination before the Warren Commission released its own report. Three days after Kennedy's death, President Johnson ordered the FBI to make a complete investigation and present the findings to him (*Hearings before the President's Commission* 1964, Vol. 5). The FBI completed its investigation in a mere two weeks, and in early

December 1963, J. Edgar Hoover submitted to the White House a four-volume report that summarized the Bureau's findings. On December 9, the *Summary Report* was submitted to the Warren Commission, and on January 13, 1964, a *Supplemental Report* consisting of one volume was sent to the Commission (Epstein 1966). These reports were considered crucial to the investigation of the assassination and were an authoritative and official summary of the facts as of January 13, 1964, before the Warren Commission began its investigation (Epstein 1966).

The FBI concluded that Lee Harvey Oswald was the lone assassin and was not aided by any conspirators but killed Kennedy for his own political and psychological motives (Federal Bureau of Investigation 1963, 22a–74). In fact, one day after the assassination, Hoover told Johnson that Oswald was the lone assassin (Kurtz 1982).

The five volumes of reports that the FBI turned over to the Warren Commission were mostly a psychological profile of Oswald and contained less than five hundred words about the assassination itself (Federal Bureau of Investigation 1963, 1–3). The Commission faced a problem in receiving the FBI's conclusions about the assassination. The purpose of the Commission was to conduct an investigation into the assassination, but only seventeen days after Kennedy's murder, it received a report from the FBI naming Oswald as the lone assassin. Commission member John J. McCloy was troubled by the fact that the FBI *Summary Report* paralleled too closely the mission of the Commission. Thus, "the Warren Commission decided to reserve judgments on the conclusions of the FBI Summary Report until all of its premises were critically appraised" (Epstein 1966, 8). The Commission decided not to make public the findings of the *Summary Report* before it published its own report. This was done with the intent to avoid confusion and rumors.

The conclusions reached by the FBI in its pre–Warren Commission investigations did not remain secret for long. Although the *Summary Report* was not delivered to the Warren Commission until December 9, 1963, the press was already announcing the FBI's conclusions as early as December 3. The conclusions reached by the FBI were summarized accurately in a *Time* magazine article of December 13 ("A Sad and Solemn Duty" 1963, 26). With lead-time for publication, it may be assumed that the editors of *Time* had the conclusions of the FBI *Summary Report* before the members of the Warren Commission did. It is not clear who in the FBI was leaking the results of the *Summary Report*, but the fact that the public was now aware of its conclusions upset Commission member Richard Russell.[6] He asked the FBI sarcastically if the whole *Summary Report* would be leaked to the press before the Commission got its copy of the report.[7] The Commission now faced a dubious task. If its findings did not agree with the FBI, doubt would be cast upon the Bureau, a most respected governmental agency in 1964. However, the Commission's decision to rely on the FBI to do its investigative work almost precluded such a possibility.

Earl Warren opposed the release of the FBI report, claiming that the only report that should be released to the public was the one that the Commission would produce.[8] The Commission members agreed with Warren, and the leak of the FBI's conclusions angered many Commission members who blamed the FBI. The FBI, on the other hand, accused the Commission of leaking the FBI's report, since copies of the report had been circulated to all Commission members. An intra-Bureau memorandum from DeLoach to Mohr on December 11, 1963, indicated that the FBI was convinced the Warren Commission was responsible for the unauthorized release of the contents of its report to the press:

Also, since copies of the report have been made available to members of the Commission, there is every indication leaks are coming from the Commission itself. It is a fact that within a matter of an hour or two after the report was made available to the Commission local radio stations were broadcasting details. We will maintain a "no comment" here.[9]

As mentioned earlier, Johnson's selection of the members of the Warren Commission may be seen as a keen attempt to placate all political factions. Whether he knew it or not, when Johnson selected Gerald Ford to be a commissioner, he chose a member who would look out not only for the interests of the GOP but for the interests of the FBI as well. Ford was the FBI's eyes and ears within the Commission. An intra-Bureau memorandum from DeLoach to Mohr on December 12, 1963, indicated Ford's willingness to cooperate with the FBI. This declassified memo revealed that Ford would keep DeLoach apprised of what was happening in the Commission's closed-door meetings, especially anything that might reflect badly on the FBI. Hoover's comment to DeLoach about this relationship was, "Well handled."[10] William Sullivan, an assistant to Hoover, put it more bluntly: "He [Ford] was our man, our informant, on the Warren Commission" (Sullivan 1979, 53).

The FBI was not always willing to give the Warren Commission all the information that it wanted. Though the media and Hoover had the American people believing that the FBI happily worked at the request of the Warren Commission, this was not the case. In a declassified FBI memorandum of March 12, 1964, the Bureau is depicted as quite clearly *not* wanting to aid in the investigation of Kennedy's assassination when the Commission relied on agencies outside of the FBI to examine evidence. The topic of discussion in this memorandum is a request by

Commission staff member David Belin that the FBI deliver the firearms evidence to a third party:

While we are, of course, mindful of the Director's instructions that we are to comply with all of the Commission's requests . . . it is our feeling that it is undesirable for this Bureau to act as the transmission belt in delivering any evidence to outside examiners pursuant to the Commission's request.[11]

Hoover's written remark on this memo is "I concur." The FBI also dragged its heels when it came to participating in a reenactment of the assassination. The FBI concluded that it would not be in the best interest of the Bureau to cooperate with the Warren Commission. However, almost as soon as the Warren Commission began its deliberations, events occurred that were to drive a wedge between these two investigative bodies forever.

Perhaps nothing put more of a strain on the already shaky relationship between the Warren Commission and the FBI than rumors that Oswald was either an FBI informant or agent. When the Commission received information regarding a possible connection between Oswald and the FBI, it faced an unexpected obstacle to what some called a "pre-planned investigation" (Epstein 1966; Lane 1966; Weisberg 1965). As Commissioner Ford stated, "Thus the matter of determining at the outset how to handle the rumor that Oswald was connected to the FBI was a test of the ability of the Commission to execute its mission" (Ford and Stiles 1965, 22). During a January 22, 1964, meeting Allen Dulles was a bit more concise with respect to this revelation: "Oh, terrible" (Transcripts of the Executive Sessions 22 January 1964, 12). Hale Boggs summed up the dilemma that now faced the Commission: "Its implications of this are fantastic, don't you think so?" (Transcripts of the Executive Sessions 22 January 1964, 12).

On January 22 and 27, 1964, the Warren Commission met to discuss allegations that Lee Harvey Oswald was an FBI undercover agent. Rumors had been circulating that Oswald had been paid $200 a month as an FBI informant from September 22 until Kennedy's assassination. He had supposedly been assigned badge number 179 by the FBI for his services. These allegations, if true, would have opened up a Pandora's Box; the Commission would have been forced to expand its investigation to determine why the FBI had covered up the matter. This investigation would have delayed the release of the *Warren Report* beyond the upcoming presidential election in November of 1964, something that President Johnson wanted to avoid. The transcripts of these meetings provide good insight into the thinking of the Warren Commission, for they reveal an aspect of faulty decision making that was present in the Commission's deliberations: groupthink (see Janis 1982).

GROUPTHINK AND DECISION MAKING

In 1972 Irving Janis introduced the concept of "groupthink" to small group decision making. After studying decision-making fiascoes of foreign policy groups, he determined there was one variable present in groups that made poor and, at times, disastrous decisions. This variable, groupthink, is defined as "a mode of thinking that people engage in when they are deeply involved in a cohesive in-group, when the members' striving for unanimity overrides their motivation to realistically appraise alternate courses of action" (Janis 1982, 174). In other words, individuals suppress their personal thoughts and beliefs to maintain the group's cohesion. To determine the presence or absence of groupthink, Janis discovered behaviors that he calls symptoms of groupthink. When these symptoms are present, the group has a greater likelihood of experiencing groupthink. These symptoms include an illusion of invulnerability, collective rationalizations, stereotyping out- or competing groups, pressure on dissenting members to conform, failure to share information with out- or competing groups, and solution-centeredness. In addition, Janis believes that symptomatic groupthink is evident only when the following antecedent conditions are in operation: a high level of group cohesion, insulation of the group, lack of impartial leadership, and the absence of norms requiring methodical procedures for dealing with the decision-making tasks of the group.

On the basis of historical records and transcripts of the Warren Commission, it becomes evident that groupthink has claimed another victim. In order to understand how this dilemma occurred, it is first necessary to examine the antecedent conditions for groupthink that were manifested in the deliberations of the Warren Commission.

The Warren Commission as a Cohesive Group

Of all the antecedent conditions for groupthink, Janis believes that a high level of cohesion is the most essential. Though some dispute this, Janis still stands by his claim.[12] Was the Warren Commission a cohesive group? At first appearance the answer is no. Two of its members—Warren and Russell—were coerced by Johnson to serve on the Commission. Johnson told Warren that a nuclear war might occur if rumors about the assassination were not put to rest, and Warren reluctantly agreed to be the Commission's chair (Warren 1977). Johnson was less diplomatic with Senator Richard Russell. When Johnson asked him to serve on the Commission, Russell flatly refused. However, when Johnson announced the formation of the Warren Commission, he named Russell as one of its members, which left Russell little choice but to accept.

Though attendance at Commission meetings was poor (as it is with most presidential commissions), the Commission was held together by Executive Order 11130, which gave it the responsibility of investigating the assassination. According to Weisberg, the Commission was cohesive in that it wanted to "appear credible and do what was regarded as necessary for acceptability or at least reduce criticism [that] could not be avoided in advance" (Weisberg 1985). The production of a credible report that the American people would accept appears to be the thread that held the Commission together.

Leadership in the Warren Commission

The role of leadership in the Warren Commission was assumed by J. Lee Rankin, the Commission's General Counsel (executive director). Weisberg claims that Rankin, not Warren, was the most powerful man on the Commission (1985). Rankin was the person on the Commission who was influential in directing the activities of the group, and all communication between governmental agencies and the Commission went through Rankin—not Warren—before it was passed on to the rest of the Commission.

The direction that Rankin gave the Commission precluded any other conclusion except that Oswald was the lone assassin. A progress report he prepared for Warren on January 11, 1964, after only three Commission meetings, indicated his feelings about the nature of the investigation. Rankin divided the investigation into six areas: (1) Assassination of President Kennedy on November 22, 1963; (2) *Lee Harvey Oswald as the Assassin of President Kennedy* (emphasis added); (3) Lee Harvey Oswald: Background and Possible Motive; (4) Oswald's Foreign Activity (Military Excluded); (5) Murder of Lee Harvey Oswald by Jack Ruby; and (6) Security Precautions to Protect the President (Records of Presidential Committees 1964).

When the *Warren Report* was released nine months later, the eight chapters of the *Report* varied little from Rankin's six areas of investigation. The significance of this memorandum is that Rankin had tried and convicted Oswald after only *three* meetings of the Commission. Such a memo would be expected after the group completed all of its investigation, but not *before their investigation had begun.* Janis (1982) believes that the leader of a policy-making group may find it all too easy to use his or her power and prestige to convince members of the group to approve of the policy alternative he or she prefers as opposed to encouraging them to engage in an open inquiry and/or a critical evaluation. It is quite obvious from Rankin's memo to Warren that he was directing the investigation in the way he preferred; there is no mention of any other investigation other than proving Oswald's guilt. Rankin never let the other commissioners consider any assassins other than Oswald when he ran the Commission's meetings.

Insulation of the Warren Commission

One of the greatest criticisms of the Warren Commission was the secrecy in which it conducted its investigation. The Commission was created to eliminate rumors about the assassination, but its decision not to release any details about its final report until its work was complete only led to greater speculation. In addition, the Commission took all of its testimony in secret, classified its transcripts and records without having the proper authority, and released virtually nothing of substance to the press (Weisberg 1985). The Warren Commission's decision to keep material uncovered during its investigation classified until the year 2039—seventy-five years after the release of its *Report*—drove a wedge of distrust between the public and the Commission that still exists today. A weekly news magazine stated:

By its very silence for so long, the commission headed by Chief Justice Earl Warren made its own task that much harder. It gave a long head start to confusion and conjecture even among the best intentioned; and it nourished a whole mythology of assassination literature, ranging from outlandish theories to cunningly plausible doubts. ("The Assassination" 1964, 32)

The Warren Commission's Decision-Making Procedure

The decision making of the Warren Commission was indicative of solution-centeredness and a lack of thorough planning for its investigation (McKinney 1990). In all session transcripts that are now declassified,[13] there are only two sessions where an agenda is mentioned, and the transcripts disclose a rather loosely organized discussion with no goal set for each meeting—there is no mention of any "methodical procedure" for the decision making in any of the transcripts of the Commission's meetings.[14] A reading of the transcripts reveals that Warren usually introduced the topic to be covered, and then the discussion following was directed by Rankin. Members did not appear to be briefed beforehand on the topic of discussion, which would be indicative of a failure on Rankin's part to circulate an agenda before the Commission met.

SYMPTOMS OF GROUPTHINK IN THE WARREN COMMISSION

On January 22 and 27, 1964, the Commission met to discuss a problem that could have extremely damaged its "Oswald as lone gunman" conclusion. As discussed earlier, rumors had been circulating that Oswald had been paid $200 a month as an FBI informant from September 1962 until Kennedy's assassination. A thorough investigation of this rumor would have probably delayed the release of the Commission's report beyond the presidential election of 1964 and would have angered President Johnson. Of all the Commission's meetings, these two were the only ones in which an obstacle to its conclusions about Oswald surfaced. Because of the strategic nature of these meetings, they were analyzed in light of Janis's groupthink hypothesis.

Collective Rationalization

In the January 22 meeting, Rankin made every effort to rationalize to the Commission that it could not be proven that Oswald was an employee of the FBI. Rankin stated at one point: "It is going to be very difficult for us to establish the fact in it. I am confident that the FBI would never admit it, and I presume their records would never show it" (Transcripts of the Executive Sessions 22 January, 1964, 3).

It is important to remember that Rankin outlined a sequence for the investigation eleven days earlier naming Oswald as Kennedy's assassin and most likely did not want to examine any evidence contrary to his preconceived solution. Allen Dulles also supported Rankin in this area in the next meeting. When Dulles was asked during the January 27 meeting if the CIA would ever admit it if a man like Oswald worked for the Agency, he responded that "The record might not be on paper. But on paper you would have hieroglyphics that only two people knew what they meant, and nobody outside of the agency would know and you would say this meant the agent and somebody else could say it meant another agent" (Transcripts of the Executive Sessions 27 January 1964, 152). Former CIA Director Dulles also admitted that CIA agents would commit perjury under oath to deny any connection to the CIA.

A hypothesis that is presented as impossible to prove would probably lead a group away from carefully examining any evidence contrary to the current thinking. This would tend to introduce a potential source of conflict that could have disrupted the Commission's investigation in the "Oswald was the assassin" mindset. In addition, it would be easier to rationalize away a problem if the problem was likely to destroy the group's current thinking, and any positive indication that Oswald had been employed by the FBI would have seriously damaged the Commission's preference for the lone assassin theory.

Stereotyping Out- or Competing Groups

The one group in direct competition with the Warren Commission was the FBI. As mentioned earlier, the FBI released its conclusions regarding the assassination just as the Warren Commission was having its first meetings. It is apparent in the transcripts that hostility existed between the FBI and the Warren Commission. In the January 27 meeting, the Commissioners let their feelings be known about FBI agents, and to a lesser extent CIA agents. Commissioner McCloy states, "I have really run into some stupid agents. . . . I have run into some very limited mentalities in both the FBI and the CIA" (Transcripts of the Executive Sessions 27 January 1964, 163). Warren comments in the same exchange that the problem lies with the undercover agents that the FBI employs. He states, "they [FBI] . . . do employ undercover men who are of terrible character" (8). Dulles agrees, calling these agents "[t]erribly bad characters" (163). In what has become the investigation of the century, it is sobering to discover that the investigating commission and its investigative agency had such little respect for each other.

Pressures on Dissenting Members to Conform

In the strange world of the "Commission's Assassin," Lee Harvey Oswald, things happened that one might want to question in more detail, yet Commission members decided to leave some stones unturned. One perplexing issue the Commission faced was the ease with which Oswald had obtained a passport to return to Russia after defecting to that country three years earlier. In the words of Chief Justice Warren:

One of the strange things that happened, and it may have no bearing on this at all, is the fact that this man who is a defector, and who was under observation at least by the FBI, they say they saw him frequently, could walk about the Immigration Office in [New] Orleans one day and come out with a passport that permitted him to go to Russia. From my observations of the case[s] that have come to us, such passports are not passed out with ease. (Transcripts of the Executive Sessions 22 January 1964, 7–8)

Dulles told Warren that this was not exactly the case, stating, "I think you are wrong on that" (Transcripts of the Executive Sessions 22 January 1964, 8). Warren continued to feel that it was a little odd for Oswald to obtain a passport to Russia so easily, and he was joined by Boggs and Cooper. Yet the transcripts reveal a concentrated effort on the part of former CIA Director Dulles to convince the Commission (especially Warren) that the State Department had no knowledge of Oswald as a defector—a defector who received $435.71 from the same State Department to finance his return trip from the Soviet Union in 1962. An examination of the transcripts of this meeting reveals that Dulles thought that there was nothing peculiar about a defector receiving a passport within twenty-four hours to return to Russia when it takes an average citizen weeks to obtain one. Dulles, with his CIA background, probably knew that in the case of a defector like Oswald, a "lookout card" should have been prepared by the State Department. A lookout card at the time was part of the State Department's method for keeping an eye on people who may not have been entitled to receive a passport due to a variety of circumstances. This card was then placed in a "lookout file." Whenever anyone applied for a U.S. passport from any city in the world, the application was checked against the lookout file to determine if a lookout card was present. If a lookout card was found, the person could be denied a passport (Meagher 1967).

If anyone deserved a lookout card it was Oswald. After arriving in Moscow in 1959, he turned in his U.S. passport, denounced his American citizenship, and claimed allegiance to the Soviet Union. He also told the U.S. Ambassador, Counsel Richard E. Snyder, that he had—or would—offer the Soviets all information on radar operation that he had acquired while serving with Marine Air Control Squadron One at the

Marine base in Atsuki, Japan. This was one of the two U.S. bases from which the famous U-2 spy planes took off in their espionage missions over Russia. However, in June 1961, Oswald told Snyder that he had learned his lesson and that Russia was not suited to him. In June 1962, his passport was returned and he journeyed back to the United States with his Russian wife, Marina. (As circumstances would have it, the State Department never issued a lookout card on Oswald and blamed this failure on "clerical error." See *Report of the President's Commission* 1964, 751, 772).

It is not clear why Dulles was so insistent that it would be easy for Oswald to get clearance to return to Russia in only twenty-four hours. Did Dulles act—in Janis's term—as a "mindguard" for the Commission, in which he did not let the Commission be privy to any information that might have expanded the nature of its investigation? Janis states that a mindguard "protects them [high officials] from thoughts that might damage their confidence in the soundness of their policies to which they are committed or are about to commit themselves" (Janis 1972, 42). The Commission's position was that Oswald was the lone assassin and there was no conspiracy. An investigation that could possibly explain Oswald's strange relationship with the State Department was something the Commission appeared to want to avoid. Dulles in fact had "mindguarded" the Commission from information that might have revealed a possible motive for Kennedy's assassination. The CIA, under Dulles's leadership, had conspired with the Mafia to assassinate Fidel Castro. If Castro had discovered the plot, retaliation would have been a likely motive for Kennedy's assassination. Yet Dulles chose not to inform the Commission of the plot ("Charged" 1976, 21). His reluctance to admit anything unusual about Oswald's trip to Russia and the circumstances under which it occurred may have been a further attempt to conceal CIA involvement in the assassination conspiracy. At the least, Dulles's comments certainly put pressure on his fellow commissioners to conform to his beliefs about Oswald's ease in obtaining his passport.

Solution Centeredness

Rankin, the Commission's General Counsel and true leader, had obviously made up his mind that a complete and independent investigation of the Oswald-FBI connection was out of the question. At the opening of the January 27 meeting, he let the group know that he favored approaching the FBI and letting them resolve the Oswald-FBI dilemma. Though several of the commissioners did not favor this approach, Rankin stated that the Commission should

go and see Mr. Hoover and tell him frankly what the rumor was, state that it was pure rumor, we haven't evaluated the facts, but ask him, first, if it is true, and secondly if he can supply us with information to establish that these facts are not true, and they are inconsistent with what would be the way of operation by the Bureau. (Transcripts of the Executive Sessions 27 January 1964, 141–42)

Each time the Commission moved away from this suggestion, Rankin became increasingly insistent that this was the only approach the Commission should take. Rankin had obviously formed a "solution" to this problem regardless of what the other Commission members said: he would rely upon the FBI to investigate itself. At the conclusion of the January 27 meeting, the Commission left the decision up to Rankin; he chose to let the FBI investigate itself in this matter.

The symptoms of illusion of invulnerability and failure to share information with out- or competing groups were not present in the transcripts analyzed. Janis does not claim that all symptoms have to be in evidence to indicate groupthink, and this appears to be the case with the Warren Commission. The symptom of illusion of invulnerability is one that is best evident when a group's deliberations concern military operations (for example, the Pearl Harbor advisory group, and Kennedy's advisors in the Bay of Pigs). However, nonmilitary decisions are not excluded from this symptom: President Nixon and his advisors felt that they could contain the Watergate break-in from the Oval Office (see Gouran 1976). With respect to a failure to share information with an out- or competing group, the Warren Commission had no choice but to share information with the FBI; the FBI produced the Commission's information/evidence base throughout its investigation.

SYMPTOMS OF DEFECTIVE DECISION MAKING

According to Janis, whenever a group exhibits the symptoms of groupthink, the group will also manifest symptoms of defective decision making. These include:

- incomplete survey of alternatives and objectives;
- failure to examine risks of preferred choices;

- failure to reappraise initially rejected alternatives;
- poor information search;
- selective bias in processing information at hand.

Incomplete Survey of Alternatives and Objectives

The Warren Commission never did discuss any alternative organizations with which Oswald may have been associated except the FBI. Considering Oswald's extremely peculiar travel background for a man of meager income (Europe, Russia, and Mexico City), his pro- and anti-Castro affiliations, his military background at a top secret air base, and his ease in obtaining a passport back to Russia after he had previously defected there, the Warren Commission at least should have had the idea to investigate whether Oswald was in the employ of some other intelligence agency of the U.S. government. Yet this possibility was never mentioned. Instead, the Commission focused only on how to discover whether Oswald was connected to the FBI.

With respect to possible alternatives for making this determination, the Commission gave itself only two: (1) rely on the FBI, and/or (2) perform an independent investigation. Members of the Commission at times voiced a desire for an independent investigation but never really felt comfortable with the possibility of embarrassing Hoover.[15] The Commission members never seemed to realize that due to their dependence upon the FBI, an independent investigation by the Commission was virtually impossible. Whenever the Commissioners mentioned an independent investigation of this issue, they failed to discuss how such an investigation could be carried out without the FBI. Rankin obviously did not want an independent investigation and sought to move this issue out of the way as soon as possible. When the information was first disclosed about Oswald having possible connections to the FBI, Rankin let the Commission know how he felt about this information during the January 27 meeting: "We do have a dirty rumor that is very bad for the Commission, the problem and it is very damaging to the agencies that are involved in it and must be wiped out insofar as it is possible to do so by the Commission" (Transcripts of the Executive Sessions 27 January 1964, 139).

One major objective that was never considered and still haunts the *Warren Report* was, "what can the Commission best do to prove to the American people that Oswald was not connected to the FBI or any other governmental agency?" Recent books have claimed that Oswald may have been an agent of the Office of Naval Intelligence, Army Intelligence, the CIA, and so on.[16] Instead of addressing that objective, however, the Commission decided not to offend Hoover by using an agency outside the FBI to investigate the Oswald-FBI connection. Consequently, the Commission never stated any clear objective related to the more important underlying issue of connections Oswald may have had with various governmental agencies, including the FBI. It becomes clear from an examination of the transcripts that Rankin either feared offending Hoover or had other reasons to let the FBI investigate its alleged connection to Oswald.

The Commission's fear of Hoover may not have been shared by all members; however, Hoover was an extremely powerful man in Washington in 1963. The commissioners were probably aware that any anti-Hoover sentiment would eventually reach the FBI's Director (it did, through Hoover's Warren Commission spy, Gerald Ford), who had a long record of lashing out at his critics. In addition, President Johnson and Hoover had a close relationship, and the commissioners may have wanted to avoid undermining the credibility of a Johnson ally (Sullivan 1979). During the January 27 meeting, Warren commented that, "I rather dislike going to the FBI and just ask them to establish to us that a rumor can't be true until we have at least looked into it" (Transcripts of the Executive Sessions, 27 January 1964, 142). Russell also expressed this desire: "I think the best way to handle it would be to try to exhaust it at the other hand before you go to the FBI. That would be my judgment" (142). Later on in the meeting McCloy seemed to be exasperated when he commented on Rankin's desire to avoid embarrassing Hoover: "Does the embarrassment supersede the importance of getting the best evidence in such a situation as this?" (147). As was established earlier, in the end the Commission left the direction of the investigation up to Rankin, who in turn let the FBI investigate itself.

On May 5, 1964, FBI agents John Fain, John Quigley, and James Hosty testified before the Commission. Each claimed that Oswald was not employed by the FBI (*Hearings before the President's Commission* 1964, Vol. 4, 429, 440, 469). On May 14, 1964, the Assistant to the Director of the FBI, Alan Belmont, testified before the Commission that "Oswald was not, never was, an agent or informant of the FBI" (*Hearings before the President's Commission* 1964, Vol. 5, 27). Also on the same day, FBI Director J. Edgar Hoover testified before the Commission, stating that "I know at no time was he [Oswald] an informant or agent or special employee or working in any capacity for the FBI" (*Hearings before the President's Commission* 1964, Vol. 5, 106). Regarding Oswald's possible connections with the FBI, the *Warren Report* concluded:

Director Hoover has sworn that he caused a search to be made of the records of the Bureau, and that the search discloses that Oswald "was never an informant of the FBI, and never assigned a symbol number in that capacity, and was never paid any amount by the FBI in any regard." (*Report of the President's Commission* 1964, 327)

The Warren Commission's investigation regarding the assassination of Kennedy will most likely be debated for years to come. All in all, there is little to refute the fact that the Commission's failure to investigate any alternatives to its conclusions regarding Oswald has contributed greatly to the controversies surrounding Kennedy's death.[17]

Failure to Examine Risks of Preferred Choices

With the exception of Rankin, most of the members of the Commission seemed to favor an independent investigation if it could proceed without offending Hoover. Yet the Commissioners were guilty of tunnel vision when they examined the risks of their preferred choices. Incredibly, the only risk that they envisioned was embarrassing Hoover, which was something all Commission members wanted to avoid. Thus, it was not so much a failure to examine the risk of a preferred choice; rather, it was the weight that they assigned this risk. No one in the Commission (at least according to what is recorded in their meeting transcripts) made a comment such as, "Yes, if we do an independent investigation, we may embarrass Hoover. But isn't it of greater importance that we get to the truth of this matter? If the FBI was negligent, shouldn't they suffer the consequences?" To the Warren Commission, damaging the credibility of the FBI appeared to carry more weight than pursuing the truth in the matter through an independent investigation. McCloy appeared to be wrestling with this dilemma, as noted earlier, but his comment regarding not being concerned about embarrassing the FBI went unheeded.

Failure to Reappraise Initially Rejected Alternatives

The one major alternative presented when the Commission members discussed the investigation of the Oswald-FBI issue was using the powers of the Attorney General, the slain president's brother Robert Kennedy, to investigate the issue. The idea was passed off as an unrealistic solution because Rankin thought it would produce more friction between Hoover and RFK. Rankin and Commissioner Cooper did not want to use the Attorney General in any investigation. Cooper stated: "I think to ask the President's brother, the dead president, to do this, it wouldn't have any backing in it" (Transcripts of the Executive Sessions 27 January 1964, 148). Probably what Cooper meant was that Robert Kennedy would have little backing from the FBI. Surprisingly, no one asked the obvious question: "Who would the American people trust more than the survivor of a slain brother to get the truth?"

Rankin's way of eliminating this discussion was simply to change the subject, and little or no conflict was apparent when Rankin used this strategy. McCloy and Cooper, who at first favored this approach, were strangely reticent when Rankin changed the topic of discussion.

It would seem today that if Robert Kennedy had conducted such an investigation, few would think he would have tried to cover up any conspiracy in his brother's murder—the men were extremely close. Robert Kennedy was a man of action, but the decision to approach him was never reappraised. As Attorney General, Kennedy had demonstrated that he could get results independent of Hoover's G-men. Without the help of the FBI, Kennedy's Justice Department lawyers had put a sizeable dent in organized crime. In 1961 when he became Attorney General, there were only 121 indictments for offenses associated with organized crime in the United States; by 1963, this number had risen almost 600 percent to 615. The number of convictions for organized crime activities rose from only thirty-five in 1960 before Robert Kennedy took office to a high of over 550 in 1963 (Blakey and Billings 1981).

This one rejected alternative that received little discussion may have been the most effective way the issue could have been investigated, and it also may have eliminated some of the plethora of conspiracy theories after the release of the *Warren Report*.

Poor Information Search

One crucial aspect of fact-finding is the consideration of the possible bias of witnesses. The Commission never conducted any investigation outside of questioning several FBI agents and eliciting the testimony of Hoover. As Dulles and Rankin constantly told the Commission members, (1) Hoover would never admit that Oswald was an FBI agent, and (2) FBI records would never show a connection between Oswald and the FBI. Yet the FBI was exactly who the Commission relied upon for the conclusion that Oswald had never been in the employ of the FBI. Thus, in the *Warren Report* the Commission used evidence that could have possibly been false, or at the very least suffered from the personal bias of the witnesses.

By relying only on the FBI, the Commission ignored the FBI's obvious bias in this matter and accepted Hoover's testimony with little question or reservation. The Commission was so fearful of not offending Hoover that it sent Hoover the transcript of his testimony for approval before it was published in the *Hearings before the President's Commission on the Assassination of President Kennedy* (1964, Vol. 4, 403–76; Vol. 5, 1–32, 97–119). When the FBI received this transcript, it edited Hoover's testimony and made many revisions. The doctored version of Hoover's testimony on the FBI-Oswald matter was then returned to the Warren Commission and published with the FBI-approved revisions. The FBI claimed that in making these changes, "apparently the court reporter did not record the Director's testimony accurately in some instances. We have made as few changes as possible, in order to preserve the intent and accuracy of the Director's testimony" (*Hearings before the President's Commission* 1964, Vol. 5, 97–119).

Selective Bias in Processing Information

The only information the Warren Commission had on hand with respect to the Oswald-FBI issue was the information relayed to them by Texas Attorney General Waggoner Carr. Rankin was responsible for any bias in processing and investigating this information once the Commission members gave him the go-ahead to investigate the FBI-Oswald connection as he saw fit. Rankin made no attempt to utilize the investigative capabilities of the Texas Board of Inquiry, which had also looked into the matter. Rankin also never contacted the *Houston Post* reporter, Lonnie Hudkins, who initially broke the story of a possible relationship between the FBI and Oswald.

Most of the Commission members in their deliberations did not demonstrate a bias in evaluating the information at hand; Russell, Boggs, and McCloy made numerous efforts to force an independent investigation. As Mark Lane points out in his recent book, *Plausible Denial*, "no investigating agency can fairly evaluate the fruits of its work" (Lane 1991, 358). Yet, in the end, the failure of the Commission members to demand an independent investigation outside the FBI probably has helped fuel the criticisms directed at the *Warren Report* and launched a small industry of conspiracy theorists.

PROBLEMS WITH PRESIDENTIAL COMMISSIONS

When Popper observed that presidential commissions are generally "too political" (Popper 1970, 56), he made a point that applies to the Warren Commission. The Commission's members were all appointed by Lyndon Johnson as one of his first acts as President following the assassination. Johnson's pressure on the Commission to complete its task before the presidential election in September 1964 left Warren and the others with only ten months to complete their report: Johnson wanted the Commission's findings on his desk by September 1. Popper claims that "[t]he present tight deadlines—usually eighteen months or less—hinder the recruitment of good staff members, and also mean that lawyers and government employees are more likely to be hired than writers or academics" (Popper 1970, 60–61). In the Warren Commission's case, someone from outside the government, not concerned with politics, may have made the group realize how much time they were devoting to worrying about embarrassing Hoover as opposed to getting at the truth of the Oswald-FBI issue. The Warren Commission, under the pressure of master politician Johnson to avoid a political issue—an unresolved presidential assassination before a presidential election, was left with only 35 percent of the *minimal* recommended time to finish its investigation and make a report.

Johnson's choice to appoint a commission made up exclusively of lawyers may have been unintentional. Many believe that the appointments of Ford and Dulles were intended to safeguard the best interests of the FBI (Ford) and the CIA (Dulles). D. Gouran points out that one of the problems with the "Nixon group" that attempted the Watergate cover-up was the similarities of its members (Gouran 1976). The Warren Commission, like the Nixon group, was a homogeneous group. M. E. Shaw claims that a group made up of homogeneous members might not be as effective as a heterogeneous group because of a restricted number of member attributes (Shaw 1976).

The danger in homogeneity might be that it will foster a lack of provocativeness within the group—the "Rabbit in the Hat Principle" might be applicable here. It states that group problem-solvers are like magicians: the only solutions (rabbits) that they can pull out of a hat are the ones that are considered (placed in the hat) (Johnson 1977). With such member similarity, the Warren Commission was restricted to the number of solutions it could propose as a result of member homogeneity (Gouran 1976). This condition could lead to a more cohesive group, but also a group that is less likely to engage in conflict. Popper (1970) states that constructive debate and dissent are needed aspects of presidential commissions or any decision-making group.

Commissioner Richard Russell initially went along with most of the Warren Commission's decisions, but by 1970 he claimed that he never believed that Oswald acted alone (Oberdoffer 1970). While the Commission was in session, Russell did demand that a disclaimer be put in the *Warren Report* before he would sign it. The sentence reads:

Because of a difficulty of proving negatives to a certainty the possibility of others being involved with either Oswald or Ruby cannot be established categorically, but if there is any such evidence it has been beyond the reach of all the investigative agencies and resources of the United States and has not come to the attention of this Commission. (*Report of the President's Commission* 1964, 22)

Yet when the *Warren Report* was released in September 1964 it was supposedly presented by a unified Commission. The public was led to believe that there was no dissent among the members of the Commission. The *New York Times* reported that the Commission was unified in its decision and stated that "Chief Justice Earl Warren and the six other members of the President's Commission on the Assassination of President Kennedy were unanimous on this [Oswald being the lone assassin] and all questions" (Lewis 1964, 1).

The pressure for a united front by a presidential commission may interfere with the needed conflict in decision making. Popper's advice that divided position statements and divided final reports should be encouraged (1970, 63) can be considered as another way of preventing groupthink. Any such deviance from the norm of a united report was not tolerated in the Warren Commission. In fact, it has been reported that Russell was promised that his dissent would appear in the transcript of the Commission's last meeting on September 18, 1964. Rankin, however, lied to him. There is no transcript of this meeting, only a brief narrative of the minutes of the Commission. According to assassination researcher Harold Weisberg, Russell was furious when he was told of the contents of this transcript (Weisberg 1974).

Whether or not the Warren Commission's conclusion was true—that there was no conspiracy and that Oswald acted alone—one cannot ignore the faulty decision making. Perhaps the greatest contribution to the tunnel vision of the Commission may be summed up in a trilogy of circumstances: (1) pressure to complete its investigation before the 1964 presidential election, (2) fear of offending Hoover and the FBI, and (3) little tolerance for deviation from the Commission's pre-planned final decision.

It is hoped that future presidential commissions will not have to operate under such constraints.

APPENDIX

President's Commission on the
Assassination of President Kennedy

Chief Justice Earl Warren, *Chairman*

Sen. Richard B. Russell	Rep. Gerald R. Ford
Sen. John Sherman Cooper	Mr. Allen W. Dulles
Rep. Hale Boggs	Mr. John J. McCoy

J. Lee Rankin, *General Counsel*

Assistant Counsel

Francis W. H. Adams	Albert E. Jenner, Jr.
Joseph A. Ball	Wesley J. Liebeler
David Belin	Norman Redlich
William T. Coleman, Jr.	W. David Slawson
Melvin Aron Eisenberg	Arlen Specter
Leon D. Hubert, Jr.	Samuel Stern

Howard P. Willens (liaison with Department of Justice)

Staff Members

Phillip Barson	Richard M. Mosk
Edward Conroy	John J. O'Brien
John Hart Ely	Stuart Pollack
Alfred Goldberg	Alfred Scobey
Murray J. Laulict	Charles Shaffer, Jr.
Arthur Marmor	Lloyd L. Weinre

NOTES

1. Dr. Cyril Wecht, comments made before the Assassination Symposium on John F. Kennedy, Dallas, Texas, 16 November 1991.

2. U.S. Department of Justice, FBI Headquarter File 62-109090, "Liaison with Commission," Nicholas deB. Katzenbach to Bill Moyers memorandum (attached to Courtney Evans to Alan Belmont memorandum), 25 November 1963.

3. U.S. Department of Justice, FBI Headquarter File 62-109060, "The Assassination of President Kennedy," Cartha DeLoach to John Mohr memorandum, 25 November 1963, p. 1.

4. Ibid, p. 3.

5. U.S. Department of Justice, FBI Headquarter File 62-109090, "Liaison with Commission," Alan Belmont memorandum, 29 November 1963.

6. U.S. Department of Justice, FBI Headquarter File 62-109090, "Liaison with Commission," memorandum to Alan Belmont, 6 December 1963, p. 1.

7. U.S. Department of Justice, FBI Headquarter File 62-109090, "Liaison with Commission," Courtney Evans to Alan Belmont memorandum, 2 December 1963.

8. U.S. Department of Justice, FBI Headquarter File 62-109090, "Liaison with Commission," Cartha DeLoach to John Mohr memorandum, 11 December 1963.

9. Ibid., 12 December 1963.

10. U.S. Department of Justice, FBI Headquarter File 62-109090, "Liaison with Commission," general memorandum, 12 March 1964.

11. U.S. Department of Justice, FBI Headquarter File 62-109090, "Liaison with Commission."

12. Some feel that Janis places too much emphasis on group cohesion for the occurrence of groupthink. See, for example, Matie Flowers, "A Laboratory Test of Janis' Groupthink Hypothesis," *Journal of Personality and Social Psychology*, 35 (1977), 888–96; Bruce C. McKinney, "Decision-Making in the President's Commission on the Assassination of President Kennedy: A Descriptive Analysis Employing Irving Janis' Groupthink Hypothesis," Ph.D. diss., Pennsylvania State University, 1985.

13. The transcript of the Executive Session of 19 May 1964 remains classified "Top Secret" as of this writing.

14. The transcripts of the Executive Sessions of 24 February and 30 April 1964 are the only sessions in which there is mention of an agenda.

15. Of all the commissioners, Chief Justice Warren seemed to be the least concerned about embarrassing Hoover.

16. See, for example, Jim Garrison, *On the Trail of the Assassins* (New York: Sheridan Square Press, 1988); Jim Marrs, *Crossfire: The Plot that Killed Kennedy* (New York: Carroll & Graf, 1989); and Anthony Summers, *Conspiracy* (New York: McGraw-Hill, 1980).

17. Though this may have been a mere coincidence, selecting these men to be on the Warren Commission was a major flaw because of a conflict of interest, with Ford looking out for the FBI and Dulles for the CIA—both agencies that failed in the protection of the President.

5

The 1970 Commission on Obscenity and Pornography

Roger A. Soenksen

In September 1970 the Commission on Obscenity and Pornography released its report. Even before the report was released the Lockhart Commission, as the Commission was commonly referred to, was embroiled in controversy regarding its recommendation to abolish all general laws that prohibit distribution of obscene materials to adults. Furthermore, the Commission advocated the restructuring of obscenity laws dealing with contexts such as public displays, unsolicited mailings, and distribution of pornographic materials to children. Finally, the report recommended that the United States initiate a nationwide sex education program. Critics immediately rejected these conclusions. Senator Edward J. Gurney's response was typical of the vitriolic attacks on the Lockhart Commission's conclusion. He said, "The legalization of pornography as recommended by the commission will open the floodgates to the quickening decay of morals undermining the country today" (de Grazia 1992, 559).

The topic of obscenity provokes many feelings. However, it was assumed by Congressional leaders that the majority of Americans believed that obscenity was wrong and was linked to such crimes as rape and incest. In fact, the bill to establish the Lockhart Commission had been initially structured to set up a commission and stamp out pornography (de Grazia 1992). Failure to produce such a commission mandate motivated Senator John McClellan (D., Ark.) to introduce a compromise resolution that declared that the traffic in obscenity and pornography was "a matter of national concern" (de Grazia 1992).

The creation of a special commission to study pornography was the result of multiple factors, including the perception that the morality of the United States was in a decaying state, pressures from religious leaders such as Cardinal Spellman, campaigns by moral advocacy groups, and concerns expressed by politicians who were alarmed over the Supreme Court's rulings inhibiting prosecution of obscenity cases. Those who advocated the study of pornography were confident in their belief that obscenity causes crime and other problems in the United States. They believed that the erosion of morality could be linked to the growing pornography industry (de Grazia 1992). Cardinal Spellman's view was representative of the attitudes of the pressure groups who thought that "pornography encourages brutality, violence, injustice, irreverence, disrespect for authority, illicit pleasure seeking, abnormality, degeneracy and other signs of mental maladjustment" (Packer 1971, 72).

Senators John McClellan and Karl Mundt spearheaded Public Law (PL) 90-100 through the Senate Judiciary Committee to establish the Commission on Obscenity and Pornography in October 1967 (Packer 1971). Congress charged the Commission with a fourfold task:

1. to analyze the laws pertaining to the control of obscenity and pornography, and to evaluate and recommend definitions of obscenity and pornography;
2. to ascertain the methods employed in the distribution of obscene and pornographic materials and to explore the nature and volume of traffic in such materials;
3. to study the effect of obscenity and pornography upon the public, and particularly minors, and its relationship to crime and other antisocial behavior; and
4. to recommend such legislative, administrative, or other advisable and appropriate action as the Commission deems necessary to regulate effectively the flow of such traffic, without in any way interfering with constitutional rights.

(Report of the Commission on Obscenity and Pornography 1970, 1)

The Law also permitted the Commission to make contracts with universities and research institutions to conduct research on the relationship between consuming obscene material and antisocial behavior.

It was felt by members of the Lockhart Commission that working groups should be formed in order to facilitate the study of obscenity. With this belief in mind the Commission was organized into four working panels: Legal, Traffic and Distribution, Effects, and Positive Approaches (*Report of the Commission* 1970).

The Legal panel was charged with reviewing case law to develop guidelines for legislative action that would not infringe on constitutional rights. The Traffic and Distribution panel looked into the demographic characteristics of those who use erotically stimulating materials and the distribution methods commonly employed. The Effects panel was instructed to develop plans for a major research effort that would investigate the following:

• What relationship, if any, exists between the availability of pornography and sex crimes.
• What effects, if any, erotic materials have on college students.
• What variations in intensity result from different kinds of erotic stimuli.

The specific research procedures used by the Effects panel included: (1) surveys utilizing adults and young people; (2) quasi-experimental studies; (3) controlled experimental studies; and (4) studies of rates and incidence of sex offenses and illegitimacy at the national level. The Positive Approaches panel looked into methods, besides legislative controls, that could be used to get people to avoid pornography, for example, sex education programs and citizen action groups.

The published report by the Commission was divided into four sections. In Part One the authors provided an overview of their findings on the volume of traffic in pornography, on its effects, on positive approaches, and on public attitudes. Part Two presented the controversial recommendations of the report, to be discussed in the next section of this chapter. Part Three detailed the research behind each topic in the overview. Part Four contained the "Separate Statements by Commission Members."

In order to adequately fund these subcommittees, Lockhart fought hard to receive congressional funding that would support each topic. Lockhart was successful in receiving an initial allotment of $643,000 for the commission's operation, as well as an additional $1,100,000; this brought the total cost of the Lockhart Commission's report to $1,743,000 (*Report of the Commission* 1970). Lockhart was fortunate to receive such a high degree of Congressional support for the investigation of pornography.

In this chapter an examination of the development of the Lockhart Commission will be conducted. Information to be presented includes membership of the Commission, the development of a policy agenda, and the major recommendations that the Commission advanced. This chapter will also examine the various arguments raised both in support of and against the recommendations of the Lockhart Commission. In particular, this chapter will pay attention to the fallacies that appeared in the reasoning of the supporters and detractors of the Commission's report. It will be helpful to examine the degree of certainty of the analysis that applies to the Lockhart Commission's final report to the President and to the Senate; to that end, this chapter will provide commentary on the Commission's flaws of reasoning. Fallacies are a type of argument that establishes a level of probability (Pfau, Thomas, and Ulrich 1987). A fallacy, therefore, because it is based on probability, may reveal weaknesses in the critical thinking process. This chapter will identify the gaps in reasoning employed by all parties affected by the Lockhart Commission's report.

Strong reasoning that avoids the weaknesses inherent in fallacies does not necessarily win emotion-charged arguments. The Lockhart Commission went to great lengths to employ scientific methodology in its study of obscenity in order to base recommendations not on emotion but on concrete data gathered by empiricists. These recommendations were rejected by the Senate and the President not because of sound reasoning but because of emotion-charged responses and fallacious reasoning. But before exploring the role of emotion and fallacy in the Commission's reasoning processes, a discussion of its membership and direction is in order.

COMMISSION MEMBERSHIP

Once Congress had articulated the specific agenda for the Commission, it was time for President Johnson to select commission members. Commission membership required that individuals appointed:

shall include persons having expert knowledge in the fields of obscenity and antisocial behavior, including but not limited to sociologists, psychologists, psychiatrists, criminologists, jurists, lawyers, and others from organizations and professions that have special and practical competence or experience with respect to obscenity laws and their application to juveniles. (Oboler 1970, 4227)

The President appointed eighteen American educators, social scientists, clergymen, and others to study pornography in the United States. The White House announced the composition of the Commission in January 1968 and stated that William B. Lockhart would be Chairman (*Report of the Commission* 1970). The first meeting was held in July 1968, and the group reaffirmed Lockhart as its chair (Packer 1971).

At the time, Lockhart was Dean of the University of Minnesota Law School and was a leading academic authority on obscenity law. When he was asked by the White House to accept an appointment to the Commission, Lockhart felt he had no choice (Packer 1971). In 1954 he had co-authored a work with Professor Robert McClure on the constitutional problems relating to obscenity censorship (Lockhart 1971). The article pointed out that "laws were aimed at protection against arousing sexual desires and thoughts, against undermining moral standards, and against inciting sexual behavior inconsistent with community standards of morality" (Lockhart and McClure 1954). Using this justification, lawmakers could develop legislation against the spread of obscenity by implementing one of two approaches. In one approach, the state attempted only to prevent distribution of the obscene work within the state, and the state took pains not to penalize either the bookseller or the publisher. A second approach used in some areas was aimed against a person who sold or distributed the work. In such cases the judiciary would declare a work obscene, but neither the private ownership of the book nor its right to exist were at issue (Lockhart 1971). In either approach, the underlying assumption was that to read obscene material would incite the reader to lustful thoughts. In essence, using Lockhart and McClure's standards, our lawmakers established a legal enthymeme that hypothesized that lustful thoughts will result in criminal behavior (Lockhart 1971).

Lockhart presented a strong plea to the Commission for social scientists to undertake extensive research into the effects of exposure to obscene materials (Sharp 1970). Lockhart believed that a social science approach to policy making was the only way to present relevant evidence to justify society's laws. Lockhart did not feel that legislation based merely on opinions, guesses, or fear concerning the harmful consequences of obscenity and pornography was a wise policy-making paradigm. The key to this emotion-charged topic had to be a rationally formulated public policy grounded in scientific study (Sharp 1970).

Lockhart should not be portrayed as a champion of smut. In fact, in testimony provided by Lockhart he remarked:

I do not like pornography. I never have. . . . But when we accepted this assignment we put aside our personal views and determined to seek and report the truth, whatever it might be, and then to form our independent judgment on what the government should do in this problem area only after we saw the scientific evidence. (Lockhart 1971, 210)

With this clear purpose in mind, Lockhart gathered his fellow commissioners in July 1968.

The process of selecting members and the mix of membership appointed to this Commission was not intended to bias the outcome of its work. Members were drawn from a variety of professional and religious fields.[1] All but one of the Commission members was appointed by Johnson. The one exception was Charles H. Keating, Jr., who was appointed by Nixon to complete the term of Kenneth B. Keating (no relation). Kenneth Keating resigned from the Commission to accept the position of Ambassador to India in June 1969. After examining the membership, Eli M. Oboler, a member of the Intellectual Freedom Committee of the American Library Association, concluded, "Certainly this is as 'representative' a group as could have been put together for such a difficult set of purposes as were set forth for the commission" (Oboler 1970, 4225). The Commission, therefore, was established to be independent and conduct a nonbiased investigation into obscenity.

In order to accomplish this goal, President Johnson deviated from the practice followed when most presidential commissions are put together by not appointing a bicameral balance in membership. The individuals who made up the Commission were appointees with no direct party linkage. This allowed them to be free of articulating positions to please specific political constituents. Furthermore, the members of the Commission were specialists. Undoubtedly, as Stanley Kauffman stated, "their views were more sophisticated in the field of pornography and obscenity than those of elected officials" (Kauffman 1970).

The key to the Commission, however, was Lockhart. It was Lockhart who dealt with Congress, lined up staff members, discussed specific studies that he proposed the Commission should undertake, and molded the scientific directions of the Commission (*Report of the Commission* 1970).

COMMISSION DIRECTION

Under Lockhart's leadership the Commission established several "ground rules" to facilitate their investigation into obscenity. Such rules were to help the commissioners utilize a scientific methodology.

Initially the Lockhart Commission believed that it would not hold any public hearings. The fear was that partial, misleading information would be released to the public if public meetings were held. However, in an unprecedented move, eight "unsanctioned" public meetings were held by Commissioners Hill and Link around the country. These meetings revealed the information that the American populace favored tighter pornography regulations. Twenty-six of the twenty-seven witnesses at a hearing at one such meeting in New York expressed concern over the ease of access to obscenity and requested remedial measures. Witnesses represented a cross section of the community, ranging from members of the judiciary to members of women's clubs. This pattern was repeated in such locations as New Orleans, Indianapolis, Chicago, Salt Lake City, San Francisco, Washington, D.C., and Buffalo (*Report of the Commission* 1970). The Lockhart Commission, in response to the publicity that these unauthorized public meetings generated, was forced to hold public meetings of its own. These public hearings were held in Los Angeles on May 4 and 5, 1970, and in Washington on May 12 and 13, 1970. Fifty-five people representing law enforcement agencies, the judiciary, the government, civic groups, publishers, film producers, and other interested groups were invited by the Lockhart Commission to testify. Thirty-one of the invited representatives did testify. Additionally, statements from private citizens who attended the sessions were heard.

The main result of these open hearings was the generation of a tremendous outcry against the scientific method that Lockhart wanted his Commission to use. The opinions of such "moral absolutists" produced by Commissioners Hill and Link had members of both houses of government beginning to worry about the recommendations that would be produced by Lockhart's group.

Part of the uncertainty of Congress was generated by the Lockhart Commission's operation without communication with any branch of the government or press. When asked about this "secrecy," two members of the Commission, child psychiatrist Edward D. Greenwood of the Menninger Foundation, and Morris A. Lipton, chairman of the Department of Psychiatry of the University of North Carolina Medical School, denied the charges, stating that it was the consensus of the Commission not to release partial information because the data gathered at that point in the overall study of obscenity was considered preliminary (Bell 1970).

However, there were leaks. What was reaching the public were the rumors spread by the lone Nixon appointee, Charles H. Keating, Jr., a Cincinnati lawyer, one of the founders of Citizens for Decent Literature, Inc., and one of the nation's foremost crusaders against pornography. Keating wrote:

I understand your Administration . . . to take a position that pornography and the pornographers must be stopped. . . . Mr. President, it is my duty to report to you that while the Presidential commission is an instrument which could very well affect your desires for a decent America, it is not, and with its present constituency it cannot be. (Witcover 1970)

Keating later wrote to President Nixon calling for immediate action to terminate Lockhart or the pornographers would take a giant step toward winning the war over obscenity and the Nixon administration would receive the blame (Witcover 1970). Such leaks, along with the emotional testimony at public hearings, put Congress on the defensive concerning the Lockhart Commission's report. Congress was allowing the myths concerning pornography held by its constituency to dictate the acceptability of the Commission's report even before anyone had an opportunity to examine the scientific approach employed by Lockhart's group.

The Commission's report initially ran into publication difficulty. A Federal District Court in Washington, D.C., issued a temporary restraining order preventing publication of the final report of the Commission. Charles H. Keating, Jr., was responsible for filing the request. The court order enjoined the Commission from circulating any copies of its report before September 18, 1970. This restraining order even precluded delivery of the report to the Government Printing Office. Mr. Keating claimed that he had not been granted sufficient access to the final drafts of the findings and recommendations, the four panel reports, and the ten volumes of research. Keating also demanded thirty to forty-five days to study the material. As Senator John McClellan said later, "Never before in the history of Congressionally created Presidential commissions have constitutional rights been so infringed upon that a commission member was compelled to seek judicial relief" (Keating 1971, 39).

The court order was eventually lifted after an agreement was worked out by attorneys for Mr. Keating and by a lawyer representing the Justice Department. Under the terms of the agreement, the Commission presented Mr. Keating with copies of the overall report, the four panels' reports, and the ten volumes of research material. In turn, Mr. Keating agreed to complete his dissent by September 29, which gave him fifteen days to prepare his entry rather than the thirty to forty-five he had requested originally. The final report was originally scheduled for release in January 1970, but the Lockhart Commission received extensions to July 31 and then to September 30.

Presidential commissions usually reach unanimous or near-unanimous conclusions. This one did not. Ten commissioners, alone or with others, wrote entries for Part Four of the report entitled, "Separate Statements by Commission Members," and six dissented from the majority recommendations. Irving Lehrman wrote a brief dissent stating that more time was needed for studying the long-range effects of sexually explicit material; therefore, he argued no action should be taken on legislative prohibitions. Two members of the panel, sociologists Otto N. Larsen and Marvin E. Wolfgang, advocated the repeal of all laws governing pornography. Specifically referring to the experience of Denmark and Sweden as well as U.S. studies, the sociologists declared that there was no evidence that the availability of pornography would result in youngsters "rushing in large numbers" to buy it. There might even be the beneficial effects, they noted, of "open discussion about sex between parents and children relatively early in young lives." Three others, Rev. Morton A. Hill, S.J., Rev. Winfrey C. Link, and Charles H. Keating, Jr., dissented vigorously from the Commission's recommendations, arguing that the action endorsed by the Commission would erode the moral fiber of America.

The remainder of this chapter will analyze the arguments advanced in the key recommendations of the Lockhart Commission as well as examine the refutation to the report contained in the dissenting opinions of Hill, Link, and Keating.

COMMISSION'S MAJOR RECOMMENDATIONS

Recommendation Allowing Adults to Consume Obscene Material

Without question the most controversial recommendation arising from the Lockhart Commission was the majority's declaration:

that federal, state and local legislation should not seek to interfere with the right of adults who wish to do so to read, obtain or view explicit sexual materials. On the other hand, we recommend legislative regulations upon the sale of sexual materials to young persons who do not have the consent of their parents, and we also recommend legislation to protect persons from having sexual materials thrust on them without their consent through the mail or through open public display. (*Report of the Commission* 1970, 57)

Lockhart and his fellow commissioners were careful to base their recommendation concerning specific legislation on a variety of research methodologies. The Lockhart Commission utilized both self-reporting instruments as well as physiological measuring devices to document the effects obscenity seems to have on adults. Results indicated that a large segment of men and women are sexually stimulated when consuming explicit sexual materials. Such research included exposure to erotic photographs, narratives, and films. Research revealed that high rates of sexual activity before exposure to obscene material were followed by high rates of sexual activity after exposure to erotic material. Conversely, low rates of sexual activity before exposure were followed by low rates of sexual activity after exposure to obscene material. Exposure, therefore, was found not to alter the variety of sexual activity experienced by adults (*Report of the Commission* 1970). Clearly, this evidence refutes the argument that heinous crimes are directly linked to the consumption of obscene materials. Such a position was the cornerstone of the arguments to regulate obscenity. These experimental studies revealed that laws regulating the consumption of obscene materials involving consenting adults was founded on myths rather than concrete evidence.

Members of the Lockhart Commission, in further supporting this recommendation, made a rhetorical error in the development of this issue. The report relied on an analogous country's response to its own obscenity issue. The country that the Lockhart Commission modeled its recommendation after was Denmark. The majority advanced the crime statistics of Denmark as persuasive evidence that explicit sexual material does not cause sex crimes. Specifically, Denmark's literary pornography was declared legally available in 1967, and pictorial sexually explicit material became available in 1969. As the material became increasingly available for public consumption, an amazing decrease in sex crimes was reported by police (*Report of the Commission* 1970). Over the period from 1966 to 1969, when a large variety of sexually explicit material was made available in Denmark, there was a 54 percent decrease in the total number of sex crimes. Excluded from this statistic were the pornography violations and other changes in the law that would influence this reduction in sex crimes (Bell 1970, 29).

The main problem with the use of Denmark for evidentiary purposes was that the Lockhart Commission constructed an argument by analogy. What the Commission was trying to prove was that because of the Denmark experience there does not appear to be a relationship between the consumption of sexually explicit material and the increase of sex crimes. Unfortunately, the Lockhart Commission failed to meet a key test in using literal analogies. The Commission failed to prove to the members of Congress or the American public that the two countries are essentially the same in their critical attributes. In this case no effort was made to relate the real world experiences of Denmark to the implementation of this controversial recommendation in the United States.

Opponents of this recommendation specifically attacked some of the key characteristics between Denmark and the United States as proof that the analysis of the Lockhart Commission was badly flawed. For example, Charles Keating indicated that Denmark's population was merely 4,700,000. Furthermore, it was argued by opponents that the long-term impact of decriminalizing the sale of obscene material was unknown due to the short interval of time that Denmark's policy had been in place (*Report of the Commission* 1970). The failure of the Denmark analogy to persuade Congress seriously hampered the Lockhart Commission's ability to get this landmark recommendation accepted.

The third type of evidence that was used to support this key recommendation was an experiment conducted at the University of North Carolina. The principal investigator was Dr. James L. Howard, an assistant professor of psychiatry at the University of North Carolina Medical School. Twenty-three volunteer students were the subject pool. The experimenters hooked up the subjects' penises to measuring devices. In addition, the experiment measured urinary acid phosphatase and heart rates. Interest in erotica was measured by observing the time spent by the subject as he examined obscene material. Over a three-week period the subjects became satiated with sexually explicit material (*Report of the Commission* 1970).

Such results were never directly refuted by the critics of the Lockhart Commission's recommendations. Instead, the investigations were ridiculed. Herbert L. Packer wrote, "This [study] seems to me a good example of how rigor and triviality are related in empirical behavioral work" (1971, 75). Keating, in attacking the empirical studies conducted by the Lockhart Commission, reduced the studies to absurdity by declaring that some fourteen tests were conducted to determine an individual's physical response to various types of obscenity. "Why," he asked, "was it necessary to conduct dozens of experiments and interviews to demonstrate the obvious—that human beings are aroused by erotic materials?" (Keating 1971, 38).

The opponents to the Lockhart Commission's empirical approach to social policy chose not to present counter studies or analytical data to offset what the fact-finding processes of the Commission had found. Critics merely attacked the reasonableness of the experimental method and in some cases utilized the caveats that the social scientists employed in their writings. An example of this tactic can be found in the Commission's disclaimer that the effects of obscenity on youth were not studied because no experimental design could be structured that would be protective of the participating subjects (*Report of the Commission* 1970). Critics pointed to the lack of data gathering in this area and proclaimed the entire study "flawed" (Keating 1971).

Perhaps the most interesting aspect of the arguments raised by critics to the recommendation that the law concerning the consumption of obscene material should be eliminated was the lack of a point-by-point refutation of the logic implied by the studies conducted on behalf of the Commission. What occurred was the rejection of scientific studies because of the social policy that logically extended from the research conclusions. The emotions of the critics fueled their arguments. Put simply, Congress did not like the results of the studies that prompted the Lockhart Commission to frame its first recommendation, so members relied on their "feeling" about the topic to continue supporting the policy of the status quo.

Recommendation for Extensive Sex Education Program

The Lockhart Commission advanced a second proposal that the United States launch a massive program of sex education to provide the youths of our society with a healthy attitude toward sex. The Commission reached this recommendation after surveying adults and young people (*Report of the Commission* 1970).

What was uncovered by carefully worded surveys was a wide divergence between what was considered to be the most desirable sources of information about sex and the actual sources of information. Consensus was reached by those queried that it was highly desirable to receive straightforward information concerning sex from parents, from school officials, and from qualified community agencies. Unfortunately, the Lockhart Commission uncovered a lack of teacher preparation in the field of sex education. The lack of training was found to be due, in part, to strong opposition from "conservative groups" who have implemented roadblocks to the institution of sex education courses in many of our schools. Furthermore, the Commission discovered religious and medical officials limiting their own participation in sex education programs due to a lack of adequate training. Parents had not developed into a source of information because they, too, lacked sex education and were embarrassed by discussing sexual matters in an open manner with their children (*Report of the Commission* 1970).

The Lockhart Commission studies showed that the most prevalent source of information about sexual matters for youths was friends. A national survey of teens verified that 67 percent of the boys and 59 percent of the girls used friends as their primary source of information about sex (*Report of the Commission* 1970, 314). So, although young individuals wanted informed sources, they were reduced to relying on friends.

The Lockhart Commission, after discovering the empirically verified manner in which adolescents were informed about sexual data, then sought to determine if a relationship existed between sex education and exposure to pornography. What was revealed upon closer examination of the data was that exposure to pornography and learning new information about sex was the result of exposure to sexual material with friends looking on. A national survey examined many individuals' exposure to ten kinds of explicit sexual depictions and descriptions. These ranged from nudity to sexual intercourse, homosexual to sadomasochistic activity, and pictorial to textual formats. Of the adults surveyed, 84 percent of the males and 69 percent of the females reported having seen at least one of these depictions. It was further reported that 49 percent of the boys and 45 percent of the girls reported having seen at least five or more of these kinds of depictions (*Report of the Commission* 1970, 315).

At this point in the report, the Lockhart Commission stated that young Americans' exposure to obscenity was the result, for the most part, of obtaining the material from a father or brother's room and then showing the material to a friend. The impact of this information was that if state laws concerning adult consumption were to be eliminated, thereby reducing restrictions, the access of young people to such material would naturally increase. The Lockhart Commission was quick to advocate, therefore, a significant recommendation concerning a formal sex education program. It was the feeling of the Commission that a sex education program would largely satisfy an adolescent's interest in accurate, reliable information and result in a decreased interest in viewing adult material that could be declared obscene. Also, the Commission went on, a comprehensive sex education program would offset any distorted view of sex a juvenile might experience if he or she were to gain access to adult material in a clandestine manner. The sex education experience, one would have to conclude, would provide young men and women with a healthy framework for understanding their sexual nature (*Report of the Commission* 1970).

The Lockhart Commission's blend of survey research and effective reasoning established a very strong position for their recommendation. Social science research had again been utilized to develop a sound public policy.

Opponents to this specific recommendation tended to refute this aspect of the Commission's proposal in one of two ways. Initially, the minority report of Commissioners Hill and Link argued that sex education was a "panacea." They went on to state that the Lockhart Commission's report left too many questions unanswered, for example, "Will these instructors not bring the hard-core pornography into the grammar schools?" (*Report of the Commission* 1970, 458). Hill and Link clearly committed the fallacy of begging the question in utilizing this approach. This reasoning flaw assumes the conclusion as part of the rationale. Such an argument did not weaken or refute the rationale for the specific social policy that the Commission had deemed necessary. The Commission majority's argument was virtually left untouched in this attack strategy by Hill and Link.

The second line of argument used by Hill and Link to attack a nationwide sex education program was to link this recommendation to the first proposal allowing consenting adults access to sexually explicit material. Hill and Link stated:

Children cannot grow in love if they are trained with pornography. Pornography is loveless; it degrades the human being, reduces him to the level of animal. And if this Commission majority's recommendations are heeded, there will be a glut of pornography for teachers and children. (*Report of the Commission* 1970, 458–59)

Hill and Link utilized the fallacy of *post hoc, ergo propter hoc,* or "after this, therefore because of this." This false attribution of pornography running wild in society is an attempt to establish a causal relationship where none exists. Lane Sunderland (1974) expands on this argument by stating that if there were no legal restraints on the sale of pornographic material to adults, the obscene material would undercut the collective opinion and moral standards of society, and the result would be an "undermining of the institution of marriage and the family."

The position advocated by critics of the Lockhart Commission's recommendation on sex education was an emotional appeal that lacked quantification or empirical examples and is evidence of the "slippery slope" fallacy. The minority objections were based on the flawed logic that if we do something, we commit ourselves to do similar actions on a larger, more dangerous scale. Opponents were reduced to claim that an increase in pornographic material for adults would weaken or potentially destroy society and the moral fiber of our youth (Sunderland 1974).

In this recommendation we again see critics of the Lockhart Commission reduced to employing emotional appeals. The research reports mentioned in this chapter are examples of the empirical approach used and in no way attempt to provide the reader with an exhaustive list of the sixty studies included in the Commission's final report. Clearly, these studies were ignored by critics and by the senators who rejected this report. Instead of relying on data gathered and the conclusions drawn from such information, congressional policy was influenced by legislators who utilized weak logic and strong emotional appeals to justify their actions.

Recommendation for Display and Advertising Regulations

After careful study, the Lockhart Commission offered a third major recommendation. This proposed statute called for states to draft laws that would control the distribution of explicit sexual materials to youths under the age of seventeen or eighteen, except with the consent of their parents, teachers, or clergymen (*Report of the Commission* 1970). This was a very difficult recommendation to advocate for two reasons. First, given the relaxation of regulations on adult consumption, it is obvious that if adults have access to sexually explicit material a child could find the material and suffer some unknown harm. Second, the commissioners feared violating the freedom of speech guaranteed by the First Amendment that has been deemed by the courts to extend to children as well as adults.

The Lockhart Commission based this third recommendation on studies that established that a large number of individuals are offended and upset when directly confronted with pictorial, obscene material (Lockhart 1971). The Commission concluded that young people should be protected from this intrusion as long as consenting adults were not blocked from access to sexually explicit material.

In order to accomplish this goal, the Lockhart Commission recommended state statutes forbidding public display of explicit sexual activity when such displays could be observed from a public street or sidewalk (*Report of the Commission* 1970). The structure of this ordinance regulated display windows, displays outside of theaters, billboards, and outdoor theater screens when visible from a highway or other property (Lockhart 1971).

A second draft regulation was designed to protect those individuals who were offended by receiving unsolicited, sexually oriented mail advertising. The Lockhart Commission in its first year devised and sent to Congress a draft of a statute that would limit exposure to a whole range of material that was offensive in nature (Lockhart 1971). Congress enacted a law to accomplish this goal just as the Lockhart Commission was preparing to release its report. The law allowed anyone not wishing to receive advertisements of pornographic material to register his or her name with the Post Office, which publishes an up-to-date list of registered names each month. Advertisers had to buy this list at cost and it became a crime to mail offensive, sexually explicit advertising to those on the list (Witcover 1970).

This recommendation to regulate displays and advertisements was largely ignored by critics of the Lockhart Commission report. The fact that the Commission sought to protect youths and adults who were uncomfortable with sexually explicit material was downplayed while opponents focused their attacks on the first two recommendations. It is indeed ironic that one of the Commission's three primary recommendations was placed into law by congressional action prior to the rejection of the complete Lockhart report.

REACTION TO THE LOCKHART COMMISSION REPORT

On October 13, 1970, the United States Senate voted 60-5 (with 35 abstentions) "declaring that the Senate rejects the findings and recommendations of the Commission on Obscenity and Pornography" (Oboler 1970, 4225). The resolution concluded:

The Senate declares that (1) generally the findings and recommendations are not supported by the evidence considered by or available to the Commission; and (2) the Commission has not properly performed its statutory duties nor has it complied with the mandates of Congress. (*Free Speech Newsletter* 1970, 7)

This resolution was presented by Senator McClellan and co-sponsored by 25 other Democratic senators and 24 Republican senators (Oboler 1970).

During the debate in the Senate on October 13, Senator McClellan included in the speech supporting his resolution the minority comments of Commissioners Hill and Link, while ignoring the majority's findings based on two years of work. Wasting no time, McClellan, in an unusual strategy, asked for immediate approval of his resolution (Oboler 1970). In essence, McClellan called upon the Senate to reject a report that the members in truth probably had not had time to read.

It was not surprising to anyone that the Senate rejected the Lockhart Commission report. It would be hard to imagine a politician in the late hours of an election campaign declaring himself or herself in favor of legalizing the sale of smut ("The Temptations of Pornography" 1970). The Senate vote, delayed several times to allow the Lockhart Commission to compile its final report, occurred just three weeks before a congressional election (Oboler 1970).

In reality, the Lockhart Commission's report was being attacked as early as two months before its release to the Senate. For example, Ron Ziegler, White House press secretary, stated that President Nixon would oppose the report if it "recommends what the newspapers say it recommends." Two weeks later, Attorney General John Mitchell declared that the Johnson-appointed commission "is not connected with the Nixon administration." Commissioners Hill and Link in September urged Congress to "file [the majority report] in the wastebasket." Even Billy Graham joined the chorus of those condemning the Lockhart Commission, calling the report "one of the worst and most diabolical ever made by a presidential commission," and one that "no Christian or believing Jew could support" ("The Temptations of Pornography" 1970, 1339).

In supporting Senator McClellan's resolution Senator Stennis stated:

Mr. President I hold that national morals are a matter of national concern. Therefore, they are a matter of concern to the Congress. The Commission report comes as a shock to the majority of American people. It should be condemned, and I do condemn it. It should be repudiated, as the Senator from Arkansas says, and I believe it will be repudiated by this body and by the American people. The fact that such a report can originate from an official commission is fair warning that we should work for practical and effective legislation for the control of obscenity and pornography. (*Free Speech Newsletter* 1970, 7)

Senator Griffin concluded that the Lockhart Commission report should be "tossed into the trash with corrupting pornography" (*Free Speech Newsletter* 1970, 7). Vice President Spiro Agnew echoed the Senate's position by proclaiming that "as long as Nixon is President, Main Street will never be Smut Alley" (de Grazia 1992, 552). Such reactions are very unusual, for in the past when Congress or the administration has not liked the results of a commission's report, the document has been ignored. It is very surprising for the Senate to take such a strong action against a commission that it set up.

The Commission's report has been ignored by legislators since the Senate voted to reject its recommendations. In 1986, Attorney General Edwin Meese spearheaded another Commission on Pornography. In its final report, a short comparison with the 1970 Commission on Pornography and Obscenity was provided. The Meese Commission (as it was popularly referred to) initially commented on the budgets and the amount of time each body had to investigate the topic of pornography in the United States. The 1970 Commission had a budget of close to $2,000,000 and two years to complete its task. The Meese Commission had only one year and a budget of $500,000. When the fluctuating value of the dollar was taken into account, the 1970 Commission had a budget nearly sixteen times as large as the Meese Commission's (*Attorney General's Commission on Pornography* 1986, 225).

The Meese report went into the substantive differences in "perspective" to help explain why its own study of obscenity was begun. The Meese Commission report stated that it had been sixteen years since the 1970 Commission's final report. It is specifically reported:

In sixteen years the world has seen enormous technological changes that have affected the transmission of sounds, words, and images. Few aspects of contemporary American society have not been affected by cable television, satellite communication, video tape recording, the computer, and competition in the telecommunications industry. . . . These technological developments have themselves caused such significant changes in the practices relating to the distribution of pornography that the analysis of sixteen years ago is starkly obsolete. (*Attorney General's Commission on Pornography* 1986, 225–26)

The Meese Commission went on to cite the numerous social, political, legal, cultural, and religious characteristics of the United States in the last sixteen years. All of this information clearly justifies this later study of pornography, but also helps to establish a framework for the different conclusions reached by these two independent investigations into obscenity.

CONCLUSION

The Commission on Pornography and Obscenity was formed and funded for two years by a congressional mandate. Society at the time was certainly greatly concerned with what was perceived as an increasing availability of sexually explicit material, and this was the primary motivation for establishing the Lockhart Commission. The Commission was asked to recommend regulations to control obscenity. Furthermore, it was asked to investigate the effects of the consumption of sexually explicit material upon the consumer and to determine if a relationship to criminal behavior exists. Finally, the Commission investigated the scope and distribution of erotic material.

In selecting the appropriate approach for the Commission to utilize, Lockhart quickly established that myths, unsupported beliefs, and unsubstantiated opinions would not be the foundation for this policy-recommending committee. Lockhart instead opted to utilize the budget of the Commission to support studies to investigate the subject of obscenity.

The outcome of this work by Commission members was the completion of around sixty studies contracted to analyze the behavioral impact of erotica. These studies led the Lockhart Commission's majority to conclude that sexually explicit material does not cause delinquent or criminal behavior. Lacking concrete evidence, the majority of the Commission concluded that there was no justification to prohibit adult consumption of obscene material.

The report from the Commission recommended that federal, state, and local legislation prohibiting the sale, exhibition, or distribution of erotica to consenting adults be repealed. The report also emphasized the need to expand sex education programs to provide an accurate picture of sexuality for children. Finally, the report offered models of statutes for federal and state regulations to control the display of sexually explicit materials. The regulations would prevent the forcing of obscene materials on those individuals who might feel uncomfortable viewing such material.

The Commission also provided a wealth of examples of fallacies. Like all presidential commissions, numerous lines of reasoning are advanced to support a specific claim. However, in this example the strong reasoning of the Lockhart Commission failed to persuade members of the Senate or the President. The emotion involved in this subject matter resulted in well-supported commission recommendations being ignored.

Unfortunately, the release of this report at election time resulted in the Senate rejecting the findings of the Commission. No matter how well supported the argument for the Commission's recommendations, no member of the Senate running for reelection wanted to run on a platform promoting obscenity. Therefore, references to this report were sparse for the next sixteen years until the Meese Commission report was released. The Meese Commission concluded that there is a direct link between violent sex crimes and the consumption of obscene material. Therefore, the Meese Commission recommended numerous mechanisms to control obscene publications and movies.

Dean William Lockhart, chairman of the 1970 Commission, expressed his hope for the future of the report, stating, "My hope and expectation is that when the research papers are studied in a calm atmosphere uncomplicated by election appeals, the results will be a far more careful appraisal of public policy in this emotion-charged area" ("Porno Politics" 1970, 453). Unfortunately, this report has become merely a footnote in reference books due to the sensitive nature of the subject matter and the controversial recommendations it advanced.

APPENDIX

1970 Commission on Obscenity and Pornography

William B. Lockhart, *Chairman*
Dr. Frederick H. Wagman, *Vice Chairman*

Edward Ellis	Thomas D. Gill
Dr. Edward D. Greenwood	Morton A. Hill
Dr. G. William Jones	Dr. Joseph T. Klapper
Dr. Otto M. Larsen	Dr. Irving Lehrman

Freeman Lewis
Dr. Morris A. Lipton
Barbara Scott
Dr. Marvin E. Wolfgang

Rev. Winfrey C. Link
Thomas C. Lynch
Cathryn A. Spelts

Staff Members

Anthony F. Abell
Paul Bender
Karen I. Green
Sylvia H. Jacobs
Lenore R. Kupperstein
Bobbie Jack Wallin

Virginia P. Banister
Jane M. Freidman
Bernard Horowitz
Weldon T. Johnson
John J. Sampson
W. Cody Wilson

NOTE

1. Of the original eighteen members, all served to the end of the Commission's existence, with the exception of Judge Kenneth Keating, who was appointed Ambassador to India by President Nixon, and who was replaced by Charles H. Keating, Jr., a Cincinnati lawyer and the head of the Citizens for Decent Literature. The other members of the Commission were as follows:

William B. Lockhart, Dean of the University of Minnesota Law School (Chairman); Edward Ellis, President of an Atlanta, Georgia, news agency; Thomas D. Gill, Chief Judge of the Connecticut Juvenile Court; Dr. Edward D. Greenwood, Child Psychiatrist, Menninger Foundation, Topeka, Kansas; Morton A. Hill, S.J., President of Morality in Media, New York City; Dr. G. William Jones, Assistant Professor of Broadcast-Film Art, Southern Methodist University; Dr. Joseph T. Klapper, Director of Social Research for the Columbia Broadcasting System; Dr. Otto M. Larsen, Professor of Sociology, University of Washington; Dr. Irving Lehrman, Rabbi of Temple Emanu-El, Miami Beach, Florida; Freeman Lewis, Vice President, Simon & Schuster; Reverend Winfrey C. Link, Methodist Church Tennessee Annual Conference; Dr. Morris A. Lipton, Professor of Psychiatry, University of North Carolina Medical School; Thomas C. Lynch, Attorney General, State of California; Barbara Scott, Attorney for the Motion Picture Association of America; Cathryn A. Spelts, Instructor in English, South Dakota School of Mines; Dr. Frederick H. Wagman, Director of Libraries, University of Michigan (Vice-Chairman); and Dr. Marvin E. Wolfgang, Professor of Sociology, University of Pennsylvania.

The staff included: W. Cody Wilson, social psychologist; Paul Bender, lawyer; John J. Sampson, lawyer; Jane M. Freidman, lawyer; Karen I. Green, clinical psychologist; Bernard Horowitz, educational psychologist; Weldon T. Johnson, sociologist; Lenore R. Kupperstein, criminologist; Virginia P. Banister, administrative officer; Sylvia H. Jacobs; Bobbie Jack Wallin; and Anthony F. Abell.

6

Factors Affecting the Decision-Making Process in the Attorney General's Commission on Pornography: A Case Study of Unwarranted Collective Judgment

Dennis S. Gouran

Since 1967, the United States has had two national commissions created to investigate pornography and to determine what, if any, constraints should be considered in relation to its production, distribution, and consumption. The first of these, the Commission on Obscenity and Pornography, was created in 1967 by Congress and reported its findings to then President Richard Nixon in 1970. Disagreeing with the Commission's recommendations and likening pornography to pollution in seriousness, the president rejected the report upon its release (Haiman 1981, 171).

Despite the rejection of the Commission's report and continuation of the Supreme Court's position that obscenity does not fall under the protection of the First Amendment, cases involving the constitutionality of state and federal laws involving obscenity contributed to a more liberal view of what constitutes obscenity. One result was an increase in the availability of pornographic material. With the rapid growth of pornography in the 1970s and early 1980s, Attorney General William French Smith in 1985 created another commission—this time known as the Attorney General's Commission on Pornography.

From almost the moment of its creation, the Attorney General's Commission on Pornography became an object of controversy, as civil libertarians, in particular, saw its investigation as politically inspired, the conclusions preordained, and the prospect of serious consequences for freedom of expression and individual rights of privacy. It would be almost an understatement to suggest that the Commission engendered a substantial amount of criticism and negative reaction. Even before the release of the *Final Report*, the National Coalition Against Censorship had published a proceedings entitled *The Meese Commission Exposed* (1986). One of the leading expert witnesses, moreover, had seriously questioned the Commission's interpretation of his own and others' research (Donnerstein and Linz 1986). At least two critics saw blatant "vigilanteeism" in the Commission's recommendations (see Yardley 1986a, 1986b; Lillienstein 1986a, 1986b). Others found the Commission to be a body pursuing misplaced concerns (for example, Saltzman 1986). And still others viewed it to be a group not to be taken seriously. This sentiment was well expressed in a newspaper article with the caption, "The Story of X," in which the report was characterized as "a well-meant, windy muddle" ("The Story of X" 1986).

Although some of this criticism was unnecessarily abusive, in light of how the Commission functioned as a decision-making body, negative reactions are understandable. However well-intentioned the Commission may have been, one is hard-pressed to find convincing evidence that many of the conclusions—either in regard to problems or solutions—reached by the members were warranted by their analysis of relevant information. The recommendations are suggested by little more than a shaky hypothesis about the social effects of pornography—a hypothesis that also has been seriously questioned by social scientists who have carefully analyzed research on pornography (see, for example, Attig 1988; Brannigan and Goldenberg 1987). The Commission's approach appears to have been one based on the presumption of a need for certain legislative proposals and for which justifications in available information were then sought. Several critics have made this charge explicitly (see Cohen 1986; Kurtz 1986a; Lynn 1986). The commissioners' behavior in this respect is consistent with that of many decision-making bodies (see Hirokawa and Scheerhorn 1986). That fact, however, does little to increase the credibility of the report or provide reasons for the public to have confidence in it.

Although scholars such as Attig, Brannigan and Goldenberg, and Donnerstein and Linz have done impressive analyses of the social science evidence on which the commission drew in reaching its conclusions, the work of such scholars does not for the most part reveal the factors that may have predisposed the members to draw conclusions from information their critics so firmly believe were unwarranted. Neither do these scholars examine in much detail the content of the Commission's report to determine how the information consulted was used. The purpose of this chapter is to identify those factors and to discuss their role in contributing to the decision-making process from which the *Final Report* of the Attorney General's Commission on Pornography emerged. Such an analysis, I hope, will more clearly establish the inappropriateness of a set of recommendations that, upon implementation, could have significant impact on the conception and exercise of free speech.

An examination of the Commission reveals several factors that seem to give legitimacy to many of the critics' concerns about the analytical and decisional process that led to its controversial report. Among these, the ones on which this analysis focuses are the Commission's understanding of its task, qualifications of the members, attitudinal influences, the failure to define critical concepts adequately, deficiencies in the information consulted, and inappropriateness of the recommendations for the type of issue examined.

THE COMMISSION'S UNDERSTANDING OF ITS TASK

In the Charter of the Attorney General's Commission on Pornography, the following statement by William French Smith appears:

The objectives of the Commission are to determine the nature, extent, and impact on society of pornography in the United States, and to make specific recommendations to the Attorney General concerning more effective ways in which the spread of pornography could be contained, consistent with constitutional guarantees. (*Attorney General's Commission* 1986, Vol. 2, 1957)

The Charter was filed on March 29, 1985, and within 15 months, the Commission had issued a nearly 2,000-page report of the results of its investigation. To the extent that the Charter obligated the members of the Commission to recommend "more effective ways in which the spread of pornography could be contained," they were more than responsive. In all, the commissioners generated 92 separate recommendations and devoted well over 300 pages of the report to a discussion of the rationale and presumptions underlying their expected impact.

The wording in Attorney General Smith's charge seems to predispose one toward a particular outcome. At least, the language does little to encourage an attitude of dispassion. Rather, it implies findings not in evidence and presumes on a priori grounds the need for a particular course of action. This runs counter to the spirit of inquiry and discovery usually associated with fact-finding bodies, and with commissions especially. More important for the present analysis, however, it helped shape the Commission's understanding of the kind of group it saw itself as being. Rather than determining primarily what, if any, problems may exist as a result of the availability and consumption of pornography, a majority of the members appeared to regard themselves as a problem-solving group.

Nothing in Attorney General Smith's statement, of course, prevented the Commission from conducting as objective a study as possible, trying to judge whether evidence about pornography establishes a need for some type of control of its distribution and consumption, or determining the probable consequences of such controls as might be indicated. In fact, the Commission Chair observed, "I believe our final report represents as intensive an examination of the multi-faceted topic of pornography as could be conducted within our time and budgetary constraints" (*Attorney General's Commission* 1986, Vol. 1, 32). Such testimony, however, is not an especially illuminating index of how well the commissioners functioned to determine the existence of a problem. Neither can one rely on such self-assessments for judging the extent to which the Commission conformed to the requirements of open-mindedness and reasoned judgment. The generation of more than 90 detailed recommendations consuming substantially more space in the report than the analysis of the problem suggests that the Attorney General's charge had at the very least accented the importance of making proposals relative to discovering and verifying the existence of problems. Although the disproportionate emphasis on solutions does not prove that the Commission was unconcerned with establishing the occurrence and scope of any ill effects of pornography, it does indicate something about the members' priorities.

QUALIFICATIONS OF THE MEMBERS

In April 1985, the Attorney General's Commission on Pornography began its work in a partial atmosphere of suspicion and doubt. This atmosphere was created by individuals concerned with actions that could threaten citizens' freedom of choice and by representatives of commercial interests who stood to lose substantial financial resources from controls that might be placed on the production, distribution, and consumption of sexually explicit material. In some quarters, the creation of the Commission was viewed as a political response to conservative groups who had supported President Reagan through two elections in the expectation that he would move the country in the direction of the social and religious values they espouse. So concerned about the motivations behind the Commission and the potential threat to civil liberties it seemed to pose were some parties that Barry Lynn, Legislative Counsel for the American Civil Liberties Union, felt obliged to attend all of the Commission's public hearings and to share his reactions even before the *Final Report* had begun taking shape (See Fields 1986a).

That the motives of the commissioners or those responsible for their appointment were directed toward the destruction of Constitutional guarantees of freedom of speech and press or rights of personal privacy is doubtful. When one considers their backgrounds, however, the question of whether as a whole they possessed sufficient expertise and were as capable of the detachment to which their roles as commissioners seemingly committed them is a legitimate and defensible one to raise.

The Commission was chaired by Henry E. Hudson, Assistant United States Attorney for the Eastern District of Virginia. His legal prominence, in part, was attributable to successful prosecution of adult book store owners during the period he served as District Attorney in Arlington, Virginia. Also serving as Commission members were Judith Becker, Associate Professor of Clinical Psychology at Columbia University; Diane Cusack, member of the City Council and former Chair of the Zoning and Planning Commission in Scottsdale, Arizona; Park Dietz, Professor of Law and Behavioral Medicine and Medical Director for the Institute of Law, Psychiatry, and Public Policy at the University of Virginia; James Dobson, former Associate Clinical Professor of Pediatrics at the University of Southern California and currently president of a non-profit organization dedicated to the preservation of the home; Edward Garcia, United States District Court Judge for the Eastern District of California; Ellen Levine, Editor-in-Chief of *Woman's Day*; Tex Lezar, a Dallas lawyer and former counsel to Attorney General Smith; the Reverend Bruce Ritter, a Catholic priest and president of a child-care agency in New York City; Frederick Schauer, Professor of Law at the University of Michigan; and Deanne Tilton-Durfee, President of the California Consortium of Child Abuse Councils (*Attorney General's Commission* 1986, Vol. 1, 3–20).

Of the 11 commissioners, then, one had been active in the prosecution of obscenity cases, two were directly concerned with the abuse of children frequently involved in the production of pornography, one had been a close associate of the Attorney General who appointed the Commission, one had been chair of a zoning and planning commission concerned with the location of adult entertainment establishments, one had established an institute concerned with the propagation of a particular set of social values, one was a federal judge with prior experience in obscenity cases, two were professors of law (one of whom also had a clinical background), and one was editor of a popular magazine concerned with women's issues.

There is little evidence that the Commission members as a group possessed substantial expertise on the subject of pornography and its effects. Judith Becker had done research concerned with male rapists and was familiar with work on the effects on behavior attributed to the consumption of pornography. Frederick Schauer is an acknowledged authority on obscenity law and First Amendment issues and has written scholarly books on the subject (see, for example, Schauer 1982). He is not acknowledged, however, for his expertise on the effects of pornography. Park Dietz had published work on pornography (for example, Dietz and Evans 1982), but there is no indication that his research has been as extensive as that of social scientists specializing in the area (for example, *Pornography and Sexual Aggression* 1984; Zillmann and Bryant 1982). In addition to the backgrounds of these three commissioners, those involved in the prosecution of obscenity cases, as well as others who through their work had come indirectly or directly into contact with the pornography industry, may well have had relevant personal experiences, a general knowledge of the subject, and a reasonable understanding of concerns about its alleged consequences.

The profiles of the commissioners in their entirety do not suggest that they were especially well qualified for the task they had been given, but do in more than one instance raise suspicion of possible bias or at least of the quality of judgment exercised. Suspicion, of course, is an insufficient basis for assuming that any of the commissioners were unable to view and assess evidence objectively. The fact is that commissions often have members who are not specialists in the issues being considered; however, the absence of substantial expertise in the subject matter renders judgments drawn from information about the effects of pornography on face value less credible than if they were formed by highly knowledgeable individuals. Moreover, there is the likelihood that the least knowledgeable participants would be susceptible to errors in judgment regarding those who presumably knew more about the subject.

ATTITUDINAL INFLUENCES

Perhaps more appropriate to the issue of detachment than expertise is what several of the Commission members revealed about their attitudes and beliefs in the individual statements they prepared for the *Final Report*. Diane Cusack, for example, asserted that the availability of sexually explicit materials challenged the understanding "held by society for thousands of years that sex is private, to be cherished within the context of love, commitment, and fidelity" (*Attorney General's Commission*

1986, Vol. 1, 36). The statement indicates a well-defined belief structure and rigid view about what constitutes acceptable sexual conduct.

Park Dietz reportedly joined the Commission primarily out of a concern with public implications of widespread distribution and consumption of pornography (*Attorney General's Commission* 1986, Vol. 1, 39). That many of the sexual practices and activities he describes pose potential or actual health hazards is hardly questionable, but the extent to which consumption of pornography is responsible for, or encourages, such behavior is an issue he fails to address. Instead, he appends an article on detective magazines that he coauthored, in which six cases of aggressive and antisocial behavior were linked to the reading of this genre of popular magazine (see Dietz, Harry, and Hazelwood 1986).

In his statement, James Dobson expresses conviction in the relationship between sexually explicit material and aggressive behavior, particularly rape, despite his acknowledgment of the absence of conclusive evidence: "[I]t is my belief, although the evidence is not easily obtained, that a small but dangerous minority then choose [sic] to act aggressively against the nearest available females. Pornography is the theory; rape is the practice" (*Attorney General's Commission* 1986, Vol. 1, 78). One wonders how Commissioner Dobson, in admitting to a lack of directly relevant information, could so clearly see a causal connection between exposure to pornography and rape. If it is true that the vast majority of consumers does not aggress or seek to aggress against women, and that most rape cases, moreover, are not associated with prior exposure to pornographic material, there would seem to be a better basis for arguing the absence of a causal connection, or at least multiple causation.

Father Ritter represented a more moderate point of view than the three preceding commissioners; however, like Commissioner Dobson, he remained convinced that existing evidence offers a compelling basis for assuming a causal connection between exposure to pornographic material and sexual abuse, most notably rape (*Attorney General's Commission* 1986, Vol. 1, 172–83). He, too, clung to the belief, despite an admission of the absence of direct evidence.

Deanne Tilton-Durfee, in her statement, seems unable to separate concerns for child abuse from suspected effects of exposure to pornographic materials. The following statement is revealing: "In my opinion, violent materials, sexual or nonsexual, are the most serious concern regarding potential negative effects on children's attitudes and behavior" (*Attorney General's Commission* 1986, Vol. 1, 186). This observation follows an extended discussion of child abuse and victimization. One can easily agree that to abuse a child, sexually or otherwise, is reprehensible and should not be tolerated, but this issue is independent of what exposure to sexually explicit material might cause one to think, feel, or do. As Haiman (1981) has noted, "[T]here remains a significant difference between arguably immoral *communication* and arguably immoral *conduct* that is as great as the gulf between verbal/pictorial pollutants of the psyche and physical pollutants of the environment" (172). In any event, it is clear that this particular commissioner held strong beliefs about the potential impact of exposure to the portrayal of violent behavior on consumers' attitudes and behavior proclivities.

Tilton-Durfee joined Commissioners Levine and Becker in an expression of revulsion at the image of women that pornography typically projects. Levine and Becker, however, prepared a separate statement contesting conclusions about the pornography/aggressive behavior/rape relationship other commissioners felt reasonable to assume (*Attorney General's Commission* 1986, Vol. 1, 193–212). Ostensibly, their willingness to endorse the recommendations of the commission stemmed from a desire to protect children from exploitation by pornographers and other related abuses.

A majority of those serving on the Attorney General's Commission appeared to have intense feelings about one or more of the aspects of pornography, and from their individual statements, one fails to discern an ability to keep values, tastes, prior beliefs, and facts disentangled. One also senses in several instances an inability to apprehend distinctions between the psychological and physical harm that might befall individuals who consume it. Throughout several of the commissioner's statements runs a theme implying that if somehow pornography could be kept out of the hands of consumers, other social problems, such as abuse of women and children, would be less serious. Why that outcome would accrue, however, is not explicitly discussed.

Critics of the Commission, by and large, have been less than charitable in their estimates of the members' objectivity or ability to suspend judgment in dealing with this complex subject. Carole Vance (1986), for example, noted that, "Prior to convening, seven of the eleven commissioners had taken public stands opposing pornography and supporting obscenity law as a means to control it" (76). More scathing was Hendrick Hertzberg (1986). Questioning the ability of three of the commissioners in particular to exercise unbiased judgment, Hertzberg wrote: "The Meese Commission lacked the financial and staff resources of its predecessor, but since its conclusions were preordained, it didn't really need them" (21). And John Baker (1986) viewed the commissioners as "[a]pparently determined from the start to prove a causal relationship between pornography and violence" (30).

Such characterizations are to a degree both excessive and unfair. Given the widespread availability of sexually explicit material, it probably would be unrealistic to assume that a commission could have been assembled without its members having some preconceptions about the connections of such material to other aspects of social behavior. And even if such observations as Lindsay Van Gelder's (1986) that the Commission's "overall drift is perceptibly to the right" (52) were accurate, the presence of preconceptions and beliefs does not automatically preclude the possibility of impartiality in resolving public policy issues. Still, the mind-sets revealed in the statements of several of the commissioners represent a gauge of how likely they might be to meet their responsibilities as impartial decision makers.

FAILURE TO DEFINE CRITICAL CONCEPTS ADEQUATELY

Although chartered as the Attorney General's Commission on Pornography (soon thereafter to be known as the Meese Commission), no definition of the object of inquiry was provided. Nor throughout the entire investigation did the members ever establish clear referents for the term "pornography." In the report, they devote seven pages to a discussion of reasons for their inability to distinguish the concept and why the attempt to do so would have reduced the inquiry to an unprofitable "definitional quagmire" (*Attorney General's Commission* 1986, Vol. 1, 227–33). The sentiment, insofar as the need for definition was concerned, was to take the position of Justice Potter Stewart that "I know it when I see it" (from *Jacobellis v. Ohio* 1964 at 197).

Given the difficulty others have had in specifying what they mean by "pornography" (see O'Neil 1972, 44–48), one has sympathy with the Commission's position. On the other hand, its many criticisms of laxness in law enforcement and looseness in the interpretations of the courts would seem to make the matter of definition more critical to the task than the commissioners acknowledged.[1] How could they expect either to judge the effects of pornographic material or produce recommendations consistent with their charge without some clear sense of what determined the scope of inquiry and the specific material to which the recommendations would apply? How, moreover, could they expect their recommendations to have intended consequences when implementation would occur in the same atmosphere of confusion and uncertainty as that which many of the commissioners appear to have believed led to the widespread availability and consumption of pornography in the first place?

The Commission's solution to the definitional problem was to divide materials into four categories: (1) sexually violent, (2) nonviolent depicting degradation, domination, subordination, or humiliation, (3) nonviolent and nondegrading, and (4) nudity (*Attorney General's Commission* 1986, Vol. 1, 304). Exactly what these terms represent is not clear either, however. Primary harms are defined in the report as "those in which the alleged harm is commonly taken to be intrinsically harmful, even though the precise way in which the harm is harmful might yet be further explored" (*Attorney General's Commission* 1986, Vol. 1, 304). The term "secondary harm" is characterized in the following way: "In other instances, however, the alleged harm is secondary, not in the sense that it is in any way less important, but in the sense that the concern is not with what the act is, but where it will lead" (*Attorney General's Commission* 1986, Vol. 1, 304).

In principle, materials of a sexually explicit nature that cause harm of either a "primary" or "secondary" nature were the focus of the Commission's inquiry. If harm could be demonstrated, then some type of legal constraint on the production, dissemination, and/or consumption of such materials, in the commissioners' judgment, would be justified.

On the surface, the Commission's approach to identifying germane materials seems sensible. The problem is that the classifications suffer from at least as much ambiguity as the term "pornography" itself. Although the report contains illustrations for each of the four categories identified, with the possible exception of nudity not involving apparent sexual acts, unequivocal assignment of materials to categories would be difficult at best.

The Commission was also divided over the ecological validity or reality of the so-called "nonviolent and nondegrading" category (*Attorney General's Commission* 1986, Vol. 1, 335–47). They disagreed as to whether such a category exists, with some commissioners taking the position that overt displays of sexual behavior are necessarily and inherently degrading. Commission members dismissed the relevance of the "nudity" category. Hence, they were left with three categories, the existence of one of which was even a question in their own minds. The ambiguity and imprecision of the categories of materials about which the Commission members were concerned surely complicated the determination of harm and development of recommendations appropriate to the prevention and treatment of such harm as might exist.

In establishing categories, some Commission members exhibited a tendency to define sexually explicit materials in terms of presumed effects. This tendency is perhaps most evident in the discussion of the "nonviolent and nondegrading" category. Commenting on the lack of evidence establishing a causal link to sexual violence for materials fitting this category, the Commission observed:

That there does not appear from the social science evidence to be a causal link with sexual violence, however, does not answer the question of whether such materials might not themselves simply for some other reason constitute a harm in themselves, or bear a causal link to consequences other than sexual violence but still be taken to be harmful. (*Attorney General's Commission* 1986, Vol. 1, 338)

The commissioners remained divided on the issue of inherent harm, but for those who subscribed to such a position, it was virtually impossible to come to any conclusion other than that pornography is harmful. For them, harm is implicit in the notion of what it is that makes certain types of material pornographic. They might almost have defined pornography as any sexually explicit material presumed to have harmful attitudinal and behavioral effects. Ostensibly, this type of question-begging (see Capaldi 1979, 97) is not something the commissioners recognized. Still, several were guilty of such thinking.[2]

The failure of the Commission to develop a clear categorization of the types of materials whose effects they sought to establish, the nebulous descriptions of "primary" and "secondary" harms, and the apparent conceptualization of these materials as inherently harmful by some members did little to facilitate proper interpretation and assessment of the information assembled or to limit the domain to which conclusions and related recommendations might legitimately apply. At this most fundamental level, then, the Commission's decision-making behavior left a great deal to be desired.

INFORMATIONAL DEFICIENCIES

In the little more than a year the Commission was given to complete its investigation and to produce a report of the findings and recommendations, the members had access to a variety of material. In addition to published research, the commissioners conducted a series of hearings at various locations around the United States,[3] in which they heard testimony from experts, self-identified victims of pornography, concerned citizens representing particular points of view, and law enforcement officials. They also acquired a sample of commercially available films, photographs, books, newspapers, and magazines. The commissioners were even taken on a guided tour of an adult bookstore by a local law enforcement official in Houston. Court rulings and past legal opinions constituted yet another source of information.

Despite the volume and diversity of information available to the Commission and the testimony taken in the public hearings, the members did not have resources to fund original research. Many witnesses, moreover, were individuals prepared to speak of bad experiences with consumers of pornography, or who saw themselves as consumers adversely affected by the exposure. This type of anecdotal material was of limited value in at least two respects. First, the sample was small. Second, it was predominately one-sided. As Commissioners Becker and Levine pointed out:

In collecting the testimony of victims, it was difficult enough to find witnesses willing to speak out about their intimate negative experiences with pornography. To find people willing to acknowledge their personal consumption of erotic and pornographic materials and comment favorably in public about their use has been nearly impossible (*Attorney General's Commission* 1986, Vol. 1, 196)

Testimony from witnesses, especially self-identified victims, was problematic in other respects. One has no way of verifying the incidents reported nor of determining whether accounts of the role pornography played were accurate. In addition, testimony was often vivid and dramatic in its presentation. Reports of battered children, abused wives, torture, and sexual assault could only serve to elicit sympathy in any but the most callous of individuals. At a psychological level, the vividness of information is memorially more available than other types of data on which one might base inferences (Enzle, Hansen, and Lowe 1975; Nisbett and Ross 1980; Nutt 1989; Walster 1966).[4] Coupled with the fact that most of the experiences reported were negative, the testimony presented to the Commission could easily have contributed to overestimates of the extent to which the consumption of pornography has the kinds of effects described by many of the witnesses (see, for example, Kanouse and Hanson 1972).

Of course, the commissioners were not exclusively reliant on testimony in their efforts to determine the effects of pornography. They, or at least staff members, consulted published social science literature. The problem with much of this information, however, was that studies of an experimental nature in particular were not, and could not be, designed to test directly some of the types of effects with which the Commission was most vitally concerned. To the extent that such studies show evidence of causality, some social scientists (for example, Attig 1988; Brannigan and

Goldenberg 1987) have suggested that the causal factor is more likely observed aggression and violence than sexually explicit material. Correlational studies, based on social statistics, moreover, were fraught with the usual difficulties attendant upon establishing causal relationships. The fact that the incidence of rape, for instance, is high in locales in which the consumption of pornography is high and lower in locales in which consumption rates are relatively lower does not establish that rape in any degree is attributable to the availability of, or exposure to, sexually explicit materials of the types the Commission had identified.

Through no particular fault of its own, the Commission did not appear to have information well suited for making clear determinations of the effects of pornography. Yet in recognizing this limitation, a majority of the commissioners still acted as if they did. The irony is evident in any number of instances in the report, but possibly clearest in the Commission's discussion of its standard of proof for establishing a causal relationship:

As we deal with causal assertions short of conclusive but more than merely some trifle of evidence, we have felt free to rely on less proof merely to make assertions about the harm then [sic] we have required to recommend legal restrictions, and similarly we have required greater confidence in our assertions if the result was to recommend criminal penalties for a given form of behavior than we did to recommend other forms of legal restriction. (*Attorney General's Commission* 1986, Vol. 1, 308)

A causal relationship either exits or it does not, and the acceptability of a causal claim is not dependent on the use to which it may be put. That is not the crucial point, however. The more important consideration is that the Commission, with only the apparent exceptions of Judith Becker and Ellen Levine, felt free beyond some unspecified minimum standard to conclude when a causal relationship may be said to exist, regardless of possible reasons for believing otherwise. This represents a kind of condition Arie Kruglanski (1986) has referred to as "Freeze-Think," that is, a type of mind-set that seems impervious to competing judgments once one has been formed.

In its discussion of the category of sexually violent material, the Commission posits a causal effect on the incidence of sexual violence among consumers. This connection is based on evidence from studies showing a relationship between exposure to the type of material in question and subsequent aggressive behavior toward women. How well research establishes this link is itself a question to be addressed at a later point. But even if the exposure/aggression relationship were firmly established, its applicability to the incidence of sexual violence is doubtful. At least, the extension appears to be unwarranted.

To establish the causal linkage, the Commission report acknowledges that certain assumptions (inductive leaps, if you will) were necessary:

Finding a link between aggressive behavior towards women and sexual violence, whether lawful or unlawful, requires assumptions not found exclusively in the experimental evidence. We see no reason, however, not to make these assumptions. The assumption that increased aggressive behavior towards women is causally related, for an aggregate population, to increased sexual violence is significantly supported by the clinical evidence, as well as by much of the less scientific evidence. They are also to all of us assumptions that are plainly justified by our own common sense. (*Attorney General's Commission* 1986, Vol. 1, 325)

It is interesting that the clinical psychologist noted for having done research with rapists disputed the claim (*Attorney General's Commission* 1986, Vol. 1, 195–207). Of perhaps even greater interest is the fact that one of the expert witnesses whose research on the relationship was cited extensively in the report also disputed the basis for concluding that his and others' work either directly or indirectly establishes the alleged causal linkage (Donnerstein and Linz 1986). Insofar as the "clinical" evidence is concerned, the Commission's assumption did not even meet the first condition for establishing a causal relationship, that is, that the alleged effect consistently follow the alleged cause (see Babbie 1986, 55).

Other effects attributed by the Commission to the class of material labeled "sexually violent" were of an attitudinal variety, including increased acceptance of the "rape myth" that women actually enjoy or privately wish for the experience, greater acceptance of the behavior of sexual offenders, reduction in sympathy for the victims of sexually aggressive and violent behavior, and increases in the belief that victims of sexual assault provoke such actions (*Attorney General's Commission* 1986, Vol. 1, 327). In support of its conclusions about the causal relationships reviewed, the Commission was heavily, if not exclusively, reliant on social science research—the same research that at other points some members were willing to discount because of its incapacity for capturing the social context in which the consumption of pornography typically occurs.

As Commissioner Hudson noted in reference to social science research on the relationship of sexually violent material and subsequent behavior of consumers, "From a purely social science perspective, there is no cogent evidence that materials in this class have predominately negative behavioral effect. There is, however, a scarcity of research material within the definitional boundaries of the Category" (*Attorney General's Commission* 1986, Vol. 1, 28). In light of how the Commission used social science research, there appears to have been substantial inconsistency. When such inquiry produced evidence of negative effects, then it seemingly had probative value. When such evidence was not produced, social science inquiry was viewed as having questionable and restricted utility.

An instance of the sort of inconsistency mentioned above is apparent in the Commission's discussion of the effects of so-called "non-violent but degrading" material. Given limited evidence of negative effects in social science research for this particular category, the commissioners noted:

The absence of evidence should by no means be taken to deny the existence of the causal link. But because the causal link is less the subject of experimental studies, we have been required to think more carefully here about assumptions necessary to causally connect [sic] increased acceptance of rape myths and other attitudinal changes with increased sexual aggression and sexual violence. And on the basis of all the evidence we have considered, from all sources, and on the basis of our own insights and experiences, we believe we are justified in drawing the following conclusion: Over a large enough sample of a population that believes that many women like to be raped, that believes that sexual violence and sexual coercion is [sic] often desired or appropriate, and that believes that sex offenders are less responsible for their acts [missing subject, sic] will commit more acts of sexual violence or sexual coercion than would a population holding these beliefs to a lesser extent. (*Attorney General's Commission* 1986, Vol. 1, 332–33)

The preceding passage is also indicative of a general deficiency displayed by commission members. Nowhere in the report does the Commission offer any indication of the percentage of the pornography-consuming public likely to be harmed in either a behavioral or an attitudinal sense. Neither does it provide so much as an educated guess about the percentage of individuals likely to become victims of consumers of pornographic materials. Yet, with data the commissioners themselves frequently distrusted and with highly ambiguous conclusions like the one above, they somehow found a basis for making 93 specific recommendations aimed at controlling a problem of unknown dimensions, which is allegedly the result of exposure to something they could not—at least, chose not to—define.

FAULTY REASONING

In addition to using questionable evidence concerning the effects of pornography, the Commission exhibited a tendency to perceive implicit causal relationships of a specific directional nature in the correlational studies consulted and was guilty of other types of faulty reasoning. To the extent that a correlation may be indicative of a cause-to-effect relationship, in many instances, one cannot be sure which of two variables is the cause and which the effect. Data suggesting, for example, a marked increase in sexually violent behavior paralleling substantial increases in the availability, distribution, and consumption of pornographic material does not establish pornography as the causal factor. One could just as easily reason that an increase in sexually violent behavior and social attitudes has been the source of an increase in the consumption of and demand for pornographic material. Similarly, data suggesting that locales having tighter controls on distribution and consumption have lower rates of sexually violent behavior do not, in and of themselves, constitute evidence of a causal connection. Such a relationship might simply indicate that communities and regions populated by individuals having less desire for pornographic materials and lower rates of sexually violent behavior are more likely to place restrictions on the production and distribution of such materials. One sociologist, in fact, related differences in both consumption of sex magazines and the incidence of sexually aggressive behavior in the cases of North Dakota and Alaska, to the relative age distribution of the residents (see Kurtz 1986b). His and his colleagues' research (see, for instance, Libby and Strauss 1980) had been cited by the Commission as evidence supporting a causal relationship. However, according to Strauss, "when proper statistical controls are introduced, the relationship between rape and pornography disappears" (Kurtz 1986b).

At a theoretical level, members of the Commission understood that correlational data are not necessarily indicative of causal relationships. They discuss this matter in some detail in the report (*Attorney General's Commission* 1986, Vol. 1, 315–17). Nevertheless, in practice, they consistently tended to view exposure to sexually explicit material as the most critical variable among many combinations of potential causal factors, each of which could independently contribute to the behavioral and attitudinal effects of interest. Only once is consumption of pornography discussed as an effect, and then in relation to new technologies. That is, the growth in availability and consumption has been the result of commercially available and relatively inexpensive video-recording equipment. However, it is this very increase in availability, according to the Commission, that has led to the problems they identified. Comparing itself to its 1970 forerunner, the Attorney General's Commission attributed the failure of the earlier Commission to identify similar effects, in large part, to pornography's more restricted circulation (*Attorney General's Commission* 1986, Vol. 1, 224–27). One needs little background in formal logic to recognize the familiar *post hoc, ergo propter hoc* fallacy and the fallacy of insufficient cause in this aspect of the Commission's discussion.

Despite the Commission's failure at any point in its investigation or in its report to establish, or even to estimate, the percentage of individuals exposed to pornography who commit acts of violence or who develop unhealthy attitudes as a result, and despite the questionability of the types of evidence consulted in providing grounds for assuming causal connections of the type reported, the members nevertheless developed numerous recommendations. Upon first examination, one wonders how the analysis of the problem could have suggested most of the remedies proposed. If one agrees with the Commission that availability and consumption are at the base of the social ills they identified, however, he or she can begin to see a logic underlying the recommendations. But in the absence of demonstrable causal connections, the likelihood that the recommendations would have measurable effects is doubtful. This is a matter that will be examined more fully in the next section of this chapter. Insofar as the present discussion is concerned, one must conclude that the Commission's identification of a problem to be solved rests on many questionable inferences requiring assumptions for which few grounds for belief are furnished. In this regard, the Commission's understanding, assessment, and use of information leaves one with little confidence in the judgments of its members.

INAPPROPRIATENESS OF THE RECOMMENDATIONS

In light of the preceding discussion, there are two ways in which one can view the recommendations of the Attorney General's Commission on Pornography. One is as a set of actions aimed at alleviation of the incidence of sexually violent behavior and alteration of the attitudes and values the Commission, to its satisfaction, determined to have been the consequence of the increased availability and consumption of pornographic material. The other, which is consistent with the Commission's Charter, is to view them simply as actions designed to curtail pornography. The report would seem to suggest that the commissioners saw the recommendations as achieving both ends because in the judgment of most of them, the harms they had identified were in large measure the causal outcome of availability and consumption. In either case, however, the presumed impact bears close scrutiny.

For purpose of this analysis, it is not possible, nor is it necessary, to examine each of the 92 recommendations presented in the *Final Report*. More central to the critique, perhaps, are the bases for believing that the recommendations, upon implementation, would have the presumed effects.

The Commission did not specifically address the question of how implementation of its recommendations would reduce consumption. In fact, the discussion of the proposals often reminds one of high school and college debaters' "plan meets needs" arguments, in which assertions serve as substitutes for evidence or probability assessments. As an example, in the Discussion of Recommendation 37, which would require retailers or distributors of sexually explicit materials to use consent forms and to maintain records of performers' ages, the Commission noted that, "This proposed legislation should afford protection to minors through every level of the pornography industry" (*Attorney General's Commission* 1986, Vol. 1, 619). The report details what would be required under the legislation, but the reasons and evidence for believing that minors would be better protected are not evident.

As another example, in Recommendation 7 the Commission encouraged the elimination from state statutes and local ordinances of the requirement that material be "utterly without redeeming social value" to be considered obscene. In this case, the members did not even make an assertion about the probable consequences. Instead, the report reviews court cases suggesting that such amendments could be made without constitutional problems (*Attorney General's Commission* 1986, Vol. 1, 491–95).

The Commission failed to make any estimate of the extent to which availability and consumption, especially, might be reduced by implementation of the recommendations. Nor did it exert much effort in assessing the extent to which the pornography industry might continue to function in violation of the proposed legislation. Still, it is not unreasonable to assume that the recommendations taken as a whole would probably reduce consumption to some degree and make pornographic materials less easily accessible. But even if the expected impact were substantial, the remaining question is whether a reduction in the availability and consumption of pornography of any magnitude would show corresponding changes in the behavior and attitudes the Commission so strongly believed pornography to encourage.

Many, in fact most, of the Commission's recommendations involve legislation aimed at the protection of children and adults forced into the production of pornographic films, magazines, and the like, and who are often physically and psychologically abused. These recommendations, of course, have few implications for the effects presumed to be causally linked to the consumption of pornography. Collectively, they might restrict the amount of certain types of material currently available, but there is no necessary reason that such protections would limit one's exposure to other classes of pornographic materials.

Other sets of recommendations involved changes in laws to facilitate prosecution of obscenity cases, the creation of nuisance and anti-display laws, and one proposal to provide civil remedies for harm attributable to pornography. In the last category, it should be noted that efforts along these lines in Indianapolis and Minneapolis met with serious opposition. Legislation was defeated in Minneapolis, and Indianapolis's act was ruled unconstitutional (Fields 1986b).

In its discussion of the recommendations, in not one case did the Commission relate the specific provisions to the behavior and attitudes of consumers or indicate how the effects on them could be reduced. The reader must presume these consequences on the basis of causal linkages the Commission felt it had established. Since the causal relationships are questionable at best, the Commission leaves little reason for believing that they represent realistic solutions to the problems of primary concern—or at least, the problems to which the members devoted most of their attention. Since the causal relationships were so strongly implanted in the minds of some commissioners, however, it is more understandable that they would expect the recommendations to have the desired effect. This type of thinking represents an excellent example of the sort of influence that Richard E. Nisbett and Lee Ross (1980) have suggested some knowledge structures exert on a variety of inferences, including those we might think of as predictive.

There is a certain irony to the Commission's advocacy of predominately legal approaches to what many of its members viewed as a public health problem. Perhaps even more ironic is the Commission's failure to draw on the findings of a report it had requested be prepared by the Surgeon General. The report, entitled *Pornography and Public Health*, reached some conclusions about the effects of pornography that were not altogether dissimilar to those of the Commission. The Surgeon General's report, however, recommended better identification of the content of sexually explicit materials and a campaign in "media literacy" to make consumers more aware of potentially harmful effects. The report also recommended social programs aimed at preventing young people from becoming involved in the production of pornography as well as assisting those with a history of involvement (see Lawton 1986). The Commission's *Final Report* predated the Surgeon General's by a little over a month, but there was no apparent reason for the Commission members' not having been able to survey preliminary drafts before completing its own.

Whether either set of recommendations would have the intended effect is difficult to judge. In principle, however, the recommendations more directly tied to the nature of the problem (assuming the problem exists) would seem to have a greater chance of succeeding (see Gouran 1988; Janis and Mann 1977; Nutt 1989). At the very least, the Surgeon General's recommendations would seem to represent a more appropriate choice.

CONCLUSION

As a decision-making group, the Attorney General's Commission on Pornography cannot be offered as a model worthy of emulation. Although the sincerity and effort of its members are not at issue, the factors examined in this chapter proved too powerful a combination for the dictates of enlightened judgment to prevail. If the experience of the Commission serves to clarify and alert us to the unwanted sources of influence that can impede even the most well-intentioned of groups in their examination of serious and significant social issues, its legacy will have been of value. This is an especially important lesson when we are dealing with as significant a social institution as freedom of expression.

APPENDIX

Attorney General's Commission on Pornography

Judge Henry Hudson, *Chairman*

Dr. Judith Veronica Becker	Ms. Ellen Levine
Ms. Diane D. Cusack	Mr. Tex Lezar
Dr. Park Elliott Dietz	Rev. Bruce Ritter
Dr. James C. Dobson	Frederick Schauer, J.D.
Judge Edward J. Garcia	Ms. Deanne Tilton

Alan E. Sears, *Executive Director*
Professional Staff

David Cayer, J.D.	Peggy Coleman, J.D.
Genevieve McSweeney Ryan, J.D.	Dr. Edna Einseidel

ACKNOWLEDGMENTS

This chapter is reprinted from *Free Speech Yearbook* 28 (1990): 104–19. Copyright Speech Communication Association. Published by permission of the author and publisher. Dennis S. Gouran is Professor and Head in the Department of Speech Communication at Penn State University. The author gratefully acknowledges the assistance of Janet Bodenman in locating information on which this study is in part based.

NOTES

1. It is somewhat surprising that the Commission did not offer a definition because one of its members, Professor Schauer, had not seemed at all reluctant to do so in other contexts (see, for example, Schauer 1982, 179).

2. If this reasoning does not beg the question, at the very least, it ignores it. That is, it suggests that if one cannot prove that pornography is not harmful, it follows that it is (see Capaldi 1979, 121–22).

3. Hearings were held in Washington, D.C., Chicago, Houston, Los Angeles, Miami, and New York (*Attorney General's Commission* 1986, Vol. 2, 1845–59).

4. During a tour of an adult bookstore in Houston, a vice officer opened the door to a peep show booth where the commissioners observed two customers involved in an act of oral copulation (Grove 1986). This was a particularly vivid and memorable scene.

7

The Rogers Commission Investigation of the *Challenger* Tragedy

Christine M. Miller

Commissions, be they appointed by the President or another governmental entity, are expected to provide nonpartisan, expert advice after conducting an independent inquiry into some state of affairs. Their activities are usually deemed newsworthy, and their findings may produce profound changes in policy. To be sure, governmental commissions are not the only source of relatively unbiased investigation and advice available, but the prestige, the scale of operation, and the national importance of the topics investigated establish the governmental commission as unique among investigatory bodies.

Surprisingly, there have been few studies of governmental commissions as investigatory entities. As Frank Popper notes, "Commissions will continue to be important, but the commission as an institution is a largely unexamined and unevaluated advisory device" (1970, 8). Popper's work on presidential commissions, coupled with a small handful of other studies of commissions detailed in the first three chapters of this book, are the only concerted efforts to examine the goals, characteristics, operating procedures, and decision-making strategies of these unique panels of inquiry.

This chapter seeks to enhance and update our understanding of how governmental commissions function by examining one of the most high-profile commissions in recent history: the commission charged with investigating the space shuttle *Challenger* accident. In the aftermath of the *Challenger* tragedy, attempts to reconstruct the decision and events prior to the disaster sought to account for how and why it occurred. The managers and engineers responsible for the launch decision justified their behaviors to the satisfaction of the Rogers Commission, a presidentially appointed independent investigatory panel.[1] The justifications offered to the Rogers Commission have served as the basis for several scholarly communication studies of the accident (Gouran, Hirokawa, and Martz, 1986; Seeger 1986; Ice 1987; Miller 1988). However, no attempt has been made to analyze the activities of the Commission itself. While the investigation conducted by Rogers and his colleagues is an invaluable account of pre- and post-launch decision making, the investigatory body itself deserves to be examined for its conduct of the inquiry.

This chapter tracks the *Challenger* investigation for the purpose of determining how the inquiry process functioned. The Commission's goals, responsibilities, and practices provide insight into why the investigation proceeded as it did. In addition, the constraints under which the Commission operated, as well as the influence of the media on the proceedings, also help explain how the commissioners reached their conclusions. Such issues are often at the core of the success or failure of any independent commission's decision-making processes. Accordingly, this chapter will examine the process by which the Rogers Commission conducted the investigation, and the constraints under which it operated. As Popper notes, commissions "can, in principle, perform great services for the President and the public, but too often they have not fulfilled their potential" (1970, 56). Examining the processes and constraints allows a determination of the extent to which the Rogers Commission fulfilled its potential.

PROCESS

The inquiry into the disaster was a cooperative effort. As Chairman Rogers put it, "This is not an adversarial procedure. The Commission is not in any way adversarial" (*Report of the Presidential Commission* 1986, 435). Given the nature of the problem, both the investigators (the Rogers Commission) and those being investigated (NASA and its contractors) were genuinely concerned with finding out the same information: what happened to cause the space shuttle *Challenger* to explode, and why it happened. Naturally, these fundamental questions led to a myriad of other questions, and as the investigation continued the complexity of the issues became patently obvious.

For its part, "the commission amassed more than 120,000 pages of materials, interviewed 160 people and conducted 13 days of hearings" (Abramson 1986, 11). Examining the transcripts from these hearings provides the best accounting of how the process functioned and how those involved conducted themselves. Specifically, the transcripts reveal what NASA's strategies seemed to be during the investigation, and they reveal what the commissioners themselves seemed to consider important in their role as investigators.

NASA Strategies

NASA was cooperative in the investigation. In fact, the space agency had quite a vested interest in and an emotional commitment to finding out what caused the deaths of the six astronauts and one teacher. Therefore, in addition to cooperating with the Rogers Commission it launched its own internal investigation. This shadow inquiry was termed "a devil's advocate team" by Associate Administrator for Space Flight Jesse Moore. When the team was formed, Moore told the Commission that it

will be a team which will set off and support my activities and think up scenarios that may have occurred on this mission that will not be intimately involved into the detailed scenario analysis that we are doing with our own teams in place here. There will be a team set off to the side and hopefully do some independent thinking to make sure we are not letting anything fall through the cracks (*Report* 1986, 62)

The internal investigation, according to NASA, was not designed to supplant the Commission's efforts. NASA administrators viewed their devil's advocate team as complementary to President Reagan's appointed board. Jesse Moore and William Graham, Acting Administrator of NASA, continually assured the Commission of full cooperation, as these excerpts from the transcripts illustrate:

CHAIRMAN ROGERS: Now, there is no feeling on the part of NASA that the work of the Commission is in any way interfering with the disclosure of information, I hope?

DR. GRAHAM: No, sir. In fact, the work of the Commission is very much in accord with the work that NASA is undertaking and conducting internally, and we find these to be in general complementary.

CHAIRMAN ROGERS: In fact, you asked me to have this public session today in order to make it clear that NASA was not trying to brush anything under the rug, isn't that right?

DR. GRAHAM: Yes, sir. I suggested to you that you consider having a public session today on specific characteristics of the SRBs, the solid rocket boosters, and any other matters you saw fit to question the NASA officials concerning. (*Report* 1986, 599–600)

MR. MOORE: [T]he activities we initiated on that tragic Tuesday at NASA are continuing. We are doing everything we possibly can . . . to fully assess and evaluate and determine the problems associated with this particular mission. . . . We are continuing to analyze the facts and circumstances . . . and we would be happy to support you and the members of this Commission in any way you deem fit. (67)

DR. GRAHAM: NASA continues to analyze the system design and data and, as we do, you can be certain that NASA will provide you with its complete and total cooperation. (5)

MR. MOORE: We plan to cooperate very fully with the Commission and provide the data to the Commission as required. (606)

CHAIRMAN ROGERS: [W]e have no reason to think that we will not get full cooperation from NASA.

DR. GRAHAM: [Y]ou can be certain that NASA will provide you with full cooperation. That is NASA's policy and my personal position as well, and that continues to be NASA's policy, and will remain that way throughout the course of this investigation. (435–36)

A cynical attitude would suggest that *promises* and *intentions* to cooperate often do not translate to practices—one need only read Professor McKinney's analysis of the relationship between the Warren Commission and the FBI to find evidence that such cynicism is justified. In the present case, as the investigation became more complex and NASA's own policies and personnel were called into question, one might wonder just how forthcoming NASA was with information. Notwithstanding Jesse Moore's proclamation that "we will be happy to provide you and [sic] additional information that you need and support your Commission in any way you deem fit" (*Report* 1986, 234), the issue of full cooperation deserves to be addressed by examining NASA's actions.

Of course, it may never be definitively established that NASA did or did not fully cooperate with the Commission, at least insofar as publicly accessible information allows such an assessment. But by and large, it can be established that *the Commission* was satisfied with NASA's cooperation, so a cynical attitude does not appear justified. After all, the Commission was a panel of independently appointed investigators made up of at least some members who did not have a vested interest in exonerating NASA of responsibility. It seems likely, then, that they would not be satisfied with anything less than full cooperation. Moreover, it may be fair to say that some of the members of the panel stood to gain professionally by finding evidence that NASA was not forthcoming with information.[2] These members may have been cynical about *promises* of cooperation, yet no one on the Commission charged that there was a gap between promise and practice. As a matter of fact, Chairman Rogers noted a few times in the transcripts that NASA "complied fully" and was "very forthcoming" (594), and he expressed his assurance that "NASA has attempted to give us the key documents"(434). Moreover, the final report details in a number of pages the procedures developed by the Commission "to assure that it received all documents requested from NASA and other sources and that all documents and other correspondence were properly processed" (214).

In addition to full cooperation, another NASA strategy for aiding the investigatory process was to ensure corrective action. It was mentioned previously that the Commission collected over 120,000 pages of information and interviewed 160 people; with such a large volume of resources, provided mostly by NASA, it is little wonder that errors in testimony or documentation might occur. Accordingly, NASA Administrator William Graham described to the Commission its strategy for detecting and correcting problems:

DR. GRAHAM: [I]n addition to trying to give you as timely and complete a volume of information as we can during our testimony, we realize that it is possible for NASA to occasionally misspeak or to delete something inadvertently, and should that occur, we will in any case be going back over the testimony and looking at it and checking it. As soon as we find something that appears to be—to warrant an amendment to the testimony or a clarification or an addition to the testimony, we will provide that to you. (437)

DR. GRAHAM: [A]ll NASA testimony that is given to the Commission will be reviewed on a word by word basis by a knowledgeable NASA technical review team. Should any error, partial, or incomplete statement, or potentially misleading statement be found in the testimony, an amendment to the testimony will be filed in order to clarify the issue of concern. That will certainly be called to your attention. (597–98)

Examining the transcripts was not the only form of feedback available to NASA and its contractors as they attempted to monitor their statements for clarity. Those who testified were also questioned separately by the media, so it was possible at times to determine when statements to the Commission were not as clear as they could have been by monitoring the media's response to an individual's testimony. Such monitoring afforded additional opportunities for clarity, as this example illustrates:

MR. MULLOY: May I clarify some testimony that I made this morning relative to the events on the 51-L [*Challenger* launch] and our observations, the rationale that we used given the O-ring erosion? Some of the questions I have had from the media indicate that it wasn't perhaps as precise a statement as it could have been. (745)

It appears in examining the transcripts that NASA's strategies for dealing with the investigatory process were positive and proactive. Agency administrators took care to assure commissioners that they were cooperating fully. This cooperation included establishing an agency shadow investigatory team to complement the work of the Commission, meeting data requests completely, and taking corrective action in instances of error or lack of precision during testimony. These strategies ultimately served NASA's aim of determining what happened to cause the crash and why it occurred.

Commission Strategies

Not surprisingly, the Commission's strategies for dealing with the investigatory process concerned what to do with the data it was presented for analysis, and how to reach conclusions warranted by the data. In other words, in order to make the process work and to answer the what-happened-and-why questions, the commissioners were fundamentally interested in evidence and reasoning. The strategies they used to evaluate the evidence and come to conclusions in which they had confidence were integral to the success of the Commission.

The Commission's approach to data analysis was fairly straightforward: collect all the data there is, don't accept the data at face value, clarify everything possible, and *then* come to a conclusion. Commissioner Sally Ride, for instance, established that she was "very sensitive to the right approaches: Collect the data, look at all the data, and then once you've looked at it all, come to your conclusions" (*Report* 1986, 389). Commissioner Richard Feynman shared this philosophy, because he believed that data can be misleading on its face and lead one to erroneous conclusions. Citing past instances of this danger, he noted that

it is the experience of Commissions who have looked into accidents that what looks obvious at first turns out later to have a little flaw, and, when you make a long list of things that are out of the ordinary, that are called anomalies, you discover that there is something that doesn't quite fit, and then the theory has to be completely changed. (*Report* 1986, 603)

To avoid such problems, it was important for the commissioners to clarify the facts and the testimony at every opportunity. The following remark by Chairman Rogers is indicative of these attempts to clarify: "All I want to do is find out what was done. If it wasn't done, tell us why and we will understand and the record will be clear. That's all." (*Report* 1986, 468–49).

Once the commissioners felt they had enough reliable data, they attempted to arrive at conclusions. The reasoning process that seemed to best characterize their deliberations was the method of residues. They largely operated from the assumption that the most reliable way of determining what went wrong and why was to test all of the available theories and eliminate those that were not supported by the best evidence possible. Chairman Rogers explained their approach in this way: "[W]e are going to be working on the exclusion theory most of the time, probably. We're not going to discover something, so we're going to have to exclude a lot of these things and say, here is what's left" (*Report* 1986, 315).

An example of the use of the method of residues as an approach to reasoning appears fairly early in the testimony, before the commissioners had excluded any possible causes of the accident. Chairman Rogers was careful to caution NASA not to be perceived as eliminating any scenarios prematurely:

CHAIRMAN ROGERS: I thought it was a little unfortunate in the paper this morning that they said that, and I don't think you really said that, that you had excluded the possibility that weather had any effect. I mean, I think weather is also going to be considered very actively by a whole lot of people, and if at the end of the road you decide or we decide to exclude it, fine, but if it appears that to begin with, particularly because apparently Rockwell did call and gave you a warning which you considered and decided that it was okay to go ahead, suppose that judgment was wrong. (*Report* 1986, 373)

Ultimately, weather was considered to be part of the reason for the explosion.

During the investigation, however, other theories, such as sabotage or White House pressure to launch *Challenger* to coincide with the State of the Union Address, were excluded from consideration for lack of compelling evidence. The final conclusions, the ones that endured through the method of residues, form the basis of the report to the President.

CONSTRAINTS

Because the Rogers Commission was a presidentially appointed board of inquiry, because the *Challenger* disaster was a public event that shook the nation, and because it was ultimately determined that the accident was preventable, the Commission faced some significant constraints during its investigation. While the constraining factors to be discussed here are not an exhaustive list, they seem to represent the most noteworthy pressures constraining the Commission's investigation.

Meeting Public Responsibility

According to Frank Popper, one function of a presidential commission is public education (1970, 9). Popper also indicates that "all commissions devote much time and effort to their public relations. At least until they submit their reports to the President, commissions often lobby for their recommendations" (36). Michael Lipsky and David Olson further note that "even while commissions pursue research and investigation, they must engage in an effort at public relations" (1977, 99). On the face of it, research, public education, and public relations might seem to be disparate goals. Indeed, Lipsky and Olson identify an inherent conflict among these goals:

All government agencies thrive on favorable public images which they more or less deliberately cultivate. Commissions, however, encounter relatively unique public relations problems. As ad hoc, temporary bodies they enjoy few sources of support aside from the political legitimacy with which they are initially endowed or attempt to nurture. And a deliberate attempt to encourage publicity may put their objectivity in question. A commission seeks to influence public opinion through its investigation and to some extent it tries to reassure the public that the controversial issue which it is charged with examining will be dealt with clearly and forcefully. There is a tension between these goals. Reassurance requires visible activities and public reminders that the agency is at work, while in the long run acceptance is gained by objectivity and systematic study. (1977, 126)

In such circumstances, commissions often have difficulty balancing their need to investigate with their need to engage in public relations. Meeting their public responsibility to deliberate without the bias of external influence conflicts with meeting their public responsibility to keep the populace informed and reassured. The result, as Lipsky and Olson point out, is that the conflict between these goals is not resolved; each receives the commission's attention (thus, perhaps, not all the attention each deserves):

Superficially, commissions seem to retreat into relatively isolated deliberations and fact-finding once they are established. Actually, however, they spend a substantial amount of time assessing and anticipating political pressures. Like agencies with more stable structures and permanent government roles, commissions respond to outside influences even as they devote themselves to research and evaluation. (Lipsky and Olson 1977, 122)

The Rogers Commission seemed to understand both the public service and the public relations function of its work. These functions can be intertwined to serve each other and to serve the constituencies involved (i.e., the public, the media, and the commission). Chairman Rogers in particular seemed to be sensitive to the public service provided by his commission's efforts. Speaking on behalf of the other commissioners, he remarked in a hearing that

while the Commission has the responsibility under its mandate from the President to investigate the accident and report its findings, the media plays a key role in the process by keeping the public informed. We believe it has performed this role well and with a high sense of responsibility. If the Commission effectively performs its duties and the media performs its role of accurately reporting the facts as they develop, the public will be well served. (*Report* 1986, 1252)

Serving the public was not simply an idle goal. Because public education and public relations depend on each other, Chairman Rogers made conscious efforts to facilitate public service. One way that the Commission met its responsibility was to establish information as open to public scrutiny. According to Rogers, "Anything that happened prior to the launch or immediately after is public property. It is all going to be in the public domain, no matter what you think" (*Report* 1986, 589). Given the media involvement in the investigation, and given the public hearings held by the Commission (issues that shall be taken up shortly), Rogers's statement points to the importance of facing public responsibility. Placing the discussion in the public domain was essential to creating the perception that the Commission was conducting its affairs properly. With the media playing its watchdog role and with many of the hearings open to the public, the Commission opened itself to a great deal of scrutiny. By meeting its public responsibility in this way, the Commission could build its credibility and increase the likelihood that its recommendations would be accepted. Releasing information into the public domain as it became available helped satisfy those who were anxious to find out the details of the accident.

Of course, just because information becomes publicly accessible does not mean that the public will understand it. Sometimes it seems that government agencies exploit this fact by using doublespeak and other obfuscation techniques. But Chairman Rogers seemed sensitive to public perception and the frustration that accompanies lack of understanding. For instance, in a follow-up comment to one witness, Rogers asked specifically that an issue be clarified to make it understandable to the public:

CHAIRMAN ROGERS: [I]t is hard to explain it to an average outsider. . . . Try to explain it. The impression is that you were directed to do it, that there was so much pressure to get this launch off that you were directed to do it, and you did it. Now, if that is not the case, try to explain it in language that the public will understand: Why you changed your mind and how you did it so quickly. (*Report* 1986, 1134)

Rogers and his colleagues were constrained by their mandate to serve the public. Arguably, the functioning and efficiency of the Commission would have been better achieved without consideration of public service. But because of their implicit charge to serve the public good and their explicit charge to report their findings, they could ill afford to ignore their public responsibility if they wanted to establish the integrity of their investigation.

Handling Media Influence

As the previous section indicated, public service and public relations are inextricably linked. Commissions need publicity to meet their public responsibility. Popper explains that "recent commissions have been distinctive only in number and in the publicity which a few have received" (1970, 8). It is probably safe to say that the Rogers Commission would fit Popper's definition of a distinctive commission by virtue of the media attention it generated.

Such media attention put pressure on the Commission. Because the media was a constraining influence, Rogers and his fellow commissioners had to understand and deal with press relations. Richard Feynman recalls that at the first meeting of the commissioners, "Mr. Rogers did discuss the importance of our relationship to the press and how we have to be very careful with the press. 'I know Washington,' he kept saying. 'We have to proceed in an orderly manner and be careful of leaks to the press' " (1988, 28).

It is interesting to note, however, that Rogers did not perceive press relations as a one-way street; in addition to cautioning his colleagues about their influence on the press, he also was cognizant of the press and its influence on his colleagues. During one of the lighter moments of an open session, Rogers commented:

CHAIRMAN ROGERS: I would also like to remind particularly those from the media that the Commission was asked to conduct a calm and deliberate investigation, which I think so far we have managed to do reasonably well. I would, though, suggest that we, because of the press attention, we are not going to continue to be available individually for individual press conferences, and I hope the media will understand that. We are going to provide as much information on a regular basis as we can, probably principally through a spokesman, and therefore we would ask your indulgence and not to intercept our progress in and out of the building.

[Laughter]

CHAIRMAN ROGERS: I realize it is a laughing matter. I realize nobody will pay any attention to it.

[Laughter]

CHAIRMAN ROGERS: Anyway, it's a good try. (*Report* 1986, 752)

The reference to providing information on a regular basis, primarily through a spokesperson, emphasizes Rogers's attempt to meet the constraints imposed by constant media attention.[3] His strategy was to keep the press reasonably informed and to help them do their jobs so that he might similarly do his own. At one point, Rogers announced, "We will attempt to advise the press of our plans as they are formulated, so that you can plan your own schedules" (*Report* 1986, 594). At another time, Rogers orchestrated press relations by declaring,

The only announcements we will make will be when we decide on meetings, where the meetings are going to be held. And if we have public meetings, we will announce the witnesses. But except for that, we won't make any announcements or comments at all. I think we have all agreed to that, and if there is any thought of deviation, why, I will talk to all of the Commission members. (*Report* 1986, 395–96)

Rogers clearly sought the cooperation of the press and his colleagues with respect to media relations.

One of the key strategies used by the Commission to meet its public responsibility and maintain positive rapport with the press was the use of public sessions. The purpose of such sessions was disclosure. For the most part, what was disclosed in public session was virtually identical to what the Commission learned in its private sessions. This was a source of consternation to Commissioner Richard Feynman, who noted that "Mr. Rogers wanted to keep the public informed, so every time we discovered something, we would quickly have an open meeting to bring out the new material. But I thought, 'It's like an act: We have to hear the same things in the open meeting as in the closed meeting, and we won't learn anything new" (1988, 30). Feynman's observation is borne out in open session testimony, as the following example indicates:

CHAIRMAN ROGERS: Mr. Mulloy, just to clarify for the record, the material you presented to us yesterday [in closed session] is not any different than the material you are presenting today, is it?

MR. MULLOY: No, sir. (*Report* 1986, 668)

To be accurate, however, it must be noted that the open sessions were also used for partial disclosure, so as not to hamper the investigation. The members of the Commission wanted to be sure that what was reported in open session was sufficiently detailed and accurate to help them educate the public and generate good public relations through the media. On the other hand, they wanted to insure that theories concerning the cause of the crash were rigorously tested according to the method of residues before they were released to the public. In other words, they did not want speculative lines of inquiry that were currently being tested for their efficacy by the Commission to be concurrently tested in the media. Therefore, there were instances of partial disclosure, as the following excerpts imply:

CHAIRMAN ROGERS: Is there something that you would like to tell us now that we should know about that it would not be wise to disclose in public at this time? We want to try to be sure that we don't do anything or say anything which injures or impairs your investigation, but, on the other hand, we want to disclose as much as we can in the public session. Is there anything that we should not disclose tomorrow, as far as you know? (*Report* 1986, 521–22)

CHAIRMAN ROGERS: Jess, consider if you will, and you don't have to decide now, whether at some time in a public session this kind of report [concerning a small boat offshore during a visit by Vice President Bush][4] would be useful.

MR. MOORE: Okay.

CHAIRMAN ROGERS: In other words, this is the kind of thing that would show care, and it would show that you have done a lot of work ahead of time and you have excluded some possibilities in public, so that would give us a basis for the report that we will make.

MR. MOORE: Yes sir. I think that if we continue to go in and get most of the details put into place and kind of get a big picture story, then I think we can talk to you about some version that is going to go public.

CHAIRMAN ROGERS: I think that you might keep in mind what kind of public sessions we can have without damaging your investigation and still reassuring the public that a lot of things are being done.

MR. MOORE: Yes, sir. (325-26)

The purpose of the public sessions was to release information about the investigation that the investigators believed could be responsibly disseminated, that is, information that the Commission believed to be reliable and accurate. Release of incomplete, speculative information ran the risk of undermining the investigation and damaging the credibility of the Commission. It is not surprising, then, that Chairman Rogers and others were "conscious of possible leaks" (*Report* 1986, 387). Given the number of people involved, as investigators, staff, and witnesses, "scooping" the Commission was a constant source of concern. This concern was articulated by Chairman Rogers during the testimony of NASA Acting Administrator William Graham. Rogers asked Graham for NASA's full cooperation in disclosing information to the Commission before such information found its way into the press:

CHAIRMAN ROGERS: I want to make it clear that obviously you can't report to the Commission every time that some newspaper is going to write a story. We wouldn't expect that. On the other hand, there are certain types of investigations which you may be aware of that seem to have particular significance, and in such event, we would hope that you would, and members of NASA would immediately let us know about it so that it didn't appear that we were taken by surprise. Do you agree with that?

DR. GRAHAM: Very much so, Mr. Chairman. I am in complete agreement with that policy, and I have transmitted that policy to the NASA staff. . . .

CHAIRMAN ROGERS: [W]e don't want to react to every newspaper story because it is inevitable there will be a lot of them, and a lot of them will be unfair and unfriendly.

I guess what concerns me a little bit about it, and I hope we don't have any further discussion publicly about it, is that this seemed to go right to the heart of the matter, and it seemed to be related to the plume [of smoke from the solid rocket booster] that was started and shown to the public, and it occurred to us that there must have been a good deal of thought in NASA about how serious a story it would be if it appeared, and therefore I would have thought that there would have been an eagerness to present it to the Commission on Thursday, and particularly on Friday, in the private session. (*Report* 1986, 439–40)

William Rogers simply didn't want the work of the Commission to be compromised by reading information salient to the investigation in the newspaper rather than hearing the information presented first in closed session. He didn't want to be surprised. But he and the other commissioners *were* surprised on occasion, and they had to respond to such surprises. As Commissioner Feynman remarked, "This gets into the *New York Times*, and so we have to have a special meeting. It's the press, you see; we have to match the press" (1988, 30). To be sure, the Commission had to remain ahead of, or at least in sync with, the press. As Popper notes, commissions must not let the media get the upper hand in the investigation or the commission loses its impact. He explains that "if the subject under study explodes into the news before the commission submits its report, or before action is taken on the report, the commission will seem a weak palliative" (1970, 10). Fundamental to the success of the Rogers Commission and other commissions is the ability to handle the media.

Leveling Blame

In addition to meeting public responsibility and handling the influence of the press, a third constraining force facing commissions is how to deal with the issue of blame. As Barth argues in his book, *Government by Investigation*, "the purpose of inquiry is information, not punishment" (1955, 23). Similarly, Popper notes that "[n]o government agency is criticized directly unless its ineptitude or misconduct has been flagrant. No constituency represented by the commission is criticized" (1970, 34).

There are many observers who thought that Popper's caveat concerning the ineptitude or misconduct of a government agency was ample justification for the Rogers Commission to break from the tradition of the majority of previous commissions; these observers felt that strong censure was not only warranted, it was mandated. During the investigation, it was made clear to the commissioners that both Congress and the public demanded to know who was to blame for sending seven astronauts to their deaths. Handling the issue of blame, then, was a constraining force operating in the inquiry into the launch decision.

Chairman Rogers understood that there were those who wanted his Commission to fix blame. But during the testimony, and later when questioned about the Commission's actions by members of Congress, he made it clear that he believed no useful purpose would be served by determining the blame issue.

CHAIRMAN ROGERS: One of the things that—when we ask questions, when we continue to ask questions, we are not really trying to point a finger. . . . I mean, I don't think anybody, if there were any errors in judgment, God knows, nobody is going to expect everything to be perfect. . . . Nobody is going to blame anybody. I mean, somebody has to make those decisions, and you were all there and made the decision. (*Report* 1986, 373-74)

CHAIRMAN ROGERS: [A]s long as there is not a dispute about the facts, then it doesn't seem to me that anybody can fault anybody. After all, we are going to have a lot of different points of view on something like this, and somebody has to make the decision [to launch]. (416)

To the extent that it was possible to conduct an investigation of this type without looking for blame, there was a conscious decision not to find fault with a specific individual or individuals: "Beginning with the findings of the Rogers Commission investigation, one could practically conclude that no one had any responsibility whatsoever for the disaster" (Boisjoly, Curtis, and Mellican 1989, 226). It is clear, though, that the Commission's decision was somewhat controversial. Kathy Sawyer of the *Washington Post* reported that "in a Senate subcommittee hearing, some panel members continued to criticize the presidential commission for not placing individual blame for the shuttle disaster more directly" (1986, A3). In a similar story, *U.S. News and World Report* noted that "some members of Congress . . . grilled Rogers for not levying individual blame—and even criminal charges—against those who gave *Challenger* the 'go' signal. . . . Rogers responded that there was no evidence of criminal misconduct by individuals and no purpose would be served by 'picking any scapegoats' " (Wellborn 1986, 10). Even a former NASA employee, budget analyst Richard Cook, believed that specific individuals should have been found culpable:

The commission's final report absolves high NASA officials of any direct responsibility for the accident. Yet it ignores substantial evidence—some of

it presented to the commission privately and some of it at public hearings—
that those officials were fully aware of the long history of problems that led
to the explosion. (1986, 13)

The blame issue constrained the Commission during its investigation,
and it haunted the Commission afterward when support for the report to
the President was sought. Finding fault with specific individuals in a
complex accident investigation is not easy,[5] and the issue is compounded
by the nature of the proceedings themselves. As Barth explains, "The line
between investigation and trial is a tenuous one. . . . When someone's
testimony is injurious to his reputation, the inquiry takes on for him the
nature of a prosecution" (1955, 72). This is precisely one of the outcomes
that Chairman Rogers attempted to avoid. For example, at one point in the
hearings Rogers decided not to swear in some witnesses from Morton
Thiokol so that the session's informality might encourage open discussion:

CHAIRMAN ROGERS: Well, this meeting today is in the nature of an
investigation and not really a hearing, so it is not necessary to swear anybody in. When we have our regular formal meetings, we will swear all our
witnesses, but this really is for us to assess the facts and to see how they will
be presented later on. So, although it is going to be recorded, it is not going
to be sworn testimony. That doesn't mean we don't want the truth, but it
means that this is not formal, this is informal and in the nature of the investigation, and we want to have you feel free to have a discussion about the
facts. (*Report* 1986, 1068–69)

Upon further reflection, however, he reversed his earlier ruling in defer-
ence to the potential for scrutiny of his actions after the fact:

CHAIRMAN ROGERS: Excuse me. I think I've changed my mind. If
you don't mind, I think all the people from Thiokol that are going to talk
today, let's swear them all in at one time, because if we don't and we have
sworn the other witnesses it may in retrospect look a little odd. (*Report*
1986, 1974)

Rogers was clearly concerned with protecting the rights of the witnesses
and with conducting an investigation that would withstand scrutiny later.
    In order to maintain the integrity of the investigation and insure that it
did not turn into a "witch hunt," Rogers had to be careful that the line
between investigation and trial mentioned by Barth was not breached. One
way that he attempted to do that was to provide a remedy to those who
believed their testimony might have injured their reputation: "The

Commission will attempt to give a right of reply as soon as possible to any person who believes he has been unfairly criticized or whose actions may have been inaccurately portrayed" (*Report*, 1251–52). This right of reply was intended to counteract the possibility that a witness would feel singled out for blame, since each witness had the option to tell his side of the story. In this way, Rogers sought to counteract the constraint imposed by the tendency to want to fix blame when tragedy occurs.

Fulfilling the Legacy

A final constraining force operating on the Commission's work was the realization that the group was making history. As Popper says, "Because commissions are so prestigious, almost all commission hearings receive considerable publicity" (1970, 36). As noted earlier, this publicity was even more pronounced in the case of the Rogers Commission because the *Challenger* disaster shocked the nation. As a result, the commissioners were conscious of the fact that their investigation would be carefully scrutinized long after their work was finished.

Chairman Rogers in particular was quite sensitive to how observers might second-guess the Commission's work. As he put it, "Anything that we do not comment on in the report will be subject to later rumors and criticisms that we didn't even investigate those things" (*Report* 1986, 312). He was also concerned that "others are going to say this is a fili-buster," and that the Commission might "appear to be ducking the issue" (574). In sum, Rogers was concerned with appearances. He wanted the commissioners and the witnesses to be thorough, and he tried to make it plain that during fact-finding the Commission was not avoiding issues or sidestepping controversies. He was quite cognizant of the fact that the Commission would be held accountable for its conclusions, as he mentioned during testimony by NASA managers:

CHAIRMAN ROGERS: I have two letters from Congress, one from the Senate, one from the House, saying they are going to not do anything while we are going through this process, but as soon as it is over with they are going to analyze the report we make, and they are going to have an overview of us. So at that time we will be in the same position you fellows are in now. We will be spending three or four or five days up there and trying to say why we said what we said in the report. And that is just the way it operates. (*Report* 1986, 590–91)

Clearly the Commission's place in history was an important consideration for the man who led the group.

It may be no exaggeration to claim that one reason why the Commission's legacy was important was due to the legacy of the Warren Commission's investigation into the assassination of President John F. Kennedy. *Los Angeles Times* reporter Rudy Abramson was not the only observer to link the two, calling the *Challenger* probe "one of the most intensive government inquiries since the Warren Commission's investigation" (1986, 1). Even Chairman Rogers summoned the comparison to infer that all of those involved should learn from the past:

CHAIRMAN ROGERS: Jess, I think on those points [concerning whether the Soviets were in the area at the time of the launch] you should have a complete file, and I don't care what you call it. We will have a section dealing with every one of these things. If we don't exclude every possibility with some convincing evidence, we're going to be subject to criticism for a long, long time. And if you remember the Warren Commission, that is exactly what they were criticized for, failing to do this and that and other things.

They did a good job and they did all the things, probably, that any commission should do, but for years they have been subject to that kind of criticism.

So each one of these things, by asking the question we don't mean you haven't done a good job. We just want the material, so that you will have it ready when we need it, to exclude these possibilities. (*Report* 1986, 315)

Rogers implies that learning from the past insures not repeating the mistakes of one's predecessors. To be sure, the Rogers Commission was one in a long line of presidentially appointed investigatory panels, and the legacy established by previous commissions constrained Rogers and his colleagues.

Notwithstanding the complaints of those who wanted the Commission to determine who was to blame for the accident, it appears that the Rogers Commission fulfilled its legacy. Even former budget analyst Cook conceded that "to the commission's credit, much of the information we now know about the launch and NASA's internal problems came out in the course of the commission hearings" (1986, 13). When President Reagan accepted the Commission's report, he "praised the investigation as a testimony to an open society" (Abramson 1986, 11). It appears that the processes that guided the Commission's investigations worked well and the constraints that challenged the Commission were managed appropriately.

APPENDIX

President's Commission on the Space Shuttle *Challenger* Accident

---

William P. Rogers, *Chairman*
Neil A. Armstrong, *Vice Chairman*

David C. Acheson	Dr. Eugene E. Covert
Dr. Richard P. Feynman	Robert B. Hotz
Major General Donald J. Kutyna, USAF	Dr. Sally K. Ride
Robert W. Rummell	Joseph F. Sutter
Dr. Arthur B. C. Walker, Jr.	Dr. Albert D. Wheelon

Brigadier General Charles Yeager, USAF (Ret.)

Dr. Alton G. Keel, Jr., *Executive Director*
Thomas T. Reinhardt, *Executive Secretary*
Special Assistants and Staff Members

Marie C. Hunter	M. M. Black
Mark D. Weinberg	Herb Hetu
John T. Shepherd	Stephen B. Hyle
Patt Sullivan	Marilyn Stumpf
Joleen A. B. Bottalico	Jane M. Green
Lorraine K. Walton	Vera A. Barnes
Virginia A. James	

NOTES

1. The following individuals served on the Rogers Commission (excerpted from the *Report to the President*, pages 202–3): William P. Rogers, Chairman: Former Secretary of State under President Nixon (1969), and Attorney General under President Eisenhower (1957–1961). Neil A. Armstrong, Vice Chairman: Former astronaut, Chairman of the Board of Computing Technologies for Aviation, Inc., Professor of Aeronautical Engineering at the University of Cincinnati from 1971 to 1980, and appointed to the National Commission on Space in 1985. David C. Acheson: Former Senior Vice President and General Counsel, Communications Satellite Corporation (1967-1974), served as U.S. Attorney for the District of Columbia (1961-1965), and a partner in the law firm of Drinker Biddle & Reath. Dr. Eugene E. Covert: Professor and Head, Department of Aeronautics and Astronautics at Massachusetts Institute of Technology, and recipient of the NASA Public Service Award in 1980. Dr. Richard P. Feynman: Professor of Theoretical Physics at California Institute of Technology, and Nobel Prize winner in Physics in 1965. Robert B. Hotz: Editor-in-Chief of *Aviation Week & Space Technology* magazine from 1953 to 1980, and member of the General

Advisory Committee to the Arms Control and Disarmament Agency since 1982. Major General Donald J. Kutyna, USAF: Director of Space Systems and Command, Control, Communications, and recipient of numerous awards as a command pilot. Dr. Sally K. Ride: First American woman in space, and astronaut on two space shuttle missions. Robert W. Rummel: Former Vice President of Trans World Airlines, space expert and aerospace engineer, and holder of the NASA Distinguished Public Service Medal. Joseph F. Sutter: Aeronautical engineer, and Executive Vice President of the Boeing Commercial Airplane Company. Dr. Arthur B. C. Walker, Jr.: Astronomer, Professor of Applied Physics, and consultant to Aerospace Corporation, Rand Corporation, and the National Science Foundation. Dr. Albert D. Wheelon: Physicist, Executive Vice President for Hughes Aircraft Company, member of the President's Foreign Intelligence Advisory Board, and consultant to the President's Science Advisory Council from 1961 to 1974. Brigadier General Charles Yeager, USAF (Retired): Former experimental test pilot, appointed in 1985 as a member of the National Commission on Space, first person to penetrate the sound barrier, and first to fly at a speed of more than 1,600 miles per hour. Dr. Alton G. Keel, Jr., Executive Director: Detailed to the Commission from his position in the Executive Office of the President, Office of Management and Budget, as Associate Director for National Security and International Affairs.

2. One commissioner in particular appeared to exploit his membership on the Commission for what resulted in professional gain: Richard Feynman. For example, his staging of an experiment to test the resiliency of O-ring material by immersing it in ice water was very widely publicized. This "stunt," as well as his insistence on publishing his thoughts on NASA and the investigation as an appendix to the Commission's report, earned him a reputation as a "maverick." Additionally, after the investigation was completed, Feynman published a book that included anecdotes from his service as a commissioner. It does not seem likely that this "maverick" commissioner would have been satisfied with anything less than full disclosure from NASA. Moreover, Feynman and other commissioners conducted on-site investigations at NASA and Morton Thiokol. Events such as these indicate a hands-on approach to the investigatory process. Such an approach places the commissioners in a position that they might discover a cover-up by NASA. Since the commissioners were not NASA employees, presumably "blowing the whistle" on NASA might result in some personal and/or professional notoriety.

3. It may be significant to note that the Rogers Commission had to contend with press coverage via print and radio, the major networks (ABC, CBS, and NBC), and the Cable News Network (CNN). The Commission, then, as opposed to others, had to conduct its affairs under the scrutiny of 24-hour television news. When the *Challenger* craft exploded, many Americans turned their attention to CNN for continuous coverage of the story. The sustained attention that the event generated seemed to ingrain it into the national consciousness. When the Commission conducted its inquiry, it was clearly constrained by the legacy of the visual image and the interest evoked by this dramatic event.

4. It was reported to the Commission that when Vice President George Bush visited the launch site prior to liftoff, the Secret Service investigated the presence of a small boat in the ocean close to the launch structure. The boat was not considered to be a threat to the Vice President, but there was some speculation after the disaster that perhaps sabotage was the cause of the explosion. NASA and the Commission subsequently ruled out that possibility. In his statement, Chairman Rogers is suggesting to

Mr. Moore that release of the information about the boat might be reassuring to the public and indicative of care in the conduct of the investigation.

5. Assigning blame is not easy in a situation such as the one faced by the Rogers Commission investigators in that blame is able to be diffused among those within the organization. The result is that individual culpability is subsumed by organizational responsibility. Boisjoly, Curtis, and Mellican articulate the phenomenon in this way:

> Modern technology has so transformed the context and scale of human action that not only do the traditional parameters of responsibility seem inadequate to contain the full range of human acts and their consequences, but even more fundamentally, it is no longer the individual that is the primary locus of power and responsibility, but public and private institutions. Thus, it would seem, it is no longer the character and virtues of individuals that determine the standards of moral conduct, it is the policies and structures of the institutional settings within which they live and work. . . . One of the most pernicious problems of modern times is the almost universally held belief that the individual is powerless, especially within the context of large organizations where one may perceive oneself, and be viewed, as a very small, and replaceable, cog. It is in the very nature of this situation that responsibility may seem to become so diffused that no one person IS responsible. . . . The problem with this emphasis on management systems and collective responsibility is that it fosters a vicious circle that further erodes and obscures individual responsibility. This leads to a paradoxical—and untenable—situation (such as in the space shuttle program) in which decisions are made and actions are performed by individuals or groups of individuals but not attributed to them. It thus reinforces the tendency to avoid accountability for what anyone does by attributing the consequences to the organization or decision making process. . . . The end result can be a cancerous attitude that so permeates an organization or management system that it metastasizes into decisions and acts of life-threatening irresponsibility. (1989, 218, 227)

The larger issue of how blame is diffused when an organization assumes collective responsibility for decisions and actions is a provocative one (see Miller 1988). For the present discussion, however, it is important to understand how this larger issue constrained the Commission's investigation and led to Rogers's decision not to identify "scapegoats."

8

The Senate Select Committee on POW/MIA Affairs: A Government Committee as Mediator

William D. Kimsey and Rex M. Fuller

Like most wars, the end of the Vietnam War was not a clean and easy affair. Most remember the tortuous Paris peace negotiations dragging on and the fragile peace that kept coming apart (see "Indochina Fighting Further Threatens Fragile Peace" 1973; "Indochina: Peace Growing More Precarious Every Day" 1973). When settlement was fully secured and POWs began returning home, there were many who believed that service men and women were being left behind in Southeast Asia. The *New York Times* reported that U.S. officials were convinced that Americans were held by the Communists after the 1973 Operation Homecoming (Shine 1973). In testimony before the House Foreign Affairs Subcommittee on National Security Policy by representatives of the National League of Families of American Prisoners and Missing in Southeast Asia, it was stated that hard evidence existed proving that the governments of North Vietnam, Laos, and Cambodia were withholding information on more than 1,300 Americans listed by the Pentagon as MIA ("POW-MIA Concern" 1973). In 1974, the United States acknowledged that 320 MIAs were in Pathet Lao–controlled territory in Laos (Clarity 1974).

In 1976 the House Select Committee on Missing Persons in Southeast Asia ended its investigations, charging that Vietnam, Laos, and Cambodia could resolve the cases of the missing Americans. In 1977, President Carter sent a delegation headed by United Auto Workers President Leonard F. Woodcock to Hanoi with the specific purpose of confronting the government of Vietnam about missing Americans. Then, during the exodus of thousands of Vietnamese boat people from Vietnam, stories of live American POWs emerged, causing the U.S. government once again to attempt to resolve the fate of missing Americans in Southeast Asia.

The Subcommittee on Asian and Pacific Affairs in 1986 heard testimony from the former head of the Defense Intelligence Agency (DIA), Lieutenant General Eugene Tighe, who repeatedly asserted before the subcommittee that "there was the 'strong possibility' that there were live Americans in Indochina" (*Tighe Report* 1987). Similarly, in 1987, General John W. Vessey, Jr., a presidential envoy to Vietnam, stated his belief that the government of Vietnam was not telling the truth about live Americans in Southeast Asia ("Vietnam Hints MIAs May Be in Bush Areas" 1987).

The U.S. Senate demonstrated renewed concern for live missing Americans in Southeast Asia in 1991 when a proposal by Senator Harry Reid was introduced requiring that the POW/MIA flag be displayed at the national Vietnam Veterans Memorial. The POW/MIA flag, designed by the National League of Families of American Prisoners and Missing in Southeast Asia, was to be flown over all federal buildings designated by the General Services Administration. The POW/MIA flag would fly until a full accounting had been made of all members of the armed forces of the United States and civilians who were known to be POWs or MIAs in Southeast Asia ("Senate Approves POW/MIA Panel" 1991, 2268).

The continuing charge by POW/MIA activists of inactivity concerning the fate of missing Americans caused President Bush and administration officials to become defensive. Colonel Milard A. Peck, head of the Defense Intelligence Agency's POW/MIA office, resigned, charging that the U.S. government was not serious about resolving the POW/MIA issue. He claimed that the U.S. government was more concerned about debunking live sighting reports than accounting for missing Americans in Southeast Asia. (See U.S. Senate Committee on Foreign Relations Republican Staff, Request for Relief Memorandum, 23 May 1991.) Photographs released to the media by POW/MIA activists alleging that they depicted missing Americans in captivity reinforced suspicions concerning a possible coverup by the U.S. government.

In a meeting with Republican senators, Secretary of Defense Dick Cheney reported that President Bush might appoint a special commission to investigate the fate of missing Americans. Senator John McCain, a prisoner of war for six years in Hanoi, suggested that General H. Norman Schwartzkopf, the commander of the U.S. forces in the Persian Gulf War, should head the President's commission ("POW/MIA Inquiry" 1991).

At a news conference on August 2, 1991, President Bush, in response to the photographs of missing Americans in Southeast Asia, said the U.S. government should "run down every single lead." However, the President warned that no hard evidence concerning live American POWs or MIAs in Southeast Asia existed. President Bush and the chairman of the House Foreign Affairs Subcommittee on Asia and Pacific Affairs, Representative Stephen J. Solarz, criticized the fabrication and dissemination of fraudulent information or materials by unscrupulous individuals exploiting the POW/MIA issue ("POW/MIA Inquiry" 1991).

Senator Robert C. Smith sponsored Senate Resolution 82, 102d Congress (appended at the end of this chapter), establishing a Senate Select Committee on POW/MIA Affairs. The purpose of the Committee was to investigate the fate of American prisoners of war and those missing in action. The chairman of the twelve-member panel was Senator John Kerry of Massachusetts, and the vice chairman was Smith. "The No. 1 focus is whether there are live Americans still held in Southeast Asia," said Senator Smith. He further stated, "A major thrust of the Committee would involve getting answers about missing Americans from the governments of Vietnam, Laos, and Cambodia" ("POW/MIA Inquiry" 1991). On November 5, 1991, the first set of hearings before the Select Committee on POW/MIA Affairs began. In January 1993 a full committee report was presented outlining the Committee's recommendations for resolving the fate of missing American service personnel.

PRESIDENTIAL COMMISSIONS
VERSUS SENATE SELECT COMMITTEES

The Select Committee was a unit of the United States Senate and, as such, represented a significantly different governmental authority, as differentiated from presidential commissions. In the opening chapters, authors offered an extended description and definitional schema of governmental commissions. Those discussions established the parameters of how such investigatory bodies function. Although the Senate Select Committee on POW/MIA Affairs is not a governmental commission per se, its charge and its function parallel such bodies, so exploring these parallels allows us to analyze the communication processes, outcomes, and values as they are operationalized by the Committee in a dispute resolution context.

In general, presidential commissions provide the President with "disinterested, expert advice" (Popper 1970, 5). Conclusions reached by a presidential commission represent recommendations submitted to the President. The President is not bound by commission recommendations.

In fact, the President is under no obligation to release a committee's recommendations to the public.

Congressional select committees, whether House Select Committees or Senate Select Committees, are created for a variety of purposes that distinguish them from presidential commissions. Whereas presidential commissions serve as advisory bodies to the President, Select Committees may serve "to highlight important policy issues, to study or investigate pressing problems, to coordinate the development of policy that overlaps the jurisdictions of several standing committees, or simply as a reward to particular legislators" (Smith and Deering 1990, 4). Select committees typically "are not permitted to report legislation" (*Congressional Quarterly's Guide to Congress* 1982, 454.) Moreover, like government commissions, they are usually temporary and have limited life expectancies.

The Senate Select Committee on POW/MIA Affairs began its work on November 5, 1991. In his opening statement Chairman Kerry defined the role and purpose of the Committee. Kerry asserted that all Americans deserve to know that the POW/MIA issue is held as the highest national priority. He recognized that "almost 19 years after the formal termination of the war in Vietnam, a part of that war is still very much with us" (*Hearings before the Select Committee on POW/MIA Affairs* 1992, 2). Kerry asserted the importance of questions regarding the status of POW/MIA cases and commented that the issue was legitimate and appropriate. Kerry pledged that over the next year the Committee would "leave no stone unturned, no question unasked, and no effort unexplored in order to try to resolve the issue" (*Hearings* 1992, 3).

Kerry ended his statement with a plea to all those who might have something to contribute to the process, asking "anyone out there who may have legitimate information about this issue to come forward and to share it with us" (*Hearings* 1992, 4). He emphasized the public nature of the Committee's hearing process and that the Committee would do all it could to produce complete answers.

Committee Vice Chairman Smith followed Senator Kerry with a statement further clarifying the Committee's role and purpose. Smith affirmed Kerry's pledge to work "together [to do] whatever it takes to find the truth" (*Hearings* 1992, 5). Smith's statement focused on the need for the nation to unify its effort in establishing the true fate of our missing service personnel in Southeast Asia. He expressed hope that the committee would garner public confidence and be, in fact, a source of truth. Smith addressed the issue of past attempts to find solutions to the

POW/MIA question by acknowledging that "there have been 10 or 11 past investigations, some executive, some congressional. In my opinion, this is not the 12th investigation, it is the first and the last. It is also the most comprehensive. We need to leave no lead uninvestigated" (*Hearings* 1992, 6–7). A question remained, however. Why was this important question left to a Senate select committee, and why did President Bush decide not to appoint a special commission as was suggested by Secretary of Defense Dick Cheney? Obviously, there are no clear answers to these questions. Conclusions and assumptions are based on pure speculation. But it is interesting to speculate about the possible motivations and ramifications these choices involved.

There are, we believe, at least three possible reasons for choosing to use the select committee process instead of a presidential commission. First, inasmuch as the objective was to discover what happened to the POW/MIAs, a select committee might have been able to produce an appearance of greater objectivity and closer identification with the concerned population than a presidential commission—as noted in earlier chapters, commissioners sometimes appear to be appointed to placate special interests of various organizations (for instance, in the Warren Commission, former head of the CIA Allen Dulles is thought to have acted on behalf of the CIA in his role as a commissioner). In this case, all committee members were elected representatives of the United States Senate. Most had done active duty military service, including several who served in Vietnam. Hence, they might be more aggressive in their investigation than commissioners who represent special interests. Moreover, a Senate select committee might be perceived by the public as more objective and less apt to succumb to possible conflicts of interest attendant to the President's commander-in-chief role. Carrying out that role requires the President to be ultimately responsible for the safe return of those who serve under his mandate. If the public perceives that the President has any motive to orchestrate the investigation so that it does not impeach a present or former commander-in-chief, then the public may consider a presidential-level investigation tainted.

Second, the Senate Select Committee Hearings would be open to the public and broadcast on C-SPAN television to the nation. One of the driving motives for the Committee was the "hope that these hearings will serve to educate both the committee and the public about the current status" (*Hearings* 1992, 4). Senator Kerry promised that the Committee would "proceed in public because clearly it must be said in public" (*Hearings* 1992, 4). As some of the case studies in this book make clear, government commissions often close their hearings to the public, and even those that receive extensive publicity conduct at least some of their affairs behind closed doors.

Perhaps the most compelling justification for consideration of this question by a select committee and not by an elite presidential commission is the fact that the real goal was the discovery of truth. We do not wish to imply that presidential commissions do not seek truth, but it should not be surprising that a book on political communication might acknowledge that "politics," in the pejorative sense that a layperson might use the word, often enters into presidential commission investigations. The case studies discussed earlier chronicle numerous incidents of political maneuvering. In this case, however, owing largely to the point made previously about the apparent objectivity of the senators, there is ample evidence to suggest that "politics" were set aside in favor of uncovering the truth and resolving the uncertainty. Senators Kerry, Smith, and others on the Committee often repeated their hope that the truth would be the eventual outcome so that wives, husbands, mothers, fathers, sons, daughters, and all loved ones could, once and for all, find peace in the knowledge of what really happened. The Committee's role was to create an environment in which anyone with information about the issue would come forward and share it.

The American people were not expecting miracles; they were not insisting on the unreasonable. All they wanted was the truth. Senator Smith included in his prepared statement in the opening session a quotation from Captain Red McDaniel, a former Vietnam War POW: "I went to Vietnam prepared to fight, prepared to be wounded, prepared to be captured, and even prepared to die . . . but I was not prepared to be abandoned" (*Hearings* 1992, 12). Nor were the families of these service men and women prepared for the doubt and speculation about their loved ones persisting twenty years after the last American troops left Vietnam. They wanted answers, and they wanted this Senate select committee to find them.

DISPUTE RESOLUTION FORMS

Before a discussion of mediation as an appropriate dispute resolution process for governmental commissions and committees can be pursued, the environment created by Alternative Dispute Resolution (ADR) methods must be established. In the first place, ADR proposes to identify paradigms for discovering conflict outcomes that preserve relationships, generate conciliation, and increase community harmony while providing fair solutions for disputes. The ADR movement has taken shape and gained clearer definition over the last few decades. Today, courts and litigators widely recognize the value of dispute resolution processes outside the traditional litigation system (Goldberg, Sander, and Rogers 1992).

The classic ADR methods are negotiation, mediation, and arbitration. Each of these methods has clear and precise defining characteristics and may be practiced as a mutually exclusive process. However, ADR practitioners have recognized the potential for applying these methods in flexible and integrated ways. This has given birth to hybrid processes including "med-arb," a combination of mediation and arbitration; "mini trial," a process mixing elements of negotiation and mediation; ombudsmen; summary jury trials; and a variety of other configurations for positive dispute resolution.

Ultimately, the aim is to define dispute resolution processes that will allow the facilitation of successful resolution without causing further damage to the disputing parties. As alternatives, these methods for dispute resolution are understood to be more flexible than traditional litigation. ADR processes accommodate a fuller range of human concerns including feelings, hopes, ambitions, and motives. Within an ADR environment, disputing parties retain more control of their dispute. Disputants understand that outcomes, solutions, and agreements are their responsibility and that success depends on their own commitment to the process.

ADR may be rightly viewed as forward-looking processes in that emphasis is placed on future activities and relationships. Whereas traditional litigation focuses on past actions and seeks to discover issues of guilt, innocence, fault, or responsibility, ADR processes typically focus on issues of future behavior and new definitions for interpersonal interaction.

Providing alternatives to traditional litigation and encouraging the utilization of ADR processes is a challenge for ADR providers because these approaches differ significantly from the arbitrary, inflexible litigation environment and because they are not widely understood. Questions about the legal certainty and the legal acceptability of agreements reached using an ADR process often linger. ADR processes encouraging cooperation and the discovery of resolutions allowing for all disputants to achieve at least some success is a principle contrary to the assumption that one party must prevail over the other in the final outcome. These same challenges were faced by the Senate Select Committee on POW/MIA Affairs when it accepted the goal of national healing and reconciliation concerning the fate of missing service personnel.

In disputes involving sensitive national interests and conflicts including international relationships, questions of process integrity and outcome
validity are critical. However, disputes of national and international interest demand not only that the resolution process be valid and beyond ethical reproach, but also that they be capable of stimulating reconciliation and
building an environment in which the disputing parties can coexist in
harmony and cooperation.

When disputes such as these come before legislative bodies and governmental commissions there is, perhaps, the naive hope that law will
prevail. There is often the widely held assumption that the issue is the discovery of past transgression and application of appropriate statute.
However, that may not be enough. In addition to pursuing the discovery
of past fact, the government's role in dispute resolution must include a
concern for future conditions. No matter what has happened in the past,
no matter what violations may have occurred, the reality is that our society
must be guided in ways that will provide for its continuation, not its dissolution.

SENATE SELECT COMMITTEES AS DISPUTE
RESOLUTION ENVIRONMENTS

Select committees established by the House of Representatives or the
Senate have the power and the legitimacy of law as their foundation.
Select committees are usually charged with pursuing the discovery of fact.
Evidence is collected in much the same way as it is collected in formal
court settings. For example, public hearings are held for developing witness testimony, depositions and interrogatories are taken by committee
staffers, and so on, all contributing to the body of evidence. However, it
is important to note that select committees are not normally permitted to
report legislation (Wormser 1982, 454). Committee members are invested
with decision-making authority, and they function as a group of independent decision makers who have the responsibility of producing an outcome based on the select committee's process.

The select committee process is designed to produce findings based
on law and on the facts of the dispute. For example, during the testimony
given by Hamilton Gayden, Tennessee Circuit Judge, concerning a
specific instance involving the attempted rescue of prisoner-of-war Major
Albro Lundy on October 16, 1991, Chairman Kerry challenged the legal
acceptability of Judge Gayden's evidence (*Hearings* 1992, 588–89).
Kerry's challenge was entirely appropriate in this dispute resolution environment.

Recognizing that the Committee's responsibility extended beyond finding the truth of past actions and included the concern for society's ability to move successfully into the future, an ADR-based procedural model may prove to be desirable. It is important that select committees retain their decision-making authority and that their fact-finding role not be compromised or restricted. Equally critical to a select committee's process is its responsibility to produce constructs that encourage coexistence and harmony.

Arbitration provides a dispute resolution process in which disputing parties retain ownership of their dispute and allows an independent decision-making authority to issue an award based on evidence presented by disputants. In arbitration, disputing parties as well as the arbitrator may collaborate to reach agreement concerning agenda, procedure, tests of evidence, standards for decision, and other issues relevant to the dispute. Of course, arbitration in the governmental commission setting will necessarily function much like court-annexed arbitration (Leeson and Johnston 1988, 77–102).

A primary distinguishing characteristic of court-annexed arbitration is that the relevant court maintains significant control over procedures and the application of substantive law. In the case of a select committee using an arbitration model, the similarity to court-annexed arbitration would be significant. The procedure for accomplishing the collection of data would be strictly controlled by legislative precedent, and tests of evidence would be clearly defined by the relevant legislative body, in this case the United States Senate. Arbitration may be an appropriate model in that the select committee, having heard the cases as presented by parties interested in the dispute, renders a decision based on the committee's best ability to craft an outcome responding to the material presented. The select committee's finding is not driven by law or by legislative statute.

A potential inadequacy inherent in the use of a select committee as an arbitrator is that the concern is principally with adjudication, or rendering an impartial, third-party judgment based on an analysis of the available data. Emphasis in arbitration is on the arbitrators' decision-making authority. The source of inadequacy is the failure to consider future ramifications that may accrue to the disputing parties.

Mediation, on the other hand, offers the opportunity to focus on future conditions and relationships. Mediators assume responsibility for facilitating negotiation between and among disputing parties. They avoid the decision-maker role. In practice, select committees acting in a mediation environment would emphasize the negotiation aspect of the process and focus on the development of communication interactions between disputing parties as well as on the development of evidence relevant to each party's position.

MEDIATION AS CONSTRUCTIVE ENVIRONMENT FOR THE SENATE SELECT COMMITTEE ON POW/MIA AFFAIRS

The role of the mediator, central to the process, was assumed by the Senate Select Committee on POW/MIA Affairs. The Committee was composed of members selected from the U.S. Senate and representing a variety of constituencies and points of view. However, as a Senate select committee, they assembled themselves as a single unit to facilitate the process and hear the evidence.

Citizens Activist Group versus the Government

Activist groups and individual citizens concerned with the POW/MIA issue represented some of the disputing parties. For purposes of discussion, these groups are referred to collectively as the Citizens Activist Group. It is this group that voiced the concern that the POW/MIA question had not been adequately addressed by the government. It was the Citizens Activist Group that believed that the Government had abandoned efforts to resolve the issues pertinent to POWs and MIAs.

The Government, as defined by the Defense Department, the Pentagon, the President, the State Department, and other government agencies, represented the other disputing party. The Government was largely interested in defending its past policies and practices. Their goal was to win approval of past decisions and to verify the correctness of past actions.

The Senate Select Committee on POW/MIA Affairs found itself located between these two groups, attempting to find some responsible solution to the POW/MIA question while bringing the disputing parties together in a spirit of national reconciliation and healing. How could these seemingly contradictory goals be simultaneously achieved?

Theoretically, mediation is located on a continuum: negotiation is at one end and litigation is at the other. The Committee attempted to capture the essential elements of mediation so that appropriate resolution and justice could be discovered and reconciliation achieved.

In the mediator role, the Committee created a setting into which members representing each group could come and present their case. In addition to developing fact-based evidence, witnesses were encouraged to share their emotions, insights, and hypotheses. Because the hearings were open to the public, the disputing parties were permitted access to each other's arguments and positions. Since the Committee attempted to provide an opportunity for all interested parties to offer presentations on both sides of the issue, communication between the disputants was maximized.

By utilizing mediation in the conduct of the hearings, the Committee preserved its authority as an independent decision maker and maintained the integrity of its role as a legislative body functioning under federal statute. Their absolute right to make independent judgments and to function autonomously was unquestioned as the senators pursued the hearing process. Chairman Kerry foreshadowed the Committee's eventual role as ADR provider when he said, "we will try to understand this issue in ways it has not been the subject of understanding previously, and with an approach which has not been applied previously" (*Hearings* 1992, 4). As mediators, the Committee allowed for full development of each party's case. Given the public nature of the process, all interested parties were involved in a communication network designed to facilitate understanding and cooperation.

MEDIATION AND THE CONFLICT OVER THE FATE
OF MISSING AMERICAN SERVICE MEN AND WOMEN

Mediation as facilitated negotiation empowers the parties in conflict to reexamine their positions. The mediator role of the Senate Select Committee on POW/MIA Affairs encouraged the parties in this dispute to reframe their view of the fate of missing American service personnel and, with the other parties in this conflict, reconstruct a new understanding of the unaccounted-for soldiers, sailors, and airmen. The Committee's initial charge, as mandated in Senate Resolution 82, 102d Congress, focused only on the war in Vietnam. However, as revelations concerning POWs sent to China and the former Soviet Union, Vietnam, Laos, and Cambodia emerged during the Committee's public hearings, the Committee's purview expanded to include missing American service personnel from World War II, the Korean War, and those lost during the Cold War.

Mediation normally involves three parties: the two parties in dispute and a neutral third party responsible for facilitating the process designed to resolve the conflict. While mediation may involve only two individuals in dispute with a single mediator, more complex disputes, such as the disagreement over POWs and MIAs unaccounted for in the war in Southeast Asia, involve multiple parties made up of many people. The parties in the conflict over the fate of missing Americans aligned themselves with either the Government or the Citizens Activist Group. The mediation process initiated by the Committee required the Government to explain its role in resolving the fate of missing American service personnel and allowed the Citizens Activist Group to tell their story of how the Government failed to do all that it could to bring home Americans left behind following the Vietnam War. As the conflict between these two groups escalated, the Government's role emerged as that of the offender while the Citizens Activist Group's role turned into that of the victim.

The mediation process employed by the Committee set in motion the process that brought about reconciliation between the U.S. government and the American people. Testimony by several parties in the Citizens Activist Group, including H. Ross Perot, the independent candidate in the 1992 presidential election, suggested that immunity ought to be granted to parties in the U.S. government who might testify as to their involvement in any coverup of the POW/MIA affair (*Hearings* 1992). The American Defense Institute, a key player in the POW/MIA activists' movement, even suggested that a policy of forgiveness and reconciliation be extended to the parties in the U.S. government as well as to the government of Vietnam (McDaniel 1992).

Parties in the Conflict

The Citizens Activist Group consisted of three constituencies. First, there were the family organizations made up of the National League of Families and the National Alliance of Families. Organized during the Vietnam War, the League focused attention on POW/MIAs. The Alliance, on the other hand, was recently formed because POW/MIA families were disconcerted with the inaction of the League. Second, there were veterans groups including the American Legion, Veterans of Foreign Wars (VFW), Disabled American Veterans (DAV), Vietnam Veterans of America (VVA), VietNow, and the Vietnam Veterans Coalition. The third group comprised concerned citizens groups such as Homecoming II, Task Force Omega, National Forget-Me-Nots, Skyhook II, Operation Rescue, Live POW Lobby, Minnesota Won't Forget POW/MIA, POW Publicity Fund, POW/MIA Grassroots Association, Heart of Illinois POW Association, Release Foundation, and Live POW Committee. The American Defense Institute, a defense policy organization, championed the cause of the Citizens Activist Group. ADI's president and founder,

Navy Captain Eugene B. "Red" McDaniel, a former Vietnam POW, considered the effect of abandoned POWs on military morale an important national defense issue.

The disputing groups are identifying as "the Government" included several U.S. government agencies involved in the POW/MIA issue. First, the National Security Council handled POW/MIA matters in the executive branch and helped formulate policy matters on POW/MIAs. Second, the Department of Defense made the Defense Intelligence Agency responsible for collecting and analyzing intelligence data on POW/MIAs. Also involved were the casualty offices for the Army, Air Force, Navy, and Marine Corps. In addition, the Central Intelligence Agency (CIA) and the National Security Agency (NSA) collected and analyzed POW/MIA data. Representatives of these governmental agencies made up the Inter-Agency Group on POW/MIA, which also included the executive director of the National League of Families.

The Senate Select Committee on POW/MIA Affairs, the neutral third party, included six Democrats and six Republicans. Senator John F. Kerry, Democrat, served as the Committee's chairman. Kerry was a naval officer on a gunboat in the Mekong Delta from 1968 to 1969. He was awarded the Silver Star, a Bronze Star with Combat V, three purple hearts, and a Vietnam Service Medal. Senator Bob Smith, Republican, served as the Committee's vice chairman. Senator Smith served in active duty in the U.S. Navy from 1965 to 1967. He received a Republic of Vietnam Campaign Medal and a Vietnam Service Medal.

The Democratic side of the Committee included Senator Tom Daschle, who served as an intelligence officer in the Strategic Air Command of the U.S. Air Force from 1969 to 1972. Senator Harry Reid sponsored the resolution to fly the POW/MIA flag at federal buildings. Senator Charles Robb served with the U.S. Marine Corps from 1961 to 1970 with a tour of duty as a commander of a combat infantry company in Vietnam. Senator Bob Kerrey served as a Navy SEAL from 1966 to 1969 in Vietnam and was severely wounded while leading a raid against enemy forces; for his heroism, he received the Congressional Medal of Honor. The final Democratic member of the Committee was Senator Herb Kohl, who served in the U.S. Army Reserves from 1958 to 1964.

The Republican side of the Committee included John McCain, a retired Navy captain who served from 1958 to 1981. He was a prisoner of war in Hanoi from 1967 to 1973. Senator Hank Brown served in the U.S. Navy from 1962 to 1966, with a 1965–66 tour as a forward air controller. Senator Charles Grassley received the Eisenhower Tribute Award for Defense Efficiency and was a three-time recipient of the Leadership Award from the Coalition for Peace through Strength. Senator

Nancy Kassebaum served as a member of the Senate Foreign Relations Committee for more than ten years. She worked closely with families of POW/MIAs and cosponsored the 1991 "Truth Bill."[1] Rounding out the Republican side of the Committee was Senator Jesse Helms, who served in the U.S. Navy from 1942 to 1945.

Introducing the Process

The Senate Select Committee on POW/MIA Affairs started its proceedings by introducing the Committee's roadmap for resolving the fate of missing service men and women left behind in Southeast Asia. The role of the Committee in introducing this process was to create a setting in which the disputing parties could pursue the negotiation of an agreement to settle their dispute. The objective of this phase was to establish a positive communication environment. Through discussion, the Committee and the parties met and reached agreements about schedules, procedures, rules, and other matters necessary for satisfactory interaction and negotiation.

Before meeting with the disputing parties, the Committee in its mediator role (1) reviewed available information about the witnesses, (2) discussed potential problems or difficulties, (3) discussed roles, duties, and responsibilities, and (4) became familiar with the physical setting. The Committee welcomed the parties and reaffirmed their participation in the process. The Committee clarified the purpose of the process and emphasized the settlement of the disagreements and resolution of differences between the Citizens Activist Group and the Government. Rules for interaction from witnesses were secured.

Win-Win or Win-Lose

One of the goals of the Committee in serving as a neutral third party in facilitating conflict resolution was to help the parties enter a collaborative negotiating process. Both parties in the dispute had already made judgments about their position in the conflict and their feelings toward the other party. Since the Government had to abide by the policies mandated by Congress, they were unable to change their position regarding the fate of missing military personnel—their position was that there were none. On the other hand, if the Government did not fulfill its responsibility of carrying out the policies, then there was room for correction. Likewise, the activists whose family members were not accounted for and citizens who believed that the U.S. government had a moral obligation not to abandon its military left behind in an unpopular war compelled parties of the Citizens Activist Group to take an unyielding position concerning accounting of missing service personnel. The pressure on the Government was to convince the American people that they had lived up to the letter of the policy concerning missing Americans in Southeast Asia. The activists, on the other hand, struggled with remaining loyal to the unaccounted-for POW/MIAs while facing pressure by the Government to give up their vigil.

Both the Government and the Citizens Activist Group, in most instances, preferred working together to resolve the POW/MIA issue. However, both parties were prepared to abandon each other in order to reach their objective. Based on the works of several conflict resolution scholars, it could be argued that the parties entering the Committee proceedings probably had a win-lose approach to the conflict (see, for example, Blake and Mouton 1964; Fisher, Ury, and Patton 1992). Their attitude was: "my position is correct, which makes your position wrong." Their strategies for dealing with the opposing party included competing with one another and trying to control the outcome of the proceedings. Each party preferred that the other give up its position in the conflict, or "see the light," thereby accommodating the other's position. Both sides were impatient with dialogue and information gathering.

The Government was protective of its credibility as it attempted to cast doubt on the activists' claims that the Government was either involved in a coverup or that the government was completely incompetent. In a win-lose posture both parties tended to be authoritarian and threatened by disagreement. In order to break the win-lose mind-set that the parties brought into the proceedings, the Committee equally empowered the parties to enter a more collaborative response to the conflict. The collaborative approach to conflict provided a potential for a win-win response in which both parties got what they wanted (i.e., there was no coverup conspiracy, yet military personnel were left behind in Southeast Asia). Each party in the conflict was able to present its position while inquiring about the demands of the other party; additionally, parties shared information, looked for alternatives, had an open dialogue, and welcomed disagreements—all characteristics of mediation.

If the parties embraced the win-win approach, then their focus would have been on resolving the conflict and not assigning blame. An examination of all options would have been emphasized. Fisher, Ury, and Patton describe the win-win approach as one of "principled negotiation" wherein the parties see themselves as problem solvers as opposed to friends or adversaries (1992).

Mediator Neutrality

The Committee needed to demonstrate to both parties' satisfaction that the Committee members were neutral. Whenever the Committee's neutrality was questioned, both Kerry and Smith were quick to respond to the witnesses' doubts about the sincerity of the Committee's efforts or the integrity of the proceedings. For example, in the opening session of the proceedings, Chairman Kerry said:

One thing that I want, and I know Senator Smith wants, is for the Committee to be judged as being absolutely neutral and fair in this process. There is a lot of data to go back and review. So this is the beginning, it is the baseline, and there is a lot of work yet to be done over the course of the next months. (*Hearings* 1992, 222)

However, Kerry's neutrality was questioned by the Citizens Activist Group near the end of the hearing process. The Citizens Activist Group alleged that his neutrality was compromised as a result of his "scripting" the Government's testimony and statements from the government of Vietnam (*CNN News Report* 1992). Mediators must remain impartial if the parties are to be equally empowered in the process of mediation. When the parties are equally empowered, then there can be movement from a win-lose to a win-win approach and response to conflict.

Equal Empowerment

A skillful mediator recognizes the parties' use of different power forms. Different power forms used by parties in a conflict may include controlling resources, inspiring fear, having special knowledge or skill, possessing high morals, occupying a position of authority, or communicating persuasively (French and Raven 1968; Raven, Centers, and Rodrigues 1975). Mediators allow each party to empower itself but not to the other party's detriment. A party entrenched in a win-lose approach might try to empower itself by undermining the process. Challenging Committee members' credentials was used by some witnesses. For instance, both former Secretary of State Henry Kissinger and Alexander Haig accused the Committee of leaks and selective use of documents. Both Kissinger and Haig's charges came after former Secretary of Defense Melvin Laird and James Schlesinger testified that President Nixon knew that POWs were left behind when Nixon summarily stated that all POWs had returned home during Operation Homecoming in 1973 ("Documents Show Existence of POWs" 1992).

Circumventing the proceedings by refusing to exchange information favorably positioned the Government to be a major power holder in the conflict. However, Senator Smith along with Committee members emphasized to the Government the importance of declassifying information. Early in the hearings Smith expressed his own frustration with access to information vital to resolve the fate of missing service personnel in Southeast Asia. He said:

The focus here, first of all, is to find out . . . if there are alive Americans in Southeast Asia. That is the number one focus—nothing else is important to us after that. The second is, as you said, Mr. Wallace, to declassify information which should not be classified. And I have been fighting that for those 7 years I have been in Congress, have had some minor successes on it on the House side. And I have supported that—subject to sources and methods. I have not had a lot of cooperation from many, both inside and outside the Government, frankly, to do that. But I believe that is a key answer, a key resolution to this problem that you are going to dispel a lot of these concerns if, in fact, we can get information out there that does not have to be classified. (*Hearings* 1992, 304)

The Committee, however, convinced President George Bush to declassify large amounts of information on POWs and MIAs. Declassifying this information greatly empowered the Citizens Activist Group.

Parties on both sides of the conflict often empowered themselves by denigrating the other party's credibility. For example, in Dr. Patricia Ann O'Grady's prepared statement, she blasted the Government's trustworthiness and competency:

Still the charade continues! Fingerprints and dental records disappear, journalists are attacked, legitimate pictures are discredited. Still you work feverishly to normalize relations [with Vietnam] so that AT&T can conduct business. LET THE EPITAPH OF OUR POWS READ: BETRAYED FOR THIRTY PIECES OF SILVER! (*Hearings* 1992, 373–74)

The Government, on the other hand, cast doubt about the POW/MIA activists' veracity. Secretary of Defense Dick Cheney made reference to fraudulent claims made by some activists in his testimony before the Committee:

I have already alluded to some of the recent experiences we have had with outright fraudulent claims. Let me elaborate to make it clear what we are up against. I know I join all of you in condemning the cruel actions by some fast operators who play on the hopes of families and friends of POW/MIAs. They doctor old pictures or forge documents solely to make a quick buck. The worst of these individuals traffic in reports obtained from unnamed sources in Southeast Asia, invite publicity to their claims of live Americans, promise great results, and often seek to raise money to keep their efforts going. It is also common practice for them to claim that their information is proof positive of government ineptitude and cover-up. In the process they raise the expectations of families desperate for any sign that a loved one is still alive. Unfortunately, when we investigate their claims we find no Americans, only unsubstantiated hearsay accounts, and too often signs of deceit and fabrication. (*Hearings* 1992, 34)

Still another approach the Committee witnessed as it observed the parties entrenched in a win-lose posture involved failure to negotiate in good faith. For instance, Senator McCain's follow-up questions to the testimony of Tracy Usry, Chief Investigator, Senate Foreign Relations Committee Republican Staff, attempted to test the integrity of Mr. Usry's assertions. McCain repeatedly assured that Usry's claims were false and unsubstantiated. McCain said to Usry:

So your allegation that the two Thai special forces identified Dooley's photograph as a fellow inmate is false. . . . You made a very serious allegation here, Mr. Usry, and I am surprised you would not even know what photograph it is. . . . So his [Tracy Usry's] allegation basically, Mr. Chairman, has been relayed to him with no basis in fact. I have now covered three or four of your allegations. You have no information about them, but are willing to publish them as fact, where clearly you do not have a basis in fact. (*Hearings* 1992, 444–45)

In the role of the Committee's devil's advocate, McCain often chastised witnesses for their disingenuous use of information and material pertaining to POWs and MIAs.

Other tactics employed by the parties to empower themselves included refusing to take "no" for an answer, breaking the rules of the proceedings, or violating the norms and special courtesies. It was not uncommon to see parties using put-downs through word associations or expressions of outrageous disbelief suggesting that the other party was either stupid or dishonest.

Recognizing the power consequences in the parties' testimony, the Committee probed for additional information from each party through follow-up questions using an I-statement approach. For instance, Committee members would often ask witnesses to clarify their statements by asking the parties to state their feelings, describe the other party's behavior, and list recommendations for resolving the fate of missing Americans in Southeast Asia. This tactic was most obvious in the testimonies involving family members of missing service personnel.

The Committee allowed witnesses to vent their feelings concerning the frustration of not knowing about their loved ones while criticizing the U.S. government for not doing more to resolve their case. For instance, Dr. Jeffrey C. Donahue, the brother of Air Force Major Morgan Jefferson Donahue, MIA in Laos since December 13, 1968, stated in response to a query by Smith:

Yes, I will take the next question. . . . I think cover-up is embodied in the policy, as we briefly stated. The U.S. government says the POW/MIA issue is humanitarian and not economic. Baloney. Fundamentally, it is economic. It has always been economic. All you have to do is look at the testimony before the U.S. Congress. . . . The second component of the cover-up in policy is that the answers to the POW/MIA issue are in Hanoi, not Washington—well, it was Washington that sent my brother over to serve, it was Washington that abandoned him, and it is Washington that is keeping him there—dead or alive. . . . There is an abandonment going on here, and so the answers aren't in Hanoi. The answer is in Washington. Someone will be accountable for them. . . . The next element of the cover-up is well, when somebody brings up this live group or proof to me, instead of the CIA which has all the data. . . . Finally—or next-to-last—we have more intelligence resources than ever dedicated to this issue—classic Executive Branch approach: let's put more bureaucrats in there; let's put up an office in Hanoi. (*Hearings* 1992, 551)

A major challenge to the Committee in its role as mediator was to work through the obstacles inherent in the language of the parties. Repeatedly, the Committee probed the witnesses' statements of fact. An interesting example can be found in the testimony of Monika Jensen-Stevenson, author of the book *Kiss the Boys Goodbye*. Jensen-Stevenson, with her professional journalist background as a reporter for the CBS television show *60 Minutes*, prepared herself to make assertions based on facts. Senator Reid said to her, "we have had a string of witnesses who said, if there was an American in Vietnam, we would know about it. . . . how . . . do you believe there would be places in Vietnam where these people could be hidden for almost 20 years?" Jensen-Stevenson responded:

Well, I'll give you two examples. One, my husband was there during the Truce Commission. He is a Canadian, so he was there with the Canadian delegation to the Truce Commission after the French/Indo-China conflict. And there was a strong speculation that the Vietnamese were bringing arms from the Chinese side. They were never able to prove that until about 5, 10 years later, when it was verified. I think it is very easy in a closed society like Vietnam to hide prisoners, arms, anything else. . . . The other thing I want to tell you is we have recently also met with the Vietnamese—not the official negotiators, but certainly high ranking. And I said, look, this Committee is going to go into session, and they are going to represent the American people and that's a lot different from the negotiators that you have been dealing with. Because the American people really want answers and the American people want to know, for example, what happened to the prisoners we know were alive, the ones our intelligence tell us were alive. What happened to Peter Cressman and what happened to Colonel Dona-hue? . . . These two examples I outlined for them. (*Hearings* 1992, 514)

The Committee spent a great deal of time laundering the witnesses' language in order to build a body of evidence that both The Government and the Citizens Activist Group could agree on. Because of the problems inherent in using language to reconstruct reality, the Committee focused on the creation of essential definitions in an attempt to build a body of evidence acceptable to all parties. For example, Senator Grassley quizzed Mr. Trowbridge of the DIA's Special Office for Prisoners of War Missing in Action concerning the definition of a prisoner of war: "I think, Mr. Trowbridge, you probably answered this, but let me ask it anyway. . . . In any of your analysis of live-sighting reports or other information, have you ever concluded that an American service person is being held against his will in Southeast Asia?" Trowbridge responded, "As a prisoner of war? I don't believe we have, sir." Grassley responded, "OK. Now, you say strictly a prisoner of war. I would say against his will. I do not know—I am not a lawyer. I do not know the true legal definition of a prisoner of war, but somebody being held against his will" (*Hearings* 1992, 420).

Data, Warrant, Claim

Both the Government and the Citizens Activist Group fell into the role of the demurrer as they agreed on the evidence but denied the sufficiency of the fact to warrant the conclusions made by the other party. Witnesses aligned with the Citizens Activist Group were constantly placed in the position of proving the negative proposition that American service personnel left behind in Southeast Asia were *not* dead. The Government, on the other hand, enjoyed the luxury of defending the status quo proposition first declared by President Nixon on March 29, 1973, when he said in a national radio and television address, "All of our American POWs are on their way home."

Norman M. Turner, Lieutenant Colonel, USAF (Retired), testified:

Who made the decision in our government that out of sight constitutes a presumption of death? What gave our government the right to place a burden of proof to the contrary on the families of the missing men . . . to prove beyond a reasonable doubt that a POW exists before the government will act? Nowhere else in our system of government does such backward thinking exist. (*Hearings* 1992, 579)

Turner then presented his warrants linking his reasons with his conclusion:

In the undeclared war over Laos, in which I flew at least 50 strike missions, our country lost almost 600 men MIA. Not one single prisoner of war was ever returned by that country. For every 600 such losses over Vietnam, we could expect to have 100 men returned. And my question is, what do you suppose happened to these folks? Why is it logical to presume that they are dead without conclusive evidence to support such a conclusion? (*Hearings* 1992, 579)

While the Government and the Citizens Activist Group found agreement over specific evidence, they were not able to reach congruent conclusions. The burden of proof was on the Citizens Activist Group to prove that the Government's analysis of live sighting reports was corrupt or to produce a live American POW. Neither occurred, and the Government's position was strengthened as a result of the Citizens Activist Group's failure.

The Government's demurring role was a major source of frustration for the Citizens Activist Group. The Government's success in undermining the challenges made by the Citizens Activist Group eventually demoralized and in some cases defeated POW/MIA activists' efforts to get the Government to change its policy on POWs and MIAs.

Defining the Conflict

In defining the conflict phase of the mediation process, the parties disclosed, as fully and as completely as possible, their perception of the conflict. Each party described its perception of the conflict. Each party's description was unrestrained and uninterrupted. The Committee summarized the party's description and asked for elaboration, clarification, and explanation as necessary for developing a complete and accurate understanding of the dispute. Each witness called came to the hearings and, at an appointed time, made an opening statement followed by the submission of written testimony for the record. Then the Committee asked follow-up questions. Witnesses were encouraged to identify facts, share feelings, and describe desired outcomes. Committee members summarized each statement as is the practice in mediation. At the conclusion of this phase, the parties and the Committee had a full understanding of the nature of the conflict. This information was used to identify a tentative agenda for discovering resolution.

After the witnesses gave testimony before the Committee, the parties' positions emerged. The Government's position could be summed up, "No evidence exists of Americans in captivity, but we can't preclude the possibility that some may still be alive." Several witnesses for the Government articulated this position, including Richard Cheney, Secretary of Defense; General John Vessey, Jr. (Retired), Special Presidential Emissary for POW/MIA Matters; and Garnett E. Bell, Chief, U.S. Office of POW/MIA Affairs–Hanoi (*Hearings* 1992, 27–35, 71–75, 226–27).

The National League of Families was the only private organization in the Citizens Activist Group that cooperated with the Government. The Executive Director of the League served on the inter-agency group. Mike McDaniel of the American Defense Institute believed that many POW/MIA families and other activist groups considered this close association with the Government a repudiation of the "activist" role of the National League of Families (McDaniel 1992). Mary Backley's testimony at the hearings expressed the League's frustration concerning accusations made against the League by activists. Chairman Kerry mirrored Ms. Backley's frustration when he said:

What you have really articulated here, what the whole League dispute articulates and the reason I think it is very important in understanding this issue, is the degree to which there is a division which has even entered among the families and that is, in its own way, a very sad commentary on the whole process. It underscores why it is so important for us to get the League so that it feels like one again, so that we get the Senate and the various administrative departments working together as one on this and so that we are resolving it and not carping each other. (*Hearings* 1992, 754)

The POW/MIA activist groups' and most of the veterans groups' position concerning the conflict with the Government was that the Government did have evidence that Americans were still alive in Southeast Asia but that such information remains hidden from the families and the American people. Recognizing these positions helped the parties rethink the conflict and find common ground upon which the parties could work toward resolution. When this happened, the Committee moved the parties toward generating options to resolve the conflict.

Solving the Problem

The problem-solving phase of the mediation process involved generating interaction and facilitating negotiation between the disputing parties. The purpose was to gain consensus regarding issues and develop strategies, procedures, and solutions acceptable to all parties that would allow them to reach a successful agreement.

The Committee and the parties identified issues in conflict, prioritized issues for discussion, explored the interests and positions of each party on a given issue, and encouraged dialogue relevant to all of the issues under discussion. The Committee provided periodic summaries of the progress made and provided positive reinforcement. They caucused, held private discussions when it was necessary to discuss classified information, overcame impasses, and explored ideas privately. At the conclusion of this phase, the parties and the Committee reached an agreement concerning each issue. They satisfied themselves that all dimensions of each issue had been considered and that the disputants had been given ample opportunity to participate. They felt confident that the strategies, procedures, and solutions were fair, ethical, and practical.

The Committee helped the parties discover areas of agreement in the conflict and moved the parties toward generating options for solutions. Common ground discovered by the Government and the Citizens Activist Group included resolving the POW/MIA issue and normalizing relations with Vietnam. Both parties wanted Vietnam to cooperate with the U.S. government by supplying all the information they had on POWs and MIAs. However, the Government and the Citizens Activist Group disagreed over the meaning of the word "cooperation." The Government focused on information concerning dead American military personnel in order to resolve the discrepancy cases.[2] The activists, on the other hand, focused on information about live POWs. This created an important impasse separating the parties. For the activists, this issue could only be resolved when the Government released all POW/MIA information and all persons possessing information received a fair hearing before the Committee. ADI's Mike McDaniel reported that "while the Citizens Activist Group believe that the Senate Select Committee investigated the POW/MIA issue fully and fairly, some doubt lingers concerning the Select Committee's neutrality." He further stated:

some activists have taken the position that the Senate Select Committee seems to want to continue the pattern of the U.S. government to debunk POW/MIA information, discredit POW/MIA activists and stifle dissent on the U.S. government policy on POW/MIAs, thus effectively silencing the voices of advocates of POW/MIAs so that the U.S. government can say the issue is resolved. (McDaniel 1992)

Most organizations in the Citizens Activist Group recommended declassifying all information pertaining to missing Americans in Southeast Asia. The National League of Families, however, was a dissenting voice. The League agreed with the position of the executive branch of the U.S. government that some information about POWs and MIAs should not be released. Likewise, the League opposed formation of the Senate Select Committee on POW/MIA Affairs and consistently sided with the U.S. government. The position of the League was that the U.S. government was doing all that it could to resolve the fate of missing Americans left behind in Southeast Asia (*Hearings* 1992, 328).

The Government plan for resolving the issue was presented in the roadmap to the normalization of relations between the United States and Vietnam (*Hearings* 1992, Appendix 1). The roadmap stated that normalization could occur only when a full and satisfactory accounting of POW/MIAs was forthcoming from Vietnam. One of the problems with that position for the Citizens Activist Group was that no provision was made for the release of POWs held in Laos and Cambodia. Another problem for the activists concerning the roadmap was the U.S. government's definition of accounting. To the government, accounting meant the return of remains or other information that facilitated reclassifying the MIAs as "Killed in Action" (KIA) (*Hearings* 1992, 230–31).

In an attempt to build a climate of reconciliation and move the conflict toward resolution, ADI introduced a plan calling on the President to send a delegation to Vietnam comprised of high-level government officials, POW/MIA activists, and representatives of companies seeking to conduct business in Vietnam. The delegation would be given the authority to offer normalization of relations in exchange for living POWs from Vietnam,

Laos, and Cambodia. The plan called for "no recriminations," with ADI leading the movement in the United States "to let bygones be bygones" (McDaniel 1992).

To bring the hearings on POW/MIA Affairs to closure and to provide for official documentation of recommendations, the implementing agreement phase started. The objective was to provide a device ensuring, to the degree appropriate and possible, that the parties accepted responsibility for putting the agreement into place and for providing documentation of that commitment. In private session, the Committee analyzed the mountain of data presented by all witnesses in the proceedings and, based upon standards of fairness, submitted a report making recommendations concerning future action. The mediator role required the Senate Select Committee on POW/MIA Affairs members to determine the merits of the parties' evidence and to recommend outcomes. However, the Committee's recommendations would not go into effect until they were submitted to Congress and debated once more and approved; presidential commissions are accorded no such final measures.

EPILOGUE

The resolution of the conflict between the Citizens Activist Group and the Government ended where the conflict started: the United States Living Casualty Policy. While no such policy officially exists, evidence presented during the Committee's hearings suggests that in every armed conflict involving the U.S. government and Communist regimes, the U.S. government has knowingly abandoned Americans. During the proceedings, Boris Yeltsin, President of Russia, sent a letter indicating that former American POWs from World War II were taken to the former Soviet Union to either renounce their citizenship or be executed ("Stalin's American Prisoners" 1992). Several hundred American soldiers were executed and others resigned themselves to Soviet citizenship. The evidence presented in the hearings also suggests that the U.S. government knew about the fate of these Americans and not only failed to secure their release but they also denied their existence.

The Government's admission that American service personnel were left behind in Southeast Asia served to vindicate claims by individuals that the Government was not telling all it knew about POWs and MIAs. This was a big win for the Citizens Activist Group. Toward the end of the hearings, the essential question turned from "did we leave people behind?" to "do you have evidence that they are alive today?" Reframing the conflict to include the new question represented an important change in the Committee's processes. While the Citizens Activist Group did make some progress with the Government's concessions on the first question, a new conflict emerged concerning the Government's position on the latter question. The Citizens Activist Group emerged from the hearings with a compromise outcome. They received answers to their questions and information that supported their suspicions about the Government. The new question, however, about whether anyone is still alive, presented yet another challenge. Should the activists give up the vigil or press on until they find out what happened to our people?[3]

In an interview with the Associated Press, Ellen Langer, a professor of psychology at Harvard University, said that the families continue to believe that their loved ones are alive. She asserted that "What constitutes evidence may be different for these families than for people who are not involved. . . . They take as the absence of positive confirmation of death that the person can be alive" (Esper 1992).

The Government emerged as a winner as well, minimizing damages to its credibility while maximizing the opportunity to reframe American perceptions of the Government's role in abandoning American service men and women. The writers can only speculate concerning the Government's motives for leaving people behind, but information presented later in the hearings suggests some support for the following rationale.

Communist regimes knew the importance of the individual in a democracy. The value of each citizen's life is clearly expressed in the Bill of Rights. Perhaps the Communists' policies were designed to exploit the weaknesses inherent in a belief system that places maximum worth on each citizen's life. Evidence presented in the Select Committee Hearings suggested that the Communists knew that keeping Americans—dead or alive—would deeply injure the nation's psyche.

Retired Russian Army General Dmitri Volkogonov, aide to Russian President Boris Yeltsin, probably said it best when he made reference to the differences between a totalitarian regime and the free society that exists in the United States. In testimony before the Committee on Veterans Day 1992, Volkogonov noted:

A concern for every individual is one of the distinguishing characteristics of a genuinely free society. . . . A totalitarian regime is not only uninterested in the fate of a single individual but is indifferent to the fate of hundreds of thousands or millions of its own citizens, as was the case with us [the Communist regime of the former Soviet Union]. ("Stalin's American Prisoners" 1992)

The authors conclude that the Government, through the Committee's mediation environment, achieved its goal. The Government was able to exorcise guilt accumulated as a result of a perceived living casualty policy during the many engagements with Communist regimes.

Where previously the Citizens Activist Group and the Government saw one another as the enemy, now there was a chance, with the Senate Select Committee on POW/MIA Affairs acting as mediator, to better understand one another and start the reconciliation process. This may be seen as a major success for the Committee. However, that success was dependent upon the Committee's ability to preserve its neutrality.

Covenants broken as a result of the U.S. government's response to the Communists' refusal to return captured Americans or their remains needed to be acknowledged by the Government. Regardless of how callous one may be, possessing knowledge that Americans were not repatriated under your watch must weigh heavily. With the Cold War over and a presumed living casualty policy becoming public knowledge, the Government, with impunity, told its story of abandoning American service personnel ("Aides Testify" 1992). The Committee provided an environment in which the Government could confess its trespasses while facilitating reconciliation with the American people.

The Committee's role was to provide dispute resolution. In its role as representative of the people, it was empowered to find the truth and finally answer questions about the fate of missing Americans after the Vietnam War. The Committee, however intentionally or unintentionally, served as mediator.

The Committee pledged in the beginning of the hearings that all persons with information about this issue and all persons with a stake in this problem would be allowed to participate in the process. Toward the end of the hearings, however, there were lingering doubts that a free investigation and open discussion of issues had been accomplished. While hearings were held publicly with live and recorded national television coverage, few were convinced that all questions had been asked or all answers provided.

As a forward-looking process, mediation provided all parties with the opportunity to be heard and to develop their arguments while focusing on the outcome that would accommodate reconciliation, healing, and national harmony. This critical analysis of the communication of the Senate Select Committee on POW/MIA Affairs allows us to better understand the function of these very special governmental bodies—Senate select committees. In addition, this discussion provides insight into the potential for governmental committees and commissions to act as dispute resolution providers working to resolve disputes and foster agreement and understanding between and among disputing parties.

NOTES

1. The "Truth Bill" was a resolution calling for full disclosure regarding any information that the U.S. government had about American military personnel who were POWs during the Vietnam War.

2. Discrepancy cases refer to cases in which American military personnel were known to be alive and in Communist hands during the war, but did not return during Operation Homecoming at the end of American involvement in the Vietnam War.

3. In a somewhat similar situation, the House Select Committee on Assassinations appeased both parties in the dispute over the assassination of President John F. Kennedy: those claiming there was a conspiracy and those who stood behind the report of the Warren Commission. Though it did conclude that the Warren Commission was right in its conclusions about the assassination, at the same time it concluded that there was a conspiracy in Kennedy's murder. The question remained whether or not the government should extend its efforts to identify the conspirators.

APPENDIX

Senate Select Committee on POW/MIA Affairs
Created by Senate Resolution 82, 102d Congress

Senator John Kerry, *Chairman,* Democrat, Massachusetts
Senator Robert C. Smith, *Vice Chairman,* Republican, New Hampshire

Senate Committee Members
Senator Thomas A. Daschle, Democrat, South Dakota
Senator Harry Reid, Democrat, Nevada
Senator Charles S. Robb, Democrat, Virginia
Senator Bob Kerrey, Democrat, Nebraska
Senator John McCain, Republican, Arizona
Senator Hank Brown, Republican, Colorado
Senator Charles E. Grassley, Republican, Iowa
Senator Nancy L. Kassebaum, Republican, Kansas
Senator Herb Kohl, Democrat, Wisconsin

Senate Resolution 82: To establish a Select Committee on POW/MIA Affairs
102d Congress 1st session

RESOLVED

Section 1.

(a) There is hereby established a select committee to be known as the Select Committee on POW/MIA Affairs (hereinafter in this resolution referred to as the "select committee"). The select committee shall be composed of ten members, who shall be evenly divided between the two major political parties and shall be appointed by the president pro tempore of the Senate upon recommendations of the majority and minority leaders of the Senate after consultation with their chairman and ranking minority member. Five of the members appointed under this subsection shall be appointed by the President pro tempore of the Senate upon the recommendation of the majority leader of the Senate and five shall be appointed by the President pro tempore of the Senate upon the recommendation of the minority leader of the Senate.

(b) The majority leader of the Senate and the minority leader of the Senate shall be ex officio members of the select committee but shall have no vote in the committee and shall not be counted for purposes of determining a quorum.

(c) At the beginning of each Congress, the Members of the select committee shall elect a chairman of the select committee and a vice chairman of the select committee: *Provided, however,* That the chairman and vice chairman of the select committee shall not be from the same political party. The vice chairman shall act in the place and stead of the chairman in the absence of the chairman.

Section 2.

(a) There shall be referred to the select committee, concurrently with referral to any other committee of the Senate with jurisdiction, all messages, petitions, memorials, and other matters relating to United States personnel unaccounted for from military conflicts.

(b) Nothing in this resolution shall be construed as prohibiting or otherwise restricting the authority of any other committee of the Senate or as amending, limiting, or otherwise changing the authority of any standing committee of the Senate.

Section 3.

The committee may, for the purposes of accountability to the Senate, make such reports to the Senate with respect to matters within its jurisdiction as it shall deem advisable. Such select committee shall promptly call to the attention of the Senate or any other appropriate committee or committees of the Senate any matters deemed by the select committee to require the immediate attention of the Senate or such other committee or committees. In making such reports, the select committee shall proceed in a manner consistent with the requirements of national security.

Section 4.

(a) For the purposes of this resolution, the select committee is authorized at its discretion (1) to make investigations into any matter within its jurisdiction, (2) to hold hearings, (3) to sit and act at any time or place during the sessions, recesses, and adjourned periods of the Senate, (4) to require, by subpoena or otherwise, the attendance of witnesses and the prosecution of correspondence, books, papers, and documents, and (5) to take depositions and other testimony.

(b) The chairman of the select committee or any member thereof may administer oaths to witnesses.

(c) Subpoenas authorized by the select committee may be issued over the signature of the chairman, the vice chairman, or any member of the select committee designated by the chairman, and may be served by any person designated by the chairman or any other member signing the subpoena.

Section 5.

No employee of the select committee or person engaged to perform services for or at the request of such committee shall be given access to any classified information by such committee unless such employee or person has (1) agreed in writing and under oath to be bound by the rules of the Senate and of such committee as to the security of such information during and after the period of his employment or relationship with such committee; and (2) received an appropriate security clearance as determined by such committee in consultation with the Director of Central Intelligence. The type of security clearance to be required in the case of any such employee or person shall, within the determination of such committee in consultation with the Director of Central Intelligence, be commensurate with the sensitivity of the classified information to which such employee or person will be given access by such committee.

Section 6.

The select committee shall formulate and carry out such rules and procedures as it deems necessary to prevent the disclosure, without the consent of the person or persons concerned, of information in the possession of such committee which unduly infringes upon the privacy of which violates the constitutional rights of such person or persons. Nothing herein shall be construed to prevent such committee from publicly disclosing any such information in any case in which such committee determines the national interest in the disclosure of such information clearly outweighs any infringement on the privacy of any person or persons.

Section 7.

The select committee is authorized to permit any representative of the President, designated by the President to serve as a liaison to such committee, to attend any closed meeting of such committee.

Section 8.

Subparagraph (c) of rule XXV of the Standing Rules of the Senate is amended by adding at the end of the following:

"POW/MIA Affairs . . . . 10."

References

Abramson, R. 1986. Panel Blames Shuttle Disaster on Poor Design, Management. *Los Angeles Times*, 10 June.

Aides Testify Nixon Knew about POWs. 1992. *Washington Post*, 23 September, A1.

Americans Outdoors. 1987. In *Report of the President's Commission on Americans Outdoors*. Washington, DC: U.S. Government Printing Office.

Antipoverty and Religious Groups Denounce Report on U.S. Hunger. 1984. *New York Times*, 10 January, A17.

The Assassination: The Warren Commission Report. 1964. *Newsweek*, 5 October, 32-40, 45-46, 57–60, 62–64.

Attig, R. B. 1988. How and Why Social Science Research Can Inform the Pornography Debate. *Free Speech Yearbook* 26:125–34, ed. S. A. Smith.

Attorney General's Commission on Pornography: Final Report, Vols. 1 and 2. 1986. Washington, DC: U.S. Department of Justice.

Babbie, E. 1986. *The Practice of Social Research*, 4th ed. Belmont, CA: Wadsworth.

Baker, J. F. 1986. An American Dilemma: The Meese Commission and After. *Publishers' Weekly*, 11 July, 30–37.

Barth, A. 1955. *Government by Investigation*. New York: Viking Press.

Baruch, J. 1983a. Out of Commission I. *Commonweal*, 21 October, 549–50.

———. 1983b. Out of Commission II. *Commonweal*, 18 November, 614–16.

Bell, D. 1966. Government by Commission. *Public Interest*, Spring, 3–9.

———. 1969. Government by Commission. *Public Interest*, Spring, 3–9. In *The Presidential Advisory System*, eds. T. E. Cronin and S. D. Greenberg, 117–23. New York: Harper and Row.

Bell, J. 1970. Porno—Could Danish Smut Laws Work Here? *Today's Health*, November, 24ff.

Benton, M., and P. J. Frazier. 1976. The Agenda Setting Function of the Mass Media at Three Levels of "Information Holding." *Communication Research* 3:261–74.

Berg, D. M. 1972. Rhetoric, Reality, and Mass Media. *Quarterly Journal of Speech* 58:255–63.

Bitzer, L. F. 1968. The Rhetorical Situation. *Philosophy and Rhetoric* 1:1–15.

Blake, R. R., and J. S. Mouton. 1964. *The Managerial Grid*. Houston: Gulf.

Blakey, G. R., and R. N. Billings. 1981. *The Plot to Kill the President*. New York: Times Books.

Bledsoe, W. C. 1989. Presidential Commissions. In *Cabinets and Counselors: Presidents and the Executive Branch*, eds. M. Nelson, M. S. Benjaminson, and S. B. Ledent, 141–54. Washington, DC: Congressional Quarterly, Inc.

Boisjoly, R. P., E. F. Curtis, and E. Mellican. 1989. Roger Boisjoly and the *Challenger* Disaster: The Ethical Dimensions. *Journal of Business Ethics* 8:217–30.

Bok, S. 1978. *Lying: Moral Choice in Public and Private Life*. New York: Vintage Books.

Boom in Blue Ribbons. 1983. *Newsweek*, 22 August, 18.

Brannigan, A., and S. Goldenberg. 1987. The Study of Aggressive Pornography: The Vicissitudes of Relevance. *Critical Studies in Mass Communication* 4:262–83.

Brummer J. J. 1991. *Corporate Responsibility and Legitimacy: An Interdisciplinary Analysis*. New York: Greenwood Press.

Burke, F., and G. Benson. 1989. Written Rules: State Ethics, Commissions and Conflicts. *The Journal of State Government*, 9 September, 194–98.

Burke, K. 1966. *Language as Symbolic Action: Essays in Language, Literature and Method*. Berkeley: University of California Press.

Burnett, N. F. 1989. Ideology and Propaganda: Toward an Integrative Approach. In *Propaganda: A Pluralistic Perspective*, ed. T. J. Smith, III, 127–37. New York: Praeger.

Bush Calls for Measures to Aid Families. 1992. *Los Angeles Times*, 29 January, A17.

Bush, G. H. 1992a. President Bush Speaks to Bush/Quayle Fundraiser, Cleveland, Ohio. *Federal News Service*, 21 May.

Bush, G. H. W. 1992b. State of the Union Address. *New York Times*, 29 January, A16.

Capaldi, N. 1979. *The Art of Deception*, 2d ed. Buffalo, NY: Prometheus Books.

Censorship, Secrecy, Access, and Obscenity. 1990. Ed. T. R. Kupeman. Westport, CT: Meckler Corporation.

Charged: A Cover-Up in Kennedy Killing. 1976. *U.S. News and World Report*, 5 July, 21.

Cicero. 1970. *On Oratory and Orators*. Ed. and trans. J. S. Watson. Carbondale: Southern Illinois University Press.

Clarity, J. F. 1974. Delay in Troop Pullout Irks Laotians. *New York Times*, 4 May, 3.

CNN News Report. 1992. 24 November.

Cobb, R. W., and C. D. Elder. 1972. *Participation in American Politics: The Dynamics of Agenda-Building*. Baltimore: The Johns Hopkins University Press.

Coffey, R. 1983. Hunger Study Ordered by "Concerned" Reagan. *Chicago Tribune*, 3 August, I1, 11.

Cohen, R. 1986. Pornography: The "Causal Link." *The Washington Post*, 3 June, A19.

———. 1992. Government and Family. *The Washington Post*, 30 January, A23.

Commentaries on Obscenity. 1970. Ed. D. B. Sharp. Metuchen, NJ: Scarecrow Press, Inc.

Commission on Obscenity Files Progress Report. 1969. *Library Journal*, 15 October, 3591–92.

Congressional Quarterly's Guide to Congress. 1982. 3d ed. Ed. M. D. Wormser. Washington, DC: Congressional Quarterly, Inc.

Connelly, M. 1992. Christopher Report: It Cuts Both Ways. *Los Angeles Times*, 4 February.

Cook, R. 1986. The Rogers Commission Failed. *Washington Monthly* 18 (November):13–21.

Coombs, W. T. 1990. *A Theoretical Extension of Issue Status Management: An Extension of the Four Argumentative Strategies.* Ph.D. diss., Purdue University.

———. 1992. The Failure of the Task Force on Food Assistance: A Case Study of the Role of Legitimacy in Issue Management. *Journal of Public Relations Research* 4:101–22.

Court Enjoins Publication of Obscenity Report. 1970. *Publishers' Weekly*, 21 September, 37.

Crable, R. E., and S. L. Vibbert. 1985. Managing Issues and Influencing Public Policy. *Public Relations Review* 11:3–16.

Critics: Censored! 1970. *Senior Scholastic*, 9 November, 6.

Cronin, T. E., and S. D. Greenberg. 1969. *The Presidential Advisory System.* New York: Harper and Row.

The Cuomo Commission Report. 1988. New York: Simon and Schuster.

Curtis, L. A. 1988. Thomas Jefferson, the Kerner Commission and the Retreat of Folly. In *Quiet Riots: Race and Poverty in the United States*, eds. F. A. Harris and R. W. Wilkins. New York: Pantheon.

Cushman, R. E. 1965. Why the Warren Commission? *New York University Law Review* 40:477–503.

de Grazia, E. 1992. *Girls Lean Back Everywhere.* New York: Random House.

Dean, A. L. 1969. Ad Hoc Commissions for Policy Formulation? In *The Presidential Advisory System*, eds. T. E. Cronin and S. D. Greenberg. New York: Harper and Row, 101–16.

Demac, D. A. 1990. *Liberty Denied: The Current Rise of Censorship in America.* New Brunswick, NJ: Rutgers University Press.

Denton, R. E., and G. C. Woodward, eds. *Political Communication in America.* New York: Praeger, 1990.

DeParle, J. 1983. Advise and Forget. *Washington Monthly*, May, 41–46.

Dietz, P. E., and B. Evans. 1982. Pornographic Imagery and the Presence of Paraphilia. *American Journal of Psychiatry* 139:1493–95.

Dietz, P. E., B. Harry, and R. R. Hazelwood. 1986. Detective Magazines: Pornography for the Sexual Sadist? *Journal of Forensic Sciences* 31:197–211.

Documents Show Existence of POWs after Nixon Said All Had Come Home. 1992. *Washington Post*, 25 September, A22.

Donnerstein, E. I., and D. G. Linz. 1986. The Question of Pornography. *Psychology Today*, December, 56–59, 65.

Downs, D. A. 1989. *The New Politics of Pornography.* Chicago: University of Chicago Press.

Drew, E. 1968. On Giving Oneself a Hotfoot: Government by Commission. *The Atlantic*, May, 45–49.

Dunne, J. G. 1991. Law and Disorder in LA: Part Two. *New York Review of Books*, 24 October, 62–64.

Edelman, M. 1967. *The Symbolic Uses of Politics*. Urbana, IL: University of Illinois Press.

———. 1971. *Politics as Symbolic Action: Mass Arousal and Quiescence*. Chicago: Markham Publishing Co.

Enemies of Porno—and of Reason: An Analysis. 1970. *Wilson Library Bulletin*, November, 232ff.

Enzle, M. E., R. D. Hansen, and C. A. Lowe. 1975. Humanizing the Mixed-Motive Paradigm: Methodological Implications From Attribution Theory. *Simulation and Games* 6:151–65.

Epstein, E. J. 1966. *Inquest: The Warren Commission and the Establishment of the Truth*. New York: Viking.

Ernst, M. L., and A. U. Schwartz. 1964. *The Search for the Obscene*. New York: The MacMillan Company.

Esper, G. 1992. Lingering Doubt. Associated Press. 17 December.

Etzioni, A. 1968. Why Task Force Studies Go Wrong. *Wall Street Journal*, 9 July, 18.

Excerpts from Final Report of the Presidential Panel on Food Assistance. 1984. *New York Times*, 11 January, A16.

Executive Order 11130. 1963. Federal Register 12789.

Expert Advice. 1983. *New Republic*, 29 August, 4.

Eyestone, R. 1978. *From Social Issues to Public Policy*. New York: John Wiley & Sons.

Federal Bureau of Investigation. 1963. *Investigation of the Assassination of President Kennedy November 22, 1963*. Washington, DC: U.S. Department of Justice.

Feynman, R. P. 1988. An Outsider's Inside View of the Challenger Inquiry. *Physics Today*, February, 26–37.

Fields, H. 1986a. Meese Panel Final Report Still Excepts Print-Only Material. *Publishers' Weekly*, 27 June, 16, 18.

———. 1986b. Meese Panel Urges More U.S. Action on Obscenity, ACLU Says. *Publishers' Weekly*, 2 May, 14.

Fisher, R., W. Ury, and B. Patton. 1992. *Getting to Yes: Negotiating Agreement without Giving In*. New York: Penguin Books.

Flitner, Jr., D. 1986. *The Politics of Presidential Commissions*. Dobbs Ferry, NY: Transnational Publishers, Inc.

Flowers, M. 1977. A Laboratory Test of Janis' Groupthink Hypothesis. *Journal of Personality and Social Psychology* 35:888–96.

Ford, G. R., with J. R. Stiles. 1965. *Portrait of the Assassin*. New York: Simon and Schuster.

Free Speech Newsletter. 1970. 21 (November).

Freeman, E. 1984. *Strategic Management: A Stakeholder Approach*. Marshfield, MA: Pitman Books.

French, J. R., and B. Raven. 1968. The Bases of Social Power. In *Group Dynamics: Research and Theory*, 3d ed., eds. D. Cartwright and A. Zander, 259–69. New York: Harper and Row.

Gamson, W. 1975. *The Strategy of Social Protest.* Homewood, IL: Dorsey.

Gans, H. J. 1979. *Deciding What's News: A Study of the "CBS Evening News," "NBC Nightly News," Newsweek and Time.* New York: Pantheon.

Garrison, J. 1988. *On the Trail of the Assassins.* New York: Sheridan Square Press.

Germond, J., and J. Witcover. 1980. *Blue Smoke and Mirrors.* New York: Viking.

Getzels, J. W., and E. G. Guba. 1954. Role, Role Conflict, and Effectiveness: An Empirical Study. *American Sociological Review* 18:164–75.

Global Competition: The New Reality. 1985. In *Report of the President's Commission on Industrial Competitiveness.* Washington, DC: U.S. Government Printing Office.

Goldberg, S. B., F. E. A. Sander, and N. H. Rogers. 1992. *Resolution Negotiation, Mediation, and Other Processes,* 2d ed. Boston: Little, Brown and Company.

Golden, J. L., G. F. Berquist and W. E. Coleman. 1989. *The Rhetoric of Western Thought,* 4th ed. Dubuque, IA: Kendall-Hunt.

Goodman, Ellen. 1992. Come Down from the Mountain, George. *Boston Globe,* 2 February, 65.

Gouran, D. 1976. The Watergate Cover-Up: Its Dynamics and Its Implications. *Communication Monographs* 43:176–86.

Gouran, D. S. 1988. Group Decision-Making: An Approach to Integrative Research. In *A Handbook for the Study of Human Communication,* ed. C. H. Tardy, 247–68. Norwood, NJ: Ablex.

Gouran, D. S., R. Y. Hirokawa, and A. E. Martz. 1986. A Critical Analysis of the Factors Related to Decisional Problems Involved in the Challenger Disaster. *Central States Speech Journal* 37:119–35.

Graber, D. A. 1982. The Impact of Media Research on Public Opinion Studies. *Mass Communication Review Yearbook* 3:555–64, eds. D. C. Whitney and E. Wartella. Beverly Hills, CA: Sage.

Graham, H. D., and T. R. Gurr. 1969. *The History of Violence in America.* New York: Bantam Books.

Grove, L. 1986. Decent Into the World of Porn. *Washington Post,* 7 June, D1, D8–9.

Grunig, J., and T. Hunt. 1984. *Managing Public Relations.* Chicago: Holt, Rinehart and Winston, Inc.

Guilty or Not? 1968. *Newsweek,* 18 March, 46–47.

Haiman, F. S. 1981. *Speech and Law in a Free Society.* Chicago: University of Chicago Press.

Hart, R. P. 1990. *Modern Rhetorical Criticism.* Glenview, IL: Scott, Foresman and Company.

Hearings before the President's Commission on the Assassination of President Kennedy. 1964. Washington, DC: U.S. Government Printing Office.

Hearings before the Select Committee on POW/MIA Affairs. 1992. United States Senate One Hundred Second Congress. Washington, DC: U.S. Government Printing Office.

Herbers, J. 1988. The Kerner Report: A Journalist's View. In *Quiet Riots: Race and Poverty in the United States,* eds. F. A. Harris and R. W. Wilkins, 16–26. New York: Pantheon.

Hertzberg, H. 1986. Big Boobs. *The New Republic* 14 (21 July):21–24.

Hirokawa, R. Y., and D. R. Scheerhorn. 1986. Communication in Faulty Group Decision-Making. In *Communication and Group Decision-Making,* eds. R. Y. Hirokawa and M. S. Poole, 63–80. Beverly Hills, CA: Sage.

Hoffman, D. 1983. Task Force on Hunger Created. *Washington Post*, 3 August, A1, C1.

Ice, R. 1987. Presumption as Problematic in Group Decision-Making: The Case of the Space Shuttle. Paper presented at the Fifth AFA/SCA Summer Conference on Argument. Alta, UT, 31 July.

Indochina Fighting Further Threatens Fragile Peace. 1973. *Congressional Quarterly Weekly Report*, 21 April, 894.

Indochina: Peace Growing More Precarious Every Day. 1973. *Congressional Quarterly Weekly Report*, 28 April, 1011.

Iyengar, S., and D. R. Kinder. 1987. *News that Matters*. Chicago: University of Chicago Press.

Jacobellis v. Ohio. 1964. 378 U.S. 184.

Janis, I. L. 1972. *Victims of Groupthink*. Boston: Houghton Mifflin.

———. 1982. *Groupthink*, 2d ed. Boston: Houghton Mifflin.

Janis, I. L., and L. Mann. 1977. *Decision Making*. New York: Free Press.

Jenkins, J. C., and C. M. Eckert. 1986. Channeling Black Insurgency: Elite Patronage and Professional Social Movement Organizations in the Development of the Black Movement. *American Sociological Review* 51:812–29.

Jenkins, J. C., and C. Perrow. 1977. Insurgency of the Powerless: Farm Worker Movements (1946–72). *American Sociological Review* 42:249–68.

Johnson, B. M. 1977. *Communication: The Process of Organizing*. Boston: Allyn and Bacon.

Johnson, T. W., and J. E. Stinson. 1975. Role Ambiguity, Role Conflict, and Satisfaction: Moderating Effects of Individual Differences. *Journal of Applied Psychology* 60:329–33.

Jordan, G. 1990. The Pluralism of Pluralism: An Anti-Theory? *Political Studies* 38:286–301.

Kanouse, D. E., and L. R. Hanson. 1972. Negativity and Evaluations. In *Attribution: Perceiving the Causes of Behavior*, eds. D. E. Kanouse, E. E. Jones, and H. H. Kelley, 27–46. Morristown, NJ: General Learning Press.

Kauffmann, S. 1970. On Obscenity. *The New Republic*, 17 October, 22ff.

Keating, Jr., C. H. 1971. The Report that Shocked the Nation. *Reader's Digest*, January, 37–41.

Kelman, S. 1987. *Making Public Policy: A Hopeful View of American Government*. New York: Basic Books, Inc.

Kennedy, E. C. 1970. Kind Words for the Porno-Researchers. *Commonweal*, December, 292–93.

Kennedy, G. 1963. *The Art of Persuasion in Greece*. Princeton, NJ: Princeton University Press.

Key Sections. 1986. *New York Times*, 26 February, A16.

Kilpatrick, J. J. 1960. *The Smut Peddlers*. Garden City, NJ: Doubleday.

Knowledge for What? 1970. *The Nation*, 31 August, 132.

Komarovsky, M. 1975. *Sociology and Public Policy: The Case of Presidential Commissions*. New York: Elsevier.

Kreps, G. L. 1991. *Organizational Communication: Theory and Practice*, 2d ed. New York: Longman.

Kruglanski, A. W. 1986. Freeze-Think and the Challenger. *Psychology Today*, August, 48–49.

Kurtz, H. 1986a. Meese Goes Toe to Toe with Straw Men. *Washington Post*, 27 July, D1, D4.

———. 1986b. The Pornography Panel's Controversial Last Days. *Washington Post*, 30 May, A13.

Kurtz, M. L. 1982. *Crime of the Century: The Kennedy Assassination from a Historian's Perspective*. Knoxville, TN: The University of Tennessee.

Lane, M. 1991. *Plausible Denial*. New York: Thunder's Mouth Press.

———. 1966. *Rush to Judgment*. New York: Holt, Rinehart, and Winston.

LAPD's Unaddressed Problems. 1992. *Los Angeles Times* 6 October: B6.

Lawton, K. A. 1986. Friends and Foes of Pornography Commission Try to Sway Public Opinion. *Christianity Today*, 19 September, 44.

Leeson, S. M., and B. M. Johnston. 1988. *Ending It: Dispute Resolution in America*. Cincinnati, OH: Anderson Publishing Company.

Leff, D. R., D. L. Protess, and S. C. Brooks. 1986. Crusading Journalism: Changing Public Attitudes and Policy-Making Agendas. *Public Opinion Quarterly* 50: 300–15.

Lewis, A. 1964. Warren Commission Finds Oswald Guilty and Says Assassin and Ruby Acted Alone; Panel Unanimous: Theory of Conspiracy by Right or Left is Rejected. *New York Times*, 28 September, 1, 14.

Lewis, F. F. 1976. *Literature, Obscenity and Law*. Carbondale, IL: Southern Illinois University Press.

Libby, R. W., and M. A. Strauss. 1980. Make Love Not War: Sex, Sexual Meanings, and Violence in a Sample of University Students. *Archives of Sexual Behavior* 9:133–48.

Lillienstein, M. J. 1986a. A Meese Commission Outrage. *Publishers' Weekly*, 9 May, 254.

———. 1986b. Meese Commission Vigilantes. *Publishers' Weekly*, 11 July, 43.

Lipsky, M., and D. J. Olson. 1977. *Commission Politics: The Processing of Racial Crisis in America*. New Brunswick, NJ: Transaction Books.

Lockhart, W. B. 1971. The Findings and Recommendations of the Commission on Obscenity and Pornography: A Case Study of the Role of Social Science in Formulating Public Policy. *Oklahoma Law Review*, May, 209–33.

Lockhart, W. B., and R. McClure. 1954. Literature, the Law of Obscenity, and the Constitution. *Minnesota Law Review* 29: n.p.

Lynn, B. 1986. Civil Liberties. In *The Meese Commission Exposed*, 11–12. New York: The National Coalition Against Censorship.

Mack, R. 1975. Four for the Seesaw: Reflections on the Reports of Four Colleagues Concerning Their Experiences as Presidential Commissioners. In *Sociology and Public Policy: The Case of Presidential Commissions*, ed. M. Komarovsky, 143–52. New York, Oxford, Amsterdam: Elsevier.

Madden, D. J., and J. R. Lion. 1976. *Rage, Hate, Assault and Other Forms of Violence*. New York: Spectrum.

Manheim, J. B. 1987. A Model of Agenda Dynamics. *Communication Yearbook* 10:499–516, ed. M. L. McLauglin. New York: Sage.

Marcy, C. 1945. *Presidential Commissions*. Morningside Heights, NY: King's Crown Press.

Marrs, J. 1989. *Crossfire: The Plot that Killed Kennedy*. New York: Carroll and Graf.

Marver, J. D. 1979. *Consultants Can Help: The Use of Outside Experts in the U.S. Office of Child Development.* Lexington, MA: Lexington Books.

McCombs, M. 1977. Agenda Setting Function of the Mass Media. *Public Relations Review* 3:89–95.

McCombs, M. E., and D. L. Shaw. 1972. The Agenda-Setting Function of the Mass Media. *Public Opinion Quarterly* 36:176–87.

McDaniel, M. 1992. Letter to Authors (Kimsey and Fuller). 16 November.

McKinney, B. C. 1985. *Decision-Making in the President's Commission on the Assassination of President Kennedy: A Descriptive Analysis Employing Irving Janis' Groupthink Hypothesis.* Ph.D. diss., Ann Arbor, MI: University Microfilms International.

———. 1990. Decision Making in the Warren Commission: A Qualitative Analysis of Solution Centeredness. *Pennsylvania Speech Communication Annual* 46: 21–45.

Meagher, S. 1967. *Accusations after the Fact.* New York: Bobbs-Merrill.

The Meese Commission Exposed. 1986. New York: The National Coalition against Censorship.

Meltsner, A. J. 1976. *Policy Analysts in the Bureaucracy.* Berkeley, CA: University of California Press.

Merton, R. 1975. Social Knowledge and Public Policy: Sociological Perspectives on Four Presidential Commissions. In *Sociology and Public Policy: The Case of Presidential Commissions,* ed. M. Komarovsky, 153–78. New York, Oxford, Amsterdam: Elsevier.

Miller, C. M. 1988. *Justifying Disaster: An Implicit Rhetorical Theoretical Analysis of the Space Shuttle Challenger Accident.* Ph.D. diss., Ann Arbor, MI: University Microfilms International.

Miller v. California. 1973. 413 U.S. 15.

Missouri Urban Families: Rhetoric versus Record. 1992. *American Political Network Daily Report Card,* 3 March.

Missouri's Governor Ashcroft: A Commission Head in Search of a Task. 1992. *American Political Network Daily Report Card,* 3 February.

Mohr, C. 1986. Pentagon Fears Delays. *New York Times,* 24 February, A12.

Molotch, H. L., D. L. Protess, and M. T. Gordon. 1987. The Media-Policy Connection: Ecologies of News. In *Political Communication Research: Approaches, Studies, Assessment,* ed. D. L. Paletz, 26–48. Norwood, NJ: Ablex.

National Advisory Commission on Civil Disorders. 1968. *Final Report.* New York: Bantam Books.

New Panel on Urban Families Gears Up. 1992. *Atlanta Journal and Constitution,* 13 March, A7.

Nichols, M. H. 1963. *Rhetoric and Criticism.* Baton Rouge, LA: Louisiana State University Press.

Nimmo, D. D. 1978. *Political Communication and Public Opinion in America.* Santa Monica, CA: Goodyear Publishing Co.

Nisbett, R., and L. Ross. 1980. *Human Inference: Strategies and Shortcomings of Social Judgment.* Englewood Cliffs, NJ: Prentice-Hall.

Nixon, R. M. 1973. March 29 Nixon Address. *Congressional Quarterly Weekly Report,* 31 March, 727.

Nutt, P. C. 1989. *Making Tough Decisions.* San Francisco: Jossey-Bass.

O'Neil, R. M. 1972. *Free Speech: Responsible Communication under Law*, 2d ed. Indianapolis, IN: Bobbs-Merrill.

Oberdoffer, D. 1990. Russell Says He Never Believed Oswald Acted Alone. *Washington Post*, 19 January, A3.

Oboler, E. M. 1970. The Politics of Pornography. *Library Journal*, 15 December, 4225–28.

Obscenity Report and Personal Response. 1970. *America*, 7 November, 366.

Obscure Honor of Serving Your Country. 1985. *Fortune*, 10 June, 132.

Official Cover-up: A Flagrant Case in Point. 1967. *Life*, 8 September, 103.

Once More, Into the Fray. 1970. *Science News*, 3 October, 284.

Organ, D. W. 1971. Linking Pins between Organizations and Environment. *Business Horizons*, 73–79.

Ouchi, W. G. 1985. Microeconomic Policy Dialogue. In *Global Competition: The New Reality, The Report of the President's Commission on Industrial Competitiveness*. Volume II. Appendix E. Washington, DC: U.S. Government Printing Office.

Packer, H. L. 1971. The Pornography Caper. *Commentary*, February, 72–77.

Page, B. I., and R. Y. Shapiro. 1983. Effects of Public Opinion on Policy. *American Political Science Review* 77:175–90.

Paletz, D. L., and R. M. Entman. 1981. *Media Power Politics*. New York: The Free Press.

Panel to Urge Continuing Arts Agencies. 1981. *New York Times*, 14 July, C12.

Pear, R. 1983a. Hunger Panel Cancels Final Meeting. *New York Times*, 13 December, B10.

———. 1983b. Food Panel Urges a Slight Aid Rise in Draft Report. *New York Times*, 25 December, A1, A27.

———. 1983c. Reagan Hunger Call. *New York Times*, 5 August, A8.

———. 1984. Antipoverty and Religious Groups Denounce Report on U.S. Hunger. *New York Times*, 10 January, A17.

Peterson, B. E. 1983. Did the Education Commissions Say Anything? *Brookings Review*, Winter, 3–11.

Pfau, M., D. A. Thomas, and W. Ulrich. 1987. *Debate and Argument*. Glenview, IL: Scott, Foresman and Company.

Pilpel, H. F., and K. P. Norwick. 1969. But Can You Do That? *Publishers' Weekly*, 6 October.

Plato. 1941. *The Republic*. Trans. with introduction and notes by F. M. Cornford. London: Oxford University Press.

———. 1956. *Phaedrus*. Trans. W. C. Hembold and W. G. Rabinowitz. Indianapolis: Library of the Liberal Arts.

Platt, A. M. 1971. *The Politics of Riot Commissions, 1917–1970*. New York: Macmillan.

Popper, F. 1970. *The President's Commissions*. New York: Twentieth Century Fund.

Porno Politics. 1970. *The Nation*, 9 November, 452–53.

Porno Report Cleared for Publication. 1970. *Publishers' Weekly*, 28 September, 58–60.

Pornography and Sexual Aggression. 1984. Eds. N. M. Malamuth and E. Donnerstein. New York: Academic Press.

Pornography—Is Smut Good for You? 1970. *Time*, 12 October, 19.

Porter, R. B. 1992. Remarks to the Surgeon-General's Conference on Children, "Parental Involvement in Education." *Federal News Service*, 12 February.

POW-MIA Concern. 1973. *Congressional Quarterly Weekly Report*, 2 June, 1384.

POW/MIA Inquiry Supported by Senate Rules Panel. 1991. *Congressional Quarterly Weekly Report*, 3 August, 2189.

Problem Officers Still on Force. 1992. *Los Angeles Times*, 6 October, B6.

Pross, A. P. 1986. *Group Politics and Public Policy*. Toronto: Oxford University Press.

Public Papers of the Presidents of the United States. 1983. Washington, DC: U.S. Government Printing Office.

Public Report of the Vice President's Task Force on Combatting Terrorism. 1986. Washington, DC: U.S. Government Printing Office.

Putnam, L. L. 1988. Understanding the Unique Characteristics of Groups within Organizations. In *Small Group Communication: A Reader*, eds. R. S. Cathcart and L. A. Samovar, 76–85. Dubuque, IA: William C. Brown.

Putnam, L. L., and C. Stohl. 1990. Bona Fide Groups: A Reconceptualization of Groups in Context. *Communication Studies* 41:248–65.

The Questions Get Tougher. 1986. *Time*. 3 March, 14.

Raven, R. C., C. Centers, and A. Rodrigues. 1975. The Bases of Conjugal Power. In *Power in Families*, eds. R. E. Cromwell and D. H. Olson, 217–34. New York: Halsted Press.

Records of Presidential Committees, Commission and Boards. President's Commission on the Assassination of President Kennedy, Alphabetical Files of Out-Going Letters. National Archives Record Group 270.

Reedy, G. 1970. That Obscenity Report. *America*, 7 November, 371–73.

Reich, R. B. 1988. *The Power of Public Ideas*. Cambridge, MA: Ballinger Publishing Co.

Remarks by President Bush to the American Legislative Exchange Council. 1992a. *Federal News Service*, 21 February.

Remarks by President Bush to the National League of Cities, Washington Hilton. 1992b. *Federal News Service*, 9 March.

Report of the Commission on Obscenity and Pornography. 1970. New York: Bantam Books.

Report of the Independent Commission on the Los Angeles Police Department. 1991. Los Angeles.

Report of the National Advisory Commission on Civil Disorders. 1968. Washington, DC: U.S. Government Printing Office.

Report of the Presidential Commission on the Space Shuttle Challenger Accident. 1986. Washington, DC: U.S. Government Printing Office.

Report of the President's Commission on the Assassination of President Kennedy. 1964. Washington, DC: U.S. Government Printing Office.

Report of the Select Committee on Assassinations. 1979. U.S. House of Representatives. 95th Congress, 2d session. Washington, DC: U.S. Government Printing Office.

Rhetoric of Evasion. 1969. *The Nation*, 13 October, 370–72.

Rich, S. 1984. 42 Groups Join in Hunger Report Criticisms. *Washington Post*, 11 January, A1.

Rockefeller, J. 1991. Press Conference by the National Commission on Children. *Federal News Service*, 21 November.

Ross, S. 1968. The Fact-Finding Charade. *The Nation*, 4 March, 306–308.

A Sad and Solemn Duty. 1963. *Time*, 13 December, 26.

Safire, W. 1968. *The New Language of Politics: An Anecdotal Dictionary of Catchwords, Slogans, and Political Usage.* New York: Random House.

Saltzman, J. 1986. A Case of Misplaced Concern. *USA Today*, November, 39.

Sawyer, K. 1986. Misguided "Group Think" Blamed in Decision to Launch Challenger. *New York Times*, 26 February.

Schauer, F. 1982. *Free Speech: A Philosophical Enquiry.* Cambridge: Cambridge University Press.

Seeger, M. W. 1986. The Challenger Tragedy and Search for Legitimacy. *Central States Speech Journal* 37:147–57.

Senate Approves POW/MIA Panel. 1991. *Congressional Quarterly Weekly Report*, 10 August, 2261, 2268.

Shafritz, J. M. 1988. *The Dorsey Dictionary of American Government and Politics.* Chicago: The Dorsey Press.

Sharp, D. 1970. *Commentaries on Obscenity.* Metuchen, NJ: Scarecrow Press.

Shaw, M. E. 1976. *The Psychology of Small Group Behavior.* New York: McGraw-Hill.

Shine, A. P. 1973. Until All Have Returned. *New York Times*, 1 March, 40.

Sidey, H. 1983. The Buck Stops Here. *Time*, 30 May, 14.

Simon, H. 1976. *Administrative Behavior.* New York: The Free Press.

Smith, B. L. R. 1992. *The Advisers: Scientists in the Policy Process.* Washington, DC: The Brookings Institution.

Smith, H. 1984. Leaky Business of Presidential Commissions. *New York Times*, 11 January, A18.

Smith, M. J. 1990. Pluralism, Reformed Pluralism and Neopluralism: The Role of Pressure Groups in Policy-Making. *Political Studies* 38:302–22.

Smith, S. S., and C. J. Deering. 1990. *Committees in Congress.* Washington, DC: Congressional Quarterly, Inc.

Sociology and Public Policy: The Case of Presidential Commissions. 1975. Ed. M. Komarovsky. New York: Elsevier.

Spreitzer, E., E. E. Snyder, and D. L. Larson. 1979. Multiple Roles and Psychological Well-Being. *Sociological Focus* 12:141–48.

Stalin's American Prisoners. 1992. *Washington Post*, 14 November, A24.

The Story of X. 1986. *New York Times*, 13 July, E28.

Studying the Study. 1968. *Time*, 15 March, 16.

Sullivan, W. C. 1979. *The Bureau: My Thirty Years in Hoover's FBI.* New York: Pinnacle.

Sulzner, G. T. 1971. The Policy Process and the Uses of National Governmental Study Commissions. *Western Political Quarterly* 24:438–48.

———. 1974. The Policy Process and the Uses of National Governmental Study Commissions. *Western Political Quarterly* 24 (September):438–48. Report in *Perspectives on the Presidency: A Collection*, eds. S. Bach and G. T. Sulzner, 206–18. Lexington, MA: D. C. Heath.

Summers, A. 1980. *Conspiracy.* New York: McGraw-Hill.

Sunderland, L. V. 1974. *The Court, the Congress and the President's Commission.* Washington, DC: American Enterprise Institute for Public Policy Research.

Task Force on Families Gets Down to Business. 1992. *Gannett News Service*, 22 May.

The Temptations of Pornography. 1970. *Christian Century*, 11 November, 1339.

That Porno Report. 1970. *National Review*, 20 October, 1097–98.

Thompson, J. B. 1984. *Studies in the Theory of Ideology*. Berkeley, CA: University of California Press.

The Tighe Report on American POWs and MIAs. 1987. Washington, DC: U.S. Government Printing Office.

Transcripts of the Executive Sessions of the President's Commission on the Assassination of President Kennedy. National Archives Record Group 272.

Tuchman, G. 1981. The Missing Dimensions—News Media and the Management of Social Change. In *Mass Media and Social Change*, eds. E. Katz and T. Szecsko, 63–82. Beverly Hills: Sage.

Turner, K. J. 1980. Ego Defense and Media Access: Conflicting Rhetorical Needs of a Contemporary Social Movement. *Central States Speech Journal* 31:106–16.

Turque, B., and D. Foote. 1991. Damned—But Defiant. *Newsweek*, 22 July, 22.

Tutchings, T. R. 1979. *Rhetoric and Reality: Presidential Commissions and the Making of Public Policy*. Boulder, CO: Westview Press.

United States Congress. 1984. *Review of the Report of the President's Task Force on Food Assistance*. Serial No. 98–54. Committee on Agriculture. Washington, DC: U.S. Government Printing Office.

United States Senate Committee on Foreign Relations Republican Staff. 1991. *An Examination of U.S. Policy toward POW/MIAs*. Washington, DC: U.S. Senate Committee on Foreign Relations, 23 May.

U.S. Department of Justice. 1963. The Assassination of President Kennedy. FBI Headquarter File 62–109060. Washington, DC: U.S. Government Printing Office.

———. 1963. Liaison with Commission. FBI Headquarter File 62–109090. Washington, DC: U.S. Government Printing Office.

———. 1986. *Attorney General's Commission on Pornography*. Washington, DC: U.S. Government Printing Office.

U.S. General Services Administration. 1990. *Eighteenth Annual Report of the President on Federal Advisory Committees, Fiscal Year 1989*. Washington, DC: U.S. Government Printing Office.

Van Gelder, L. 1986. Pornography Goes to Washington. *Ms*, June, 52–54, 83.

Vance, C. S. 1986. The Meese Commission on the Road. *The Nation* 2 (9 August):76–82.

Vibbert, S. L. 1984. Education as a Political Issue: Management of the Issue's "Status." Paper presented at the annual meeting of the Central States Speech Association. Chicago, IL.

Victims of Crime. 1982. In *Report of the President's Task Force on Victims of Crime*. Washington, DC: U.S. Government Printing Office.

Vietnam Hints MIAs May Be in Bush Areas. 1987. *The Washington Times*, 11 August, A1.

Wagner, S. 1970. Porno Report Becomes Political Football. *Publishers' Weekly*, 12 October, 34–35.

Walster, E. 1966. Assignment of Responsibility for an Accident. *Journal of Personality and Social Psychology* 3:73–79.

Warren, E. 1977. *The Memoirs of Earl Warren*. Garden City, NY: Doubleday.

Weick, K. E. 1979. *The Social Psychology of Organizing*, 2d ed. Reading, MA: Addison-Wesley Publishing Co.

Weisberg, H. 1965. *Whitewash: The Report on the Warren Report*. Hyattstown, MD: Harold Weisberg.

———. 1974. *Whitewash IV: JFK Assassination Transcript*. Frederick, MD: Harold Weisberg.

———. 1985. Letter to Author (McKinney). 6 February.

Wellborn, S. N. 1986. Flak Fills the Sky over NASA. *U.S. News and World Report*, 23 June, 10.

White, K. 1992. Bush Appoints Governor Ashcroft to Head Panel on Families. *Gannett News Service*, 28 January.

Why Children's Commissions Fail. 1991. *Newsweek*, 8 July, 20.

Wilkinson, T. 1991. Report was Watered Down. *Los Angeles Times*, 15 September.

Willwerth, J. 1991. Will Gates Give Up the Fight At Last? *Time*, 22 July, 18.

Witcover, J. 1970. Civil War Over Smut. *The Nation*, 11 May, 550–53.

Wolanin, T. R. 1975. *Presidential Advisory Commissions*. Madison, WI: University of Wisconsin Press.

Yardley, J. 1986a. The Porn Commission's Hidden Agenda. *Washington Post*, 14 July, C2.

———. 1986b. Vigilante Injustice and the Sleazy "Sophisticates." *Washington Post*, 23 June, D2.

Yet Another Study. 1992. *Christian Science Monitor*, 13 February, 20.

Zillmann, D., and J. Bryant. 1982. Pornography, Sexual Callousness, and the Trivialization of Rape. *Journal of Communication* 32:10–21.

Zink, S. D. 1987. *Guide to the Presidential Advisory Commissions 1973–84*. Alexandria, VA: Chadwyck-Healy Inc.

Index of Government Commissions

Advisory Committee on Television and Social Behavior, 48
Attorney General's Commission on Pornography, 4, 9, 15–16, 17, 19, 25–30, 49, 119, 123–43

Board of Tea Experts, 39
British Royal Commissions, 7

Christopher Commission. *See* Independent Commission on the Los Angeles Police Department
Civil Rights Committee, 57
Commission on Budget Concepts, 65
Commission on Children, 34–35, 36
Commission on Federal Coal Leasing, 37
Commission on Obscenity and Pornography, 5, 12–13, 19, 26–29, 103–22, 139
Commission on Public Lands, 5, 15
Committee for the Preservation of the White House, 38
Committee on Population and Family Planning, 58
Cuomo Commission on Trade and Competitiveness, 7, 13–14, 17–18

Eisenhower Commission. *See* National Commission on the Causes and Prevention of Violence

Federal Communication Commission, 6
Federal Condor Advisory Committee, 7

Grace Commission. *See* President's Private Sector Survey on Cost Control

Independent Commission on the Los Angeles Police Department, 5, 7, 21–24, 53, 56, 58, 63
Inland Waterway Commission, 5
International Screw Threads Standards Commission, 39
Interstate Commerce Commission, 6

Katzenbach Commission. *See* President's Commission on Law Enforcement and the Administration of Justice
Kerner Commission. *See* National Advisory Commission on Civil Disorders

Lockhart Commission. *See*
      Commission on Obscenity and
      Pornography

Meese Commission. *See* Attorney
      General's Commission on
      Pornography

National Advisory Commission on
      Civil Disorders, 5, 11–12, 16–
      17, 53, 59, 61, 64, 65, 67, 69
National Advisory Commission on
      Libraries, 65
National Bipartisan Commission on
      Central America, 45
National Commission on the Causes
      and Prevention of Violence, 9–
      10, 19, 52, 62, 69
National Commission on Marijuana
      and Drug Abuse, 5, 52, 61
National Commission on Tech-
      nology, Automation, and
      Economic Progress, 47, 56
National Conservation Commission,
      5

Panel on Mental Retardation, 9, 58
President's Commission on
      Americans Outdoors, 48–49
President's Commission on the
      Assassination of President
      Kennedy, 4, 5, 9, 17, 49, 56,
      60, 61, 75–101, 148, 162,
      171
President's Commission on Campus
      Unrest, 5, 52
President's Commission on Industrial
      Competitiveness, 48, 57
President's Commission on Law
      Enforcement and the
      Administration of Justice, 5,
      62, 69
President's Commission on Postal
      Organization, 69

President's Commission on the Space
      Shuttle *Challenger* Accident, 4,
      9, 55, 56, 57, 61, 65, 145–65
President's Commission on Urban
      Families, 33–38, 43–44
President's Commission on White
      House Fellowships, 38
President's Private Sector Survey on
      Cost Control, 49
President's Water Resource Policy
      Commission, 56
Public Lands Commission. *See*
      Commission on Public Lands

Roberts Commission (Pearl Harbor
      disaster), 80
Rogers Commission. *See* President's
      Commission on the Space
      Shuttle *Challenger* Accident

Scranton Commission. *See*
      President's Commission on
      Campus Unrest
Shafer Commission. *See* National
      Commission on Marijuana and
      Drug Abuse

Task Force on Arts Funding, 44–45
Task Force on Education, 57, 59, 68
Task Force on Hunger/Food
      Assistance, 43–44, 55, 58, 61–
      62, 63, 67, 68
Task Force on Private Sector
      Initiatives, 45
Task Force on Victims of Crime, 48
Tea Tasting Board, 7

Vice President's Task Force on
      Combatting Terrorism, 6–7

Warren Commission. *See* President's
      Commission on the Assassina-
      tion of President Kennedy
Winegrape Varietal Names Advisory
      Commission, 39

Subject Index

Agenda setting, 64

Attorney General's Commission on
  Pornography, 9, 15–16, 28, 49,
  128–31, 131-33, 138–39,
  139–42; begging the question,
  fallacy of, 125, 133; charge,
  125; final report, 4, 19, 124,
  125; funding, 119; ideological
  analysis, 25–30; informational
  deficiencies, 133–37; link
  between obscenity and crime,
  129, 133, 135, 136; member
  qualifications, 17, 126–28; *post
  hoc, ergo propter hoc,* fallacy of,
  139; social science research, 124,
  133, 136–37; 1970 Commission on Obscenity and Pornography, dismissal of, 29, 119–20,
  139

Bush, George, 6–7

Christopher Commission. *See*
  Independent Commission on the
  Los Angeles Police Department

Commission on Obscenity and
  Pornography, 104, 104–5, 106–
  8, 108–9, 109, 112; begging the

question, fallacy of, 115; charge,
  104; decriminalization and control, relationship between, 13,
  112; final report, 12, 103, 105,
  110, 118–20, 123; funding,
  105, 119; link between
  obscenity and crime, 103, 104,
  105, 107; Meese Commission,
  comparison to, 119; minority
  report, 12, 28–29, 110–11; *post
  hoc, ergo propter hoc,* fallacy of,
  116; recommendations, 111–17;
  sex education, 114, 115; slippery
  slope, fallacy of, 116; social
  science research, 19, 104, 105,
  107, 109, 111, 113, 115

Commissioners, 59, 60, 65; characteristics of, 36–38, 66–67, 68; and
  role conflict, 60–61

Commissions, 5–6, 38, 39, 49, 69–
  70; charge of, 16–17, 52, 61;
  and constituencies, 57–58, 59–
  60, 66, 67, 68; and contexts,
  55–56, 70; and credibility, 17,
  37; definition of, 10, 51; final
  reports of, 19, 49, 56, 59, 62,
  64, 65, 67, 68; life span of, 38,
  52, 56, 70; and membership,

36–38, 54, 59–61; naming of,
17–18, 63; and rhetorical
strategies, 44–47, 47–48, 48–
49; and rhetorical study, goals
of, 14, 39, 41, 44
Commissions, characteristics of: ad
hoc/temporary, 38, 52; advisory,
53; investigatory, 52–53, 61,
66–67; mobilization power, 65;
outside/independent, 53–54;
qualified and objective, 54
Commissions, functions of: advising,
39, 53; conflict management,
41; crisis response 9, 39;
education, 9, 41, 64; issue
avoidance, 10, 40, 63; policy
analysis and influence, 8, 61, 62,
63–66, 68–70; problem
solving, 41; symbolic
reassurance, 9, 40, 61, 62–63,
67–68, 70; window dressing, 8,
40
Commissions, and rhetorical study
assessment standards: commission background, 15–16, 42–
43; commission charge, 16–17;
commission impact, 20, 41, 44,
49; commissioners and staff, 17–
18, 60; final report, 19, 49
Cuomo Commission on Trade and
Competitiveness, 7–8; the
American Formula, 13–14; the
New American Formula, 14

Dean, Alan, 7

Edelman, Murray, 62, 63, 64, 66
Eisenhower Commission, 9–10, 19

Federal Bureau of Investigation: and
involvement with Warren
Commission, 80–81, 81–83,
89, 92, 97
Flitner, David. On commissions:
education by, 64; functions of,
7–10, 61, 65; impact of, 20, 63;
importance of, 4; and pressure
for unanimity, 18; and reas-

surance, 53, 62; and respectabil-
ity, 65; timing of, 52, 56

Groupthink, 60, 85, 91; conditions
of, 85–86, 86–87, 87–88;
symptoms of, 88–89, 89–91,
92; and symptoms of defective
decision making, 93–95, 95–
96, 97

Hart, Roderick, 12, 19; on assessing
speech situations, 15; on functions of rhetoric, 13–14

Independent Commission on the Los
Angeles Police Department, 5,
7–8, 53, 58, 63; argumentative
analysis, 21–24; charge, 16, 22

Janis, Irving. See Groupthink
Johnson, Lyndon, 11, 17; commissions appointed by, 5, 9, 17,
108; and Warren Commission,
76, 77–78, 83, 85–86, 98

Keating, Charles H., Jr., 108, 109–
10, 112, 113
Kerner Commission. See National
Advisory Commission on Civil
Disorders

Lockhart Commission. See
Commission on Obscenity and
Pornography
Los Angeles Police Department, role
in Rodney King beating investi-
gation. See Independent Com-
mission on the Los Angeles
Police Department

Meese Commission. See Attorney
General's Commission on
Pornography

National Advisory Commission on
Civil Disorders, 55, 64, 67;

charge, 16–17, 46; final report, 11, 46, 59
National Commission on the Causes and Prevention of Violence, 9–10, 19
Nixon, Richard, 5, 12

Oswald, Lee Harvey, 75, 90, 90–91; relationship to the FBI, 84, 88–89, 92–98

Plato, 31–33
Popper, Frank. On commissions: characteristics of, 77, 78; creation of, 77, 98; critiques of, 79, 98, 99, 158; public education function of, 152; and publicity, 154, 158, 161; and reasons to study, 145
POW/MIAs. *See* Senate Select Committee on POW/MIA Affairs
President's Commission on the Assassination of President Kennedy, 56, 77, 78–86, 98, 99; Gerald Ford and the FBI, 83, 94; investigation by Attorney General Robert Kennedy, 95–96; Lee Harvey Oswald and the FBI, 84, 88–89, 92–98; relationship to FBI, 81–85, 92, 93, 96–97, 148; single bullet theory, 49, 79, 88–89, 99; staff, 78–79, 86–87
President's Commission on the Space Shuttle *Challenger* Accident, 151, 152–54, 156–57, 161–62; commission investigatory strategies, 150–51; comparison to Warren Commission, 162; "devil's advocate team," 147–48; leveling blame, 158–61; media influence, 56, 154–58; NASA investigatory strategies, 147–50; scope of investigation, 146, 149
President's Commission on Urban Families, 33–38, 43–44

Rodney King beating investigation. *See* Independent Commission on the Los Angeles Police Department
Rogers Commission. *See* President's Commission on the Space Shuttle *Challenger* Accident
Roosevelt, Theodore, 5, 15
Ruby, Jack, 74–75, 86, 99

Senate Select Committee on POW/MIA Affairs, 171–72, 176, 179, 179–80, 182–86, 187–89, 189–91; Alternative Dispute Resolution (ADR), 172–74, 180; "Citizens Activist Group," 176, 178–79; committee charge, 169, 170, 177; comparison of Select Committees to government commissions, 169–70, 191, 193–94; fraudulent claims of POW/MIA sightings, 169, 182–83; history of investigations into POW/MIA issue, 167–69, 171; Select Committees and dispute resolution, 174–76, 177; United States Living Casualty Policy, 191–93; Win-Win or Win-Lose orientations, 180–81
Sulzner, George, 10, 63, 65

Thompson, John, 25–29
Tutchings, Terrence, 18, 57, 63

Warren Commission. *See* President's Commission on the Assassination of President Kennedy
Wolanin, Thomas. On commissions: characteristics of, 6, 54, 61; and consensus, 59; education by, 64; functions of, 8–10; impact of, 63, 65; and impartiality, 67; timing of, 52, 56; and vagueness of charge, 52

About the Editors and Contributors

NICHOLAS F. S. BURNETT is currently Associate Professor and Director of Forensics at California State University in Sacramento.

W. TIMOTHY COOMBS is currently Assistant Professor at Illinois State University.

REX M. FULLER is currently a Professor at James Madison University.

DENNIS S. GOURAN is currently Professor and Head of the Department of Speech Communication at the Pennsylvania State University.

WILLIAM D. KIMSEY is currently Professor and Director of the James Madison University Center for Mediation.

BRUCE C. MCKINNEY is Assistant Professor of Communication Studies at the University of North Carolina at Wilmington. His research interests include the Kennedy assassination and the Warren Commission, and mediation and conflict resolution.

CHRISTINE M. MILLER is Assistant Professor of Communication Studies at California State University, Sacramento. Her area of specialty is rhetorical criticism. She also conducts research in political communication and visual communication.

W. DAVID SNOWBALL is currently Divisional Chair of Fine Arts and Humanities at Augustana College in Rock Island, Illinois.

ROGER A. SOENKSEN is currently a Professor at James Madison University.